THE COLOR OF WELFARE

HOW RACISM UNDERMINE

The Color o

THE WAR ON POVERTY

WELFARE

Jill Quadagno

New York • *Oxford* • Oxford University Press • *1994*

Oxford University Press

Oxford   New York   Toronto
Delhi   Bombay   Calcutta   Madras   Karachi
Kuala Lumpur   Singapore   Hong Kong   Tokyo
Nairobi   Dar es Salaam   Cape Town
Melbourne   Auckland   Madrid

and associated companies in
Berlin   Ibadan

Copyright © 1994 by Oxford University Press, Inc.

Library of Congress Cataloging-in-Publication Data
Quadagno, Jill S. The color of welfare: how racism undermined the war on poverty /
Jill Quadagno.
p. cm.   Includes bibliographical references and index.
ISBN 0-19-507919-1
1. United States—Social policy. 2. Economic assistance,
Domestic—United States. 3. Poor—United States.
4. United States—Race relations. I. Title.
HN59.Q28   1994
305.5'69'0973—dc20   93-41892

1 3 5 7 9 8 6 4 2
Printed in the United States of America
on acid-free paper

PREFACE

When David Duke, former Ku Klux Klan Grand Wizard, was elected to the Louisiana State House of Representatives, he declared, "This isn't a victory for me, it is a victory for those who . . . choose to work hard rather than abuse welfare ."[1] Unspoken but understood was that the hard workers were white, the welfare abusers African American. As president, one of Ronald Reagan's favorite anecdotes was the story of a Chicago welfare queen with "80 names, 30 addresses, 12 Social Security cards and a tax-free income of over $150,000."[2] While less direct in his message, President Clinton's promise to reform the welfare system was his most popular issue, a sure-fire applause getter in his speeches.[3]

Although welfare reform is the policy issue that most readily translates into a racial code, other social programs—urban renewal, job training, school choice—elicit similar connotations. Politicians say they are talking about social programs, but people understand that they're really talking about race. There is good reason for Americans to understand coded messages about social policy as substitutes for discussions of race, for real linkages between race and social policy exist. But the linkages are more complex than the messages delineated in recent political campaigns. This book explains these intricate connections.

Race first became intertwined with social policy during Franklin Delano Roosevelt's "New Deal." The New Deal achieved dual objectives: It initiated a floor of protection for the industrial working class, and it reinforced racial segregation through social welfare programs, labor policy, and housing policy. These impediments to racial equality remained intact until the 1960s when the civil rights movement made the struggle for equal opportunity the predominant social issue of the decade. When Lyndon Baines Johnson decided to wage a "War on Poverty," the federal resources of the antipoverty programs fueled this struggle. Community action programs brought African Americans into local politics; job-training programs forced the skilled trade unions to integrate and more importantly, established affirmative action. And demands for more and better housing were coupled with the first fair-housing legislation. As social programs came to promote equal opportunity, they created a political backlash that gave rise to an ascendant "New Right" of fiscal and social conservatives intent on rolling back the welfare state and restoring traditional values. Proposals for a guaranteed annual income for the working poor and national child-care support fell victim to this backlash. Now fifty years after the New Deal and thirty years after the War on Poverty, persistent racial segregation undermines support for national social programs and impedes the nation's ability to guarantee basic social protection to all its citizens.

It has taken me more than six years to piece together this complex story. I began this project in 1988 when a National Science Foundation grant allowed me to spend a semester as a visiting professor at Harvard University. There I was privileged to co-teach a course on "Gender and the Welfare State" with Theda Skocpol. Our frequent discussions helped shape the direction of this book. I presented two of the chapters during my stay that semester and returned three years later to present another chapter.

When I was about halfway through the book, Robert Alford came to Florida State to present a talk. I volunteered to take him to breakfast before his departure. I was wondering how I would pass nearly three hours with a relative stranger. I needn't have worried. His penetrating questions forced me to articulate my own arguments and, more importantly, to think about whether my evidence really sustained those arguments. And that stranger became a friend. Since our first breakfast, we have maintained a dialogue by phone, letter, Bitnet, and conversations during his subsequent visits to Florida State. A generous man, he read the entire book and gave me more than twenty pages of comments.

My colleague, John Myles, has read nearly everything I have written for the past ten years. I have discussed every aspect of this book with him, from such major issues as developing the main arguments to the more mundane but important matter of thinking up a title. He read the entire book more than once and Chapter 1 at least five times. Many of the insights are his. The errors are mine.

For most of my career, I have admired Frances Fox Piven from afar. One of the great pleasures of this project has been the opportunity to get to know her personally. Fran read most of the chapters and provided detailed comments. I am grateful for her friendship and for her intellectual guidance.

Finally, I benefitted enormously from the comments of my close friend, Joane Nagel. She read the manuscript when I thought I was finished and told me I still had a lot of work to do. It wasn't what I wanted to hear, but she was right. Readers who find my central thesis clear can thank Joane. Those who don't can blame me.

Many other friends and colleagues have also contributed to this effort. I appreciate the comments of Bruce Bellingham, Leslie Innis, Marjorie Abend-Wein, Pamela Barnhouse Walters, Edward Berkowitz, G. William Domhoff, David James, Sonya Michel, James Max Fendrich, and Larry Isaac. James Orcutt took his skilled editorial pen to the introduction. I also benefited greatly from conversations with Patricia Yancey Martin, William Tuttle, and Ann Schofield and from the gracious hopitality of Courtney Cazden during my stay in Cambridge. I owe a particular debt to Oxford's reviewers, Joel Blau and Michael Katz. My graduate students, Debra Street and Catherine Fobes, read major portions of the book and told me bluntly where I was unclear. I also gained from presenting portions of the book in progress to the Indiana University Workshop in Political Economy and to the Florida State University Workshop in Political Economy. I thank the Mildred and Claude Pepper Foundation for funding a conference held at Florida State in March 1989, which allowed me to work through the ideas presented in Chapter 7.

As always I am in the debt of archivists. Much of the historical research was done at the National Archives. Aloha South has been my main contact at the National Archives since 1983. She has taken an active interest in my work, has advised me on where to find documents I'm interested in, and has prepared materials in advance so that I could begin working as soon as I arrived in Washington. Federal policy precludes me from giving her any token of appreciation, even a copy of the book. All I can do once again is say, "Thank you, Aloha."

I especially appreciate the support of my editor at Oxford University Press, David Roll. His interest and encouragement have been inspiring, and his helpful suggestions and comments have improved the manuscript immensely.

Last, but never least, I thank my husband, David. He followed me to Florida State so I could accept my present position, even though the move clearly enhanced my career more than his. He cared for our son while I was at Harvard, he has kept the household running for the past six years, and he tolerates our large and poorly behaved dog even though he hates pets. I dedicate this book to him.

Tallahassee   J.Q.
October 1993

CONTENTS

THE COLOR OF WELFARE

INTRODUCTION

The Equal Opportunity Welfare State

On April 29, 1992, three hours after an all-white jury acquitted four white police officers in the brutal beating of black motorist Rodney King, the streets of Los Angeles erupted in flames as enraged ghetto residents took to the streets. In the eyes of a stunned nation, and especially its black citizens, the verdict was incomprehensible. How could anyone discount the videotaped horror of King being clubbed and kicked 56 times in 81 seconds? Six days later, when the flames had been reduced to smoldering rubble, President George Bush declared that what had triggered the riot was not frustration at an unjust system, not the despair of grinding poverty and blocked opportunity, but rather the failure of the liberal social programs of the 1960s.

An astonished Bill Clinton, his Democratic rival in the 1992 presidential race, scornfully asked why Bush had to return to the 1960s to find a scapegoat when Republicans had held the presidency for 20 of the past 24 years. Weren't the causes nearer at hand? As inexplicable as Bush's comment seemed, it accurately captured the idea that during the 1960s social policy became linked to race in consequential ways. I agree. In this book, I show why I think this aspect of American welfare state development warrants reflection. That's what this book is about.

I have long been interested in how racial issues have shaped the American welfare state. In my previous book, *The Transformation of Old Age Security,* I explained why cotton production in the South hinged on racial oppression and showed how racial issues were an integral part of New Deal policymaking. I explained why southern congressmen refused to support any welfare programs that would place federal funds in the hands of black sharecroppers. And I argued that because Franklin Delano Roosevelt needed southern support to get his programs through Congress, he agreed to exclude African Americans from the core programs of the Social Security Act.

I was interested in these issues because they helped me understand why, compared to most European nations, the United States was slow to legislate national welfare programs and why it lacked programs other countries enacted as a matter of course—national health insurance, family allowances, or paid parental leave. At that time I was convinced that the limits had been imposed by the South. I also believed that by the 1960s the decline of cotton production had made race irrelevant to policymaking. I was wrong on both counts.

My subsequent research on Lyndon Johnson's War on Poverty has convinced me that race was still the defining feature of the American welfare state in the 1960s. To be sure, the solid South had not vanished entirely, but it was no longer the bastion of resistance it had been in the 1930s. Race had not, however, become less pivotal to policymaking. Indeed, it had moved from the periphery to the center. No longer a regional embarrassment, racial inequality had become a national malady. What the War on Poverty represented was a well-intended but poorly executed effort to treat that malady.

Racial inequality was brought north in the upheaval caused by a massive migration of blacks out of the South, then forced upon the American conscience by a civil rights movement that demanded equality of opportunity. This book is about how policymakers tried to respond to those demands by reconstructing the racial welfare state of the New Deal. It is also about how these attempts foundered on a deep racial divide. Finally it is about the price the nation still pays for failing to fully incorporate African Americans into the national community. That price is a welfare state that lacks the basic protection other industrialized nations take for granted.

The argument I develop here differs from other interpretations of the American welfare state. Several leading political theorists contend that the United States has been a welfare state laggard because of a tradition of liberal values, while others focus on the weakness of the working class or the peculiarities of American statemaking. I find all these interpretations partially correct; yet they pay insufficient attention to a key ingredient—race.

Theories of American Exceptionalism

According to a long-standing tradition in political theory, Americans oppose all forms of government intervention because of an encompassing liberal culture in which individual rights are sacred, private property is honored, and state authority is distrusted. For example, Roy Lubove argues that the strength of this liberal culture was responsible for the failure of most early proposals for national welfare legislation. A commitment to voluntarism "enabled groups of all kinds to exert an influence and seek their distinctive goals without resorting to the coercive powers of government." Gaston Rimlinger makes similar claims: "in the United States the commitment to individualism—to individual achievement and self-help—was much stronger than . . . in England. . . . The survival of the liberal tradition, therefore, was . . . stronger and the resistance to social protection more tenacious." [1]

The belief that liberal values weaken American support for social legislation remains a prominent argument. In *The Continental Divide*, Seymour Martin Lipset asks why the American welfare state is less advanced than that of its nearest neighbor, Canada. Lipset attributes the difference to an American ethos consisting of antistatism, individualism, populism, and egalitarianism. According to Lipset, "the evidence (that values explain the difference) is abundant and clear." [2]

The problem with explaining welfare state development in terms of liberal values is that Americans have tolerated major exceptions to that antigovernment ethos—notably an extensive Civil War pension system in the nineteenth century, numerous state-level welfare programs in the "Progressive Era" and the 1920s, and the persistent and ardent efforts by voluntary associations to win both public and private benefits.[3] If Americans are ideologically opposed to state intervention, then why have so many worked so steadfastly toward this end? In his book *The Democratic Wish,* James Morone attempts to resolve this seeming contradiction between distrust of government and the willingness of the people to endorse programs that expand it. He claims that Americans not only have a powerful dread of public power but also a yearning for a democratic ideal founded on consensus, citizenship participation, and a hearkening to the principle of community. Yet the search for direct democracy invariably builds bureaucracy until the suspicion of government materializes.[4] When it does, Americans revolt against the intrusion of the state, but new forms of government intervention remain as a permanent legacy to those communal ideals.

Morone's theory of a democratic wish explains exceptions to antistatism by recognizing that the American creed includes both a distrust of state authority and an ethos that esteems community. But his claim that the contradiction is between community and bureaucracy overlooks the fundamental tensions that have shaped the welfare state. These are tensions that reside in competing definitions of "liberty": liberty as the *positive* freedom to act on one's conscious purposes and to develop one's capacities versus the *negative* freedom from external constraints on speech, behavior, and association.[5] In the chapters that follow, I will demonstrate how efforts to use government intervention to extend positive liberties to African Americans clashed with the negative liberties of whites to dominate local politics, to control membership in their unions, and to choose their neighbors. I will then show how these conflicts established a racial fault line in public policy that subsequently provided the rationale for welfare state retrenchment.

A second prominent explanation of American exceptionalism is that a weak working class, or, more specifically, the absence of a labor-based political party, has impeded the formation of a more generous welfare state.[6] This argument is derived from comparative research, which suggests that the most advanced welfare states originated in countries where a labor-backed party fought for new social legislation. The American labor movement, by contrast, not only failed to initiate social welfare legislation, at times it actively opposed it.[7] Given the weakness of working class organizations, American capitalists have been able to impose limits on social policies that would interfere with private efforts in the market.[8]

I agree that the character of working-class politics has shaped the American welfare state. But I contend that the core issue is how working-class politics have been weakened by racial divisions, both in the workplace and in the community. In the workplace, trade union discrimination has been a barrier to labor organizing, while in the community, neighborhood segregation has impeded class solidarity.[9] These racial barriers to class solidarity originated in private practices but became embedded in the state when welfare programs were enacted. New Deal labor legislation that granted workers the right to organize also allowed trade unions to discriminate against blacks. New Deal housing policy reinforced neighborhood racial segregation. When issues of residential and workplace discrimination became pivotal to the civil rights movement, antipoverty programs dealing with labor policy and housing policy became involved in the struggle for equal opportunity. The use of the welfare state to pursue social justice aroused working-class resentment and undermined support for the welfare state.

Finally, polity-centered theorists argue that a unique sequence of democratization and industrialization impeded the development of the welfare state. Specifically, they claim that because the United States democratized before it industrialized, the American working class never coalesced around a struggle for basic democratic rights. Instead, working-class politics developed around political parties that dispensed favors, jobs, and other benefits through patronage systems. Patronage served as a substitute for broad, programmatic appeals to the electorate based on such issues as national welfare programs. Abuses of patronage further alienated voters from supporting any public provisions that might fuel graft and corruption.[10]

This account accurately describes early twentieth-century political history. What it neglects is a key piece of the puzzle: instead of being one of the first nations to democratize, the United States was among the last.[11] While the North was at least formally democratic in the twentieth century, African Americans in the South were denied basic democratic rights—the right to vote, the right to work without coercion, and the right to a modicum of economic security.[12] Not until the Civil Rights Act of 1964 prohibited discrimination in employment and the Voting Rights Act of 1965 banned practices that disfranchised African Americans was democracy formally bestowed on a nationwide basis. Still lacking was the right to economic security. The War on Poverty represented an effort to bypass the racially biased New Deal network of welfare agencies and to provide economic security to blacks. Thus, the United States did engage in a struggle for democracy. But it took place in the twentieth century, not the eighteenth, and the revolutionaries were African Americans, not the working class.

The Welfare State as a System of Stratification

Implicit in theories of welfare state origins are assumptions about outcomes. The most common assumption is that the welfare state can overcome divisions and create social solidarity. But as I noted above, the welfare state may also create or reinforce social cleavages. Gosta Esping-Anderson argues that both outcomes are possible: "The welfare state is not just a mechanism that intervenes in, and possibly corrects, the structure of inequality; it is, in its own right, a system of stratification. It is an active force in the ordering of social relations." Social programs, according to Esping-Anderson, "help determine the articulation of social solidarity, divisions of class and status differentiation."[13]

These outcomes can be classified according to three ideal types that Esping-Anderson calls "welfare state regimes": liberal, conservative and universal.[14] The first, the "liberal" regime, entails minimal intervention in the market. Rather, liberal regimes foster "the competitive individualism that the market supposedly cultivates."[15] To discourage welfare dependency that could undermine work incentives, liberal regimes rely on social programs with complex eligibility rules such as means-testing, residency requirements, and family responsibility clauses. In making welfare recipients a stigmatized class, liberal regimes promote social cleavages. "Conservative" regimes maintain traditional status relations by providing different programs for different class and status groups.[16] In nineteenth-century Germany, for example, Bismarck's pension plan constructed a myriad of social insurance schemes, each with its peculiar rules, finances, and benefit structures. Workers' pension plans were distinct from those of miners, civil servants' from those of other white collar employees.[17] Finally, "universal" regimes promote status equality by endowing all citizens with similar rights, regardless of social class or occupation. The prototype of the universal regime is Sweden's welfare state, which provides benefits to all as a right of citizenship. High-quality benefits cut across class and status cleavages and solidify support for the welfare state.

The United States is usually described as the classic "liberal" regime because of its heavy reliance on means-tested social-assistance programs. Means-testing supposedly draws rigid class distinctions between the deserving and undeserving poor. I argue, however, that the means-tested programs of the American welfare state had less to do with maintaining class divisions than with maintaining racial segregation. And I will demonstrate that the War on Poverty represented a different sort of regime entirely. The social programs enacted during the 1960s ushered in what I call an "equal-opportunity welfare state." By this I mean that the primary objective of social policy became the pursuit of equality of opportunity and that the resulting cleavages stemmed from racial conflict, not class conflict.

The equal-opportunity welfare state emerged from the collision between the War on Poverty and the civil rights movement. But its origins lay in the policy legacy of the New Deal. In tracing the historical linkages between these two great "bangs" of policymaking, I combine theories of American exceptionalism with theories of welfare state regimes. Instead of emphasizing the distinct characteristics of each period, I emphasize the dialectical interaction between them. I use the term "dialectical" because it eliminates any suggestion of a linear progression in the development of the welfare state. Rather it implies that policies enacted in one era contain inherent contradictions that must be faced in another. The dialectic in the New Deal was the contradiction between an American ethos that embodied ideals of liberty, justice, and equality of opportunity and a series of policy decisions that repudiated that ethos.[18] The War on Poverty represented an effort to resolve that contradiction.

Theda Skocpol and Ann Orloff say much the same thing, although neither uses the word "dialectical." They call these interactive processes "policy feedbacks." Skocpol argues that "tracing these feedback processes is crucial for explaining the further development of social provision after initial measures are instituted."[19] Policies have feedback effects both because they transform or expand the capacity of the state and because they "affect the social identities, goals, and capabilities of groups that subsequently struggle or ally in politics."[20] I agree—but with one crucial qualification. Whereas Skocpol and Orloff emphasize aspects of the policies themselves, I argue that the central element in national welfare policymaking is the social dynamic driving those policies. In the American case, that dynamic has been race. Race was a key component in battles over New Deal policymaking, and racial conflict over the New Deal legacy propelled the War on Poverty. The racial backlash unleashed in that turbulent decade left an enduring legacy that hampers efforts today to reconstruct America's cities and to complete its unfinished domestic agenda.

Race in the U.S. Welfare State

The process of democratization consists of the extension of civil, political, and social rights. Compared to European nations, the United States instituted social rights late in its history. The first national welfare programs were enacted during the New Deal. In Chapter 1 I explain how the New Deal not only extended social rights but also reinforced the racial divide in American democracy. I begin by showing how southern congressmen took advantage of their committee power to shape the structure of the Social Security Act of 1935. Instead of universal old age and unemployment insurance for workers, the act created two tiers of racially-segregated benefits. I also show how the New Deal legitimated racial discrimination in employment and housing. Finally, I argue that by 1960 that unwieldy legacy had become an impediment to effective government. The problem facing Lyndon Johnson was how to reorient the nation's social policy agenda so that it could eradicate, rather than reinforce, racial inequality. His solution—the War on Poverty—poured funds for education, housing, and community action into urban ghettos. These policies and resources helped fuel the struggle for equal opportunity.

Community action originated as a program to consolidate social services and improve service provision. In transferring resources directly from the federal government to the poor, it rapidly became an agent in the struggle for political rights. Chapter 2 shows how the civil rights movement absorbed community action programs, using them to redistribute political power from local machines to black organizations and black leaders. In Mississippi, community action created new patronage networks that bypassed the entrenched power structure and instead funneled federal money, and thus power, to African Americans. In Newark, civil rights leaders captured the local community action agency and used it to protest police brutality, the lack of access to city jobs, and an urban-renewal plan that would have destroyed the homes of many black families. Such outcomes weren't universal, however. In cities like Chicago, where entrenched political machines resisted any intrusion on local government rule, community action merely fueled the machine. Although community action increased the political participation of African Americans overall, often at the expense of white ethnic politicians, the ghettoization of urban politics reduced political support for funds to cities and limited what these new leaders could accomplish.

The War on Poverty also included programs for job training. At first these programs sought only to make poor, black men employable. However, as I demonstrate in Chapter 3, civil rights activists then demanded that trained apprentices be hired for the good construction jobs controlled by the skilled trade unions. When the unions refused to admit black men, federal officials devised a program of affirmative action that threatened the unions' most cherished prerogative: the right to select candidates for apprenticeships. In the ensuing struggle, the indifference of the skilled trades toward African Americans turned to open hostility, and their support for the Democratic party was converted into antagonism toward its policies. Affirmative action opened previously closed sectors of the labor market to minorities and women, yet job-training programs were mainly oriented to the poor and to minorities. This narrow focus diverted the government from adding a new tier to the welfare state—social programs for managing the labor market and supporting the needs of service sector workers.

As the civil rights movement turned north, it confronted angry residents of crowded, decaying urban ghettos whose housing needs became inextricably linked to the effort to end housing segregation. Federal officials tried to, but could not, adequately satisfy complex and sometimes competing demands for better housing for the poor, more housing for African Americans, and fair housing for all Americans. Chapter 4 demonstrates how angry suburban homeowners resisted opening their communities to minorities, forcing federal officials to retreat from a commitment to low-income housing and to back away from fair-housing laws.

By 1968 the civil rights movement was torn apart by internal conflicts, public opinion turned against demonstrations that triggered violence, and federal officials moved to quell riots and demonstrations with troops and guns rather than with social programs. In the 1968 election an alienated new majority bitterly rejected the party of the people, which had failed to deliver on its implicit social contract to incorporate the excluded and to support the working class. As the newly elected Republican president Richard Nixon ascended to office, he pondered how to reach the "forgotten Americans" and reconstruct an electoral majority around working-class disaffection. His solution was to drive out the "special interests" that had throttled urban policy and, instead, orient social programs toward the ascendant sunbelt and suburbia. As political analyst Kevin Phillips explains, the Republican party decided to offer "policies able to resurrect the vitality and commitment of Middle America—from sharecroppers and truckers to the alienated lower middle class." These policies would "do far more for the entire nation than the environmental manipulation, social boondoggling, community agitation and incendiary promises of the Nineteen-Sixties." [21]

Nixon's policies were not initially designed to roll back the welfare state. Indeed, he spent more for social programs than Johnson did. Rather, he recognized a unique political opportunity to woo an alienated working class by moving racial issues to the periphery of the welfare state. Reforming the welfare system by replacing Aid to Families with Dependent Children (AFDC) with a guaranteed annual income promised to solve a number of political problems in one package. As I show in Chapter 5, Nixon's proposed Family Assistance Plan (FAP) could have reduced the skyrocketing welfare rolls and appeased the working poor who resented the government's support of the nonworking poor. But a guaranteed annual income also seemed capable of resolving a problem that federal officials believed was responsible for urban unrest—the dissolution of the two-parent black family. By shoring up their incomes, the FAP might also have restored the ability of black men to become household heads. Despite such intriguing possibilities, the FAP threatened to undermine wages in the South and thus alienate the Republican party's most promising new constituency—white, southern Democrats, the target of Nixon's "southern strategy" in the 1968 election. But southern employers feared the benefits would eliminate incentives for low-wage workers. Even urban welfare mothers opposed the FAP for fear the new program would reduce their benefits. Realizing that the political costs of a guaranteed income were greater than any benefits it might bestow, Nixon rescinded his support for the revolutionary welfare reform proposal, and poor working mothers lost the chance for a social wage to subsidize their low-wage labor.

For women in the expanding service sector of the economy, the lack of secure and high quality child care hindered their ability to work. But a day-care program held unanticipated political hazards that might have splintered, rather than united, working-class support for the Republican party. In Chapter 6 I trace day care's inauspicious origins and untimely demise. When the federal government began paying for day care in 1962, it tied child care to AFDC. The Comprehensive Child Development Act of 1971 would have partially severed child care from welfare and made more children eligible for support. However, it only minimally served the middle class. As the day-care bill moved through Congress, it activated other political issues that had nothing to do with providing adequate child care. For civil rights activists the day-care bill presented an opportunity to revive the dying community action program; for social conservatives the bill threatened the traditional family by encouraging mothers to work. The program's broad-based, bipartisan supporters could not override the influence of the two extremes. When Nixon chose to cater to the nascent voice of the "Moral Majority," women lost a program that would have enhanced their right to work unhampered by the burden of child-care responsibilities.

Nixon finally found a spending program that nearly everyone agreed was worth improving—Social Security. Under Johnson, officials in the Social Security Administration proposed an increase in Social Security benefits and guaranteed automatic cost-of-living adjustments. In Chapter 7 I show how Nixon welcomed this chance to consolidate middle-class support around a welfare program, for few would deny that the elderly had the right to economic security after a lifetime of labor. I also take this opportunity to analyze debates about the merits of targeted programs in the context of our one universal program—Social Security.

During the 1960s, other nations added social benefits that allowed them to engage in long-range economic planning, move unemployed workers rapidly into new jobs, and provide the supports necessary for a postindustrial economy centered around a service sector comprised of female workers. The United States instead was waging a struggle to extend democratic rights. A tired and divided nation then turned away from its unfinished task. By 1970 Americans had social insurance for the elderly, the disabled, and the unemployed and health insurance for the elderly and the very poor but little else. Between 1935 and 1970 fundamental changes had occurred in the structure of the industrial working class. Whereas in the postwar era an unskilled male worker could expect to earn adequate wages to support a family and obtain the accoutrements of a middle-class lifestyle, by 1970 low-wage services were replacing the high-paying manufacturing base. During the same period the labor-force participation of women increased rapidly. Where a wife's income supplemented her husband's, working families were able to maintain their standards of living. But households headed by single women were almost guaranteed a life below the poverty line.

The War on Poverty did little for the working poor and for women in the expanding service sector. The long-term legacy of coupling social policy to racial issues has diminished America's ability to stem the decline of the inner cities and to protect the family, whether it consists of two working parents or of single mothers. The failure to expand the welfare state to meet the needs of the new working class is linked to the failure to dissolve the urban ghetto. In Chapter 8 I argue that the nation must devise programs to protect the family, whatever its form, but that racial segregation provides an unstable foundation for a successful welfare state.

Finally, in Chapter 9 I reexamine theories of American exceptionalism. I argue that the motor of American history has been the continual reconfiguration of racial inequality in the nation's social, political, and economic institutions. It is this characteristic that has impeded the development of a comprehensive welfare state. I conclude that overcoming racial inequality remains America's unfinished task.

ONE

Unfinished Democracy

According to the British sociologist T. H. Marshall, democratization has proceeded in three stages with the granting of civil, political, and finally social rights. In Europe the struggle for civil rights emerged out of a feudal heritage where serfdom locked workers to the land. The transition from servile to free labor introduced the notion of citizenship as the right to pursue the occupation of one's choice freely, without compulsion, subject only to requirements for training. By the beginning of the nineteenth century, the principle of individual economic "freedom" was accepted as axiomatic.[1]

Throughout the nineteenth century in most European nations, only monarchs, bureaucrats, and aristocrats could vote. Limited political rights were granted to some men on the basis of property ownership and education. These constitutional monarchies were gradually replaced by representative governments and popular sovereignty. Political democratization in the form of universal suffrage advanced through the dismantling of restrictions on voting based on property ownership or literacy. By 1920 adult males had full voting rights in seventeen nations, while nine had given women the vote.[2] Political rights not only meant the right to vote but also the right to a voice in a collective process of decision-making.[3]

The third phase of democratization began in the late nineteenth century with the construction of national welfare states. Programs of social protection granted social rights: "the right to a modicum of economic welfare and security, the right to share to the full in the social heritage and to live the life of a civilized being according to the standards prevailing in the society."[4] Much of the industrialized world has instituted three kinds of social rights. Some protect the poor against the exigencies of the capitalist marketplace. They include programs to compensate workers against losses for injuries on the job, against unemployment, and against old age. Others, geared to an economy based on mass production, not only provide income security for the working class but also stable product markets for mass-produced goods.[5] Examples include old-age insurance, family allowances, and national health insurance. Finally, social rights stabilize the labor supply, especially among female workers in the expanding service sector.[6] These include job training and employment-referral systems, day-care provisions, paid parental leave, and full-employment policies.

The combination of civil, political, and social rights is the foundation of democracy. While other nations added these rights gradually over centuries, the United States pursued an idiosyncratic path. That path began when the first principles of civil rights—the belief in equality and the right to liberty—were enshrined in the Bill of Rights and the Declaration of Independence. Americans, Thomas Jefferson wrote, had inherent and inalienable rights to "life, liberty and the pursuit of happiness."[7] From the first moments of the birth of the fledgling state, however, practice compromised principles. In theory, the concept of inalienable rights meant free labor markets and the absence of servile, or unfree, labor. In practice, lovers of freedom tolerated its total suppression among slaves, who had no claim on rights and whose masters owned both their labor and their progeny.

Political democracy was an extension of civil liberty, and most Americans enjoyed it early. Even as colonists under British rule, when the franchise was based on property ownership, between 50 and 80 percent of white males qualified to vote.[8] At the end of the revolutionary period, many states extended male suffrage by moving from property qualifications to tax qualifications for voting. By 1840 most adult white males could vote, and voter turnout ranged from 68 to 98 percent. Government also became more directly representative of the people who participated through mass political parties, rotation of political leaders, local community rule, and the choosing of presidential candidates by party conventions instead of wealthy elites.[9] But democracy remained incomplete. Women couldn't vote until 1920, and, of course, slaves were denied even the most rudimentary privileges of citizenship.

Though precocious in extending civil and political rights to white males, America lagged behind Europe in developing social rights through a national welfare state. Until 1935 the United States had no national social programs. Instead, it had only scattered, meagerly funded, state-level programs of workers' compensation, old-age pensions, and mothers' pensions that left decisions about eligibility to the discretion of local welfare authorities.[10] Not until the Depression challenged the foundations of this "rugged individualism" did the concept of social rights emerge as a shared ideal. When that finally happened, the presence of a "nation" within a nation, that is, of the South as a politically and economically distinct entity, imposed limits on what could be done. Instead of a "universal" welfare state that could create solidarity among workers, the New Deal welfare state instituted a regime that reinforced racial inequality.

Creating the Racial Welfare State Regime

Franklin Delano Roosevelt took office in 1932 with a mandate to inaugurate a new era in government intervention. The cornerstone of his New Deal was the Social Security Act of 1935, which provided old-age insurance and unemployment compensation for the industrial labor force. Under the old-age insurance program, workers paid payroll taxes of 1 percent on the first $3,000 earned, matched by their employers, in exchange for a $15 pension upon retirement. Under the unemployment insurance program, states levied a payroll tax on employers to protect workers against downturns in the business cycle. Although the unemployment program was technically voluntary, generous tax credits that offset most of the payroll tax provided incentives to employers to participate.[11]

The Social Security Act also included two means-tested social

assistance programs, Aid to Dependent Children and Old Age Assistance, in which state expenditures were matched by federal
funds. These programs provided minimal support to those outside
the wage labor pool. Old-age assistance paid eligible elderly men
and women a maximum grant of $30 a month, though most
states, especially those in the South, paid less. Aid to Dependent
Children was restricted to single-parent families and paid benefits
only to children.

The Social Security Act laid the groundwork for a national
welfare state and established some benefits as an earned right.
Through such measures, the New Deal liberalism of the Democratic party came to mean active, positive intervention for the public good. Public support was high for programs that protected the
many against the abuses of the few and taxed the few for the
benefit of the many.

Government intervention did not extend to support for civil
rights, however, as Roosevelt sought to stabilize his unwieldy coalition of northern workers and white southerners by refusing to
back legislation abolishing lynching or poll taxes and by weaving
racial inequality into his new welfare state.[12] This was accomplished by excluding agricultural workers and domestic servants
from both old-age insurance and unemployment compensation
and by failing to provide national standards for unemployment
compensation.[13] These omissions were not random. Rather, they
reflected a compromise reached with southern Democrats over the
structure of the welfare state.

The Repression of Rights

By 1935 the North was industrialized and democratic. It had two
active political parties, and its citizenry had full civil and political
rights. The South was neither industrialized nor democratic. Its
economy was driven by cotton production, which flourished
through a sharecropping system that locked tenants—both black
and white—to the land. Sharecropping was a system of servitude
that denied to African Americans the first civil right, "the right to
follow the occupation of one's choice in the place of one's
choice."[14] Sharecropping operated without cash. Planters loaned
money to croppers for seeds, equipment, food, and rent. Often at

year's end a cropper family owed more than it had earned in the entire year. Debt kept sharecroppers nearly enslaved.

Politically, the South was an oligarchy. Such measures as poll taxes and literacy tests introduced at the end of the nineteenth century had not only disfranchised African Americans but most poor whites as well. Disfranchisement reduced opposition to the Democratic party majority and allowed one-party politics to reign. With no competition for elective office, southern Democrats earned seniority in Congress and thus were able to control key committees in the House and Senate.[15] This power allowed them to exert a negative, controlling influence on national politics.

Although Roosevelt's electoral victory did not hinge on southern support, he needed southern Congressmen to move his programs past the key House and Senate committees. They opposed any program that would grant cash directly to black workers, because direct cash could undermine the entire foundation of the plantation economy. In 1935 more than three-quarters of African Americans still lived in the South. Most sharecropped. Those not sharecropping worked as day laborers when planters needed extra hands at picking time. The going rate for day laborers was two dollars per one hundred pounds of cotton, a day's labor for a strong worker. Outside the cotton fields black women worked as maids, earning perhaps $2.50 a week.[16] Federal old-age insurance paid directly to retired black men and women, even at the meager sum of $15 a month, would provide more cash than a cropper family might see in a year.

Because of southern opposition, agricultural workers and domestic servants—most black men and women—were left out of the core programs of the Social Security Act. Instead they were relegated to the social-assistance programs, where local welfare authorities could determine benefit levels and set eligibility rules. Even in these programs, southern Congressmen vigilantly defended "states' rights." They demanded that two clauses be removed from the old-age assistance legislation, one compelling the states to furnish assistance at "a reasonable subsistence compatible with decency and health" and another requiring states to designate a single state authority to administer the plan. Southerners simply would not allow the federal government to dictate standards or set benefit levels. They sought control over any social program that might threaten white domination, so precariously balanced on cotton production.

The unemployment insurance program also perpetuated racial inequality by charging Employment Service offices with implementing the legislation. Established in 1933, the U.S. Employment Service was a federal–state organization that provided job placement for the unemployed. In administering unemployment insurance, however, Employment Service offices devoted little attention to job placement. Instead, they spent most of their time figuring benefits. When they did connect workers to jobs, they did so in a highly prejudiced manner, either excluding minority clients entirely or offering them the most menial, low-paying jobs.[17]

Racial inequality was not confined to the South, however. By legitimating discrimination in work and housing, New Deal legislation reinforced racial barriers in other parts of the nation. Skilled craft workers had been organized into unions since the nineteenth century. Most became members of the American Federation of Labor (AFL) and its affiliates. But unskilled workers in the expanding mass-production industries—iron and steel, autos, rubber, and meat packing—had fought a losing battle against employers over the right to organize. When the National Labor Relations Act, or Wagner Act, of 1935 granted workers the right to organize unions and bargain collectively with employers, unskilled workers clamored to join unions.[18] The issue of race contributed to the already fractious relationship between them and their skilled comrades.

Throughout its history, the AFL had discriminated against black workers. Some affiliates, like the Brotherhood of Railway Carmen, banned black workers by ritual or constitutional provision. Others granted black unions separate charters or established segregated locals as second-class members under the supervision of white workers. Only the United Mine Workers, an AFL affiliate comprised mainly of unskilled workers, had integrated unions.[19]

On November 9, 1935, unskilled workers walked out of the AFL convention and founded the Committee for Industrial Organization (CIO). Among their grievances was the refusal of the AFL to address union discrimination. They knew that industrial unionism required inter-racial cooperation. After all, African Americans comprised more than 18 percent of iron and steel workers, 68 percent of tobacco workers, 40 percent of meat packers, and 9 percent of coal miners. Without their participation, any union of the unskilled would fail. From its inception the CIO opened its doors to black workers on an equal basis.[20] Following a massive organizing campaign, by 1940 the CIO had more than 500,000 black members.

Black leaders had little enthusiasm for the Wagner Act, because it legalized closed shops. Since black workers were excluded from most skilled trade unions, they feared that the closed shop provision would permanently lock them out of these jobs. The National Association for the Advancement of Colored People (NAACP) tried to have a clause barring discrimination by labor unions written into the Wagner Act, but the AFL refused to support the legislation if the clause was included. The final legislation permitted labor organizations to exclude African Americans, denied the status of "employee" to black workers engaged in strike breaking, and permitted the establishment of separate, racially segregated unions.[21] From 1936 to 1955, when the AFL merged with the CIO, the skilled trade unions maintained policies of racial exclusion and segregation with the tacit approval of the federal government.

The New Deal also preserved and reinforced patterns of racial segregation through housing policy. The government first intervened in the housing market to restore the confidence of lenders in average homebuyers, thousands of whom had defaulted on loans. The National Housing Act of 1934 sought both to stimulate a depressed economy and to calm the fears of bankers. It authorized low down payments, set up extended loan maturities (as long as 40 years), and regulated interest rates so that working-class families could afford mortgage payments. The Act also established the Federal Housing Administration (FHA) to insure lending institutions against loan defaults. The FHA was to behave like a conservative bank, only insuring mortgages that were "economically sound." In practice, economic soundness was translated into "redlining": a red line was literally drawn around areas of cities considered risky for economic *or* racial reasons. Redlining meant that most black families were ineligible for federally insured loans. Until 1949 the FHA also encouraged the use of restrictive covenants banning African Americans from given neighborhoods and refused to insure mortgages in integrated neighborhoods.[22] Thanks to FHA, no bank would insure loans in the ghetto, and few African Americans could live outside it.

What housing the federal government did provide to African Americans was racially segregated. The Housing Act of 1937 allowed local housing authorities to use proceeds from tax-free bonds to build public housing projects. Federal subsidies would pay the difference between the housing costs and what tenants could afford to pay in rent.[23] From the start, public housing authorities located new projects in racially segregated neighborhoods and selected tenants by race.[24] Thus, federal housing provided secure loans for the middle class and subsidized rentals in public housing for the poor. The working poor, much of black America but also white families outside the industrial labor force, were left out in the cold.

The New Deal thus united the industrial working class around a party that provided income security against job loss, injury, and old age to working men and their families. At the same time it left intact—indeed reinforced—the rigid color line. The extension of social rights thus had paradoxical consequences for racial equality. In the words of T. H. Marshall, it granted a modicum of economic welfare and security to whites while denying to others the full perquisites of democracy.[25]

Destabilizing the New Deal

The New Deal also encouraged farmers to replace workers with machines through farm subsidies and other benefits to agriculture. Many farmers used their subsidies to purchase machinery, and increased reliance on machines reduced labor needs. Farm subsidies were thus passed on to black sharecroppers in the form of evictions.[26] Throughout the 1940s evicted sharecroppers migrated in large numbers to northern cities. In 1940 77 percent of African Americans lived in the South; by 1970 only 53 percent still did.[27] Their departure toppled the political and economic structure underlying the cotton South and dismantled the system of tenancy that had given southern planters a stranglehold on black labor.

The presence of black migrants in northern cities moved racial inequality from the periphery to the center of national politics.

The nation as a whole now confronted the puzzle of incorporating African Americans into the national political economy. At first political analysts believed that this incorporation would occur naturally. In the past large-scale population shifts had not only created political upheavals but also new opportunities. Perhaps African Americans, like other newly arrived immigrant groups, would use these opportunities to move up the equal-opportunity ladder and out of the inner cities.[28] The problem was that racial segregation had limited opportunities, and after more than a century of deprivation, black people were unwilling to wait further for their share of the American dream. While elsewhere the extension of democratic rights had proceeded fitfully over centuries, in the United States it took less than a decade to complete the process of democratization for those on the wrong side of the color line. First across the South and then sweeping the North, a social movement arose demanding that the nation immediately grant to all its citizens the basic perquisites of a democratic society—civil, political, and social rights.

The Search for Rights

The civil rights movement began in the 1950s with an assault on the South's racial order. The first victory came in 1954 when the Supreme Court, in the Brown vs. Topeka decision, struck down the doctrine of "separate but equal" and ordered the schools to integrate. Instead of abiding by the law, however, southern attorney generals advocated that desegregation proceed "with all deliberate speed," and the Supreme Court agreed that local school authorities could determine the pace.[29] Whites not only mobilized against school desegregation officially through legal action but also through a reign of terror that included economic coercion, violence, and murder. But white resistance failed to dampen the ardor of those inspired by the promise of equal opportunity. In December 1955, Rosa Parks, a black woman from Montgomery, Alabama, refused to move to the back of a bus. Her subsequent arrest was the catalyst in a year-long battle in which the black population took on the entire white power structure and desegregated the public transportation system.[30]

Martin Luther King emerged from that struggle as the most important black leader in America, and the organization he led, the Southern Christian Leadership Conference (SCLC), became a powerful locus of mobilization for the civil rights movement. The SCLC adopted Ghandi's strategy of nonviolent protest, which became an effective political weapon in the struggle for rights. By pitting peaceful demonstrators against often violent opponents, nonviolence turned northern whites against this egregious violation of American values.

College students then formed their own organization, the Student Nonviolent Coordinating Committee (SNCC), which rapidly displaced the SCLC as the most militant.[31] Beginning with a lunch counter protest in the Woolworth's in Greensboro, North Carolina, students mounted a series of sit-in campaigns in 1960 and 1961. The effort to integrate lunch counters expanded to include all public accommodations—restaurants, theaters, department stores, hotels, and hospitals.[32] SNCC's only rival for most militant was the Congress on Racial Equality, or CORE, a northern-based civil rights organization. Both SNCC and CORE members willingly exposed themselves to dangers other organizations avoided and were burned, beaten, and murdered for their efforts. From buses to bathrooms, the civil rights movement defied every aspect of the Jim Crow laws that sustained racial inequality and made a mockery of democracy.

The civil rights movement brought to the forefront of national politics not only the brutality of racial oppression but also the instability of the New Deal compromise. The sacrifice of African Americans for the support of southern Democrats had ensnared the party in an unresolvable conflict. In 1935 black voters were irrelevant to Democratic party fortunes. By 1960 the pattern of black settlement had altered the political landscape. The black migration was not so much a general exodus from the South as a selective move out of areas where the political participation of African Americans was most limited. Thus, it was also a move from no voting to voting. From 1940 to 1960, 87 percent of the migrants settled in seven northern industrial states: New York, New Jersey, Pennsylvania, Ohio, California, Illinois, and Michigan. Because of the population-based, proportional system of voting and the winner-take-all provision, these states held the key to electoral success in presidential contests.[33] In that year's presidential election, black voters gave John Kennedy the winning margin in New Jersey, Michigan, Illinois, Texas, and South Carolina. Had Kennedy lost these states, Richard Nixon would have won the election.[34] In becoming a powerful electoral force in national elections, the southern migrants posed a political problem for the Democrats. How could the Jim Crow party of the solid South woo black voters without alienating white southerners? In fact, it could not.

President Kennedy could not confront this problem directly, for the Democrats needed the South. So he procrastinated on civil rights even as the movement gained momentum. In 1961 CORE joined with SNCC and the SCLC to organize "freedom rides" into the deep South. The riders would travel together, eat together, and use the whites-only restrooms. As the nightly news brought the sight of freedom riders being beaten and arrested into living rooms across the nation, the federal government sat back and did nothing. Indeed, federal officials attempted to halt one freedom ride. Only when the public, shocked by the attacks on the nonviolent freedom riders, demanded that the government protect them did Kennedy mobilize the National Guard.

What seemed by now the only viable solution was legislation to force the South to do what it refused to do voluntarily. Still, Kennedy vacillated. Instead, he initiated two limited programs for the poor. In 1961 he established the Area Redevelopment Agency to increase employment in depressed areas like Appalachia by providing loans and subsidies to small businesses. The following year he supported the Manpower Development and Training Act to retrain workers displaced by automation.[35] Such measures did not even begin to address the dilemma of incorporating African Americans. In fact, they mostly benefitted whites. Then in 1962 Kennedy asked his Council of Economic Advisors to suggest more comprehensive ways to address the poverty problem.

Scholars have since debated what the attention to poverty signified. Why poverty, Robert Haveman asks, when "there was no organized interest group demanding new programs for the poor . . . there was no history of party platforms that had assigned this problem particularly high priority, and there was no apparent surge of public opinion designating poverty to be the central domestic problem."[36] The answer of many social scientists is that

Kennedy's concern with poverty was an oblique response to the civil rights movement. Frances Fox Piven and Richard Cloward, for example, argue that the focus on poverty was Kennedy's way out, a means of evading forceful action on civil rights while maintaining the political support of African Americans who had given him his majority in the 1960 election.[37] Further, the civil rights movement had shifted from integration to economic problems just as Kennedy launched his wave of rhetoric about economic injustice.[38]

Margaret Weir disagrees. She argues that the antipoverty programs had no link to the civil rights movement or to the electoral concerns of Democrats over the black vote. She finds no evidence "that an attack on poverty was conceived as a political strategy for strengthening black loyalty to the Democratic party or that it was even initially intended to focus on African Americans. Instead, the president's vague request . . . appears to have been motivated by a more general desire to devise some policies that would give his administration a stamp of originality and energy."[39]

This debate about origins, which has dominated much of the literature, matters little. In fact, it obscures the crucial linkages that unquestionably did develop between the War on Poverty and the civil rights movement once the programs began operating. Programs targeted to the poor, and especially the black poor, were rapidly subsumed by the civil rights movement. As a result, the more traditional objectives of social policy to provide income stability and guarantee product markets became secondary to the grander struggle for racial justice. Instead of instituting a new group of social programs to stabilize the labor supply of a service-driven economy and support a labor force increasingly comprised of women, the welfare state became a vehicle of equal opportunity.

The Equal-Opportunity Welfare State

Kennedy's antipoverty program had barely begun when he was assassinated. No one will ever know whether he would have pursued the course he set, a minor program aimed at poor whites, or whether history would have propelled him instead along the path his successor, Lyndon Baines Johnson, took. What we do know is that when Johnson ascended suddenly to the presidency he began steering the ship of state toward the familiar liberalism of Roosevelt's New Deal, the liberalism of government intervention to eliminate social ills, but also toward an unknown destination as the federal government sought to end racial discrimination.

Under Johnson's leadership, in 1964 Congress passed the Civil Rights Act and then in 1965 the Voting Rights Act. The Civil Rights Act, which barred discrimination on the basis of race, color, religion, sex, or national origin, destroyed Jim Crow in public accommodations and helped end a decade of paralysis in school desegregation. The Voting Rights Act, which made illegal discriminatory voting regulations, rapidly enfranchised both the mass of southern African Americans and, ironically, a greater number of southern whites—ironically because southern whites would later become an important constituency in the rise of the New Right and the backlash against Johnson's "Great Society." [40]

These victories eliminated barriers to integration and to voting in the South but did little for the African Americans, legally free but unequal, living in squalor in urban ghettos. For those relegated to decrepit housing in the worst sections of cities, forced to send their children to inferior schools, and locked out of opportunities for jobs with upward mobility, the civil rights movement now demanded protection from want and some guarantee of economic security—the social rights of full citizenship. The time had come for the government to provide adequate housing for those displaced by urban renewal; adequate income for mothers raising young children alone; access to jobs in retail establishments, banks, and other businesses; and entry into the white building trades unions, which controlled the good construction jobs. What could dissolve these more intransigent barriers to equality? No one knew. And as this uncertainty became apparent, the cities erupted in explosive upheavals that drove home the message that legal emancipation was an insufficient response to the quest for equality.

Meeting demands for full democratic rights meant confronting the New Deal compromise, which had forsaken racial equality for a stable political coalition between the industrial working class and the South. That coalition was rapidly disintegrating. When the civil rights effort focused on discrimination in the South, the majority of northern whites supported it. In 1964 68 percent of northern whites supported the administration's effort to integrate the South. When the civil rights movement moved North, support waned. By 1966 52 percent of northern whites believed the government was pushing integration too fast.[41]

How could the federal government unify the nation when its major social programs were designed to maintain racial cleavages? President Johnson seemed to have an answer when, on January 8, 1964, in his State of the Union message, he promised to wage an "unconditional war on poverty."[42] Less than eight months later, on August 20, Congress passed the Economic Opportunity Act, an ambitious group of programs for job training, community action, health care, housing, and education. Johnson began preparing his antipoverty programs just months after the 1963 march on Washington where African Americans dramatically proclaimed the need for freedom (the vote) and jobs. The bill passed during the summer of 1964, as urban riots swept across Harlem, Bedford Stuyvesant, Rochester, Jersey City, Paterson, Elizabeth, Chicago, and Philadelphia.[43] Perhaps the timing was merely coincidental. However, the structure of the War on Poverty suggests otherwise.

The social institutions created by the New Deal were incapable of incorporating African Americans into the national political economy.[44] Rather the New Deal legacy could only frustrate the antipoverty effort with its network of local welfare offices, Employment Services, and housing authorities that stretched from governors' offices down into even the most remote rural townships, creating physical and social barriers to efforts to help blacks. An alternative model did exist, however, in two private projects funded by the Ford Foundation: the Grey Areas project and Mobilization for Youth. Both projects emphasized control by local community organizations, and both were founded on the belief that "the first task of community action was to enable (the poor) to assert themselves by placing the means to reform in their own hands."[45] Only by releasing social programs from the old-line agencies could the apathy and resistance existing institutions generated be transcended.[46]

Johnson's task was not merely to extend the New Deal by expanding social rights but also to eliminate the barriers to equality of opportunity it had created. Community action could circumvent the entrenched bureaucracies, which were "too preoccupied with day to day operations" and consumed by an "inertia dedicated to preserving the status quo."[47] Johnson made community action the centerpiece of his War on Poverty. Directed by a new agency, the Office of Economic Opportunity, community action would bypass old-line agencies and provide services directly to the poor. Its manpower programs operated outside the Department of Labor. Its Headstart program operated outside the established educational system. Johnson also created a new Department of Housing and Urban Development to consolidate the unwieldy hodgepodge of federal housing agencies.

While the New Deal had excluded African Americans, the War on Poverty would favor them. While the New Deal had conspired with southern elites to deny political and social rights to African Americans, the War on Poverty would integrate them into local politics, local job markets, and local housing markets. If the plan was not laid out so succinctly at the start, it was the *modus operandi* by the time the programs began running. As Kennedy's advisor Adam Yarmolinsky recalled: "We were busy telling people it *wasn't* just racial because we thought it'd be easier to sell that way, and we thought it was less racial than it turned out to be."[48]

While the War on Poverty began as a top-down effort, civil rights activists rapidly seized the opportunity that the local initiatives had created, pushing the Great Society mandate one step further. The War on Poverty would do more than eliminate impediments. It would extend equal opportunity to African Americans and complete the task of fully democratizing American society.

TWO

Fostering Political Participation

The Economic Opportunity Act of 1964, the keystone of Johnson's War on Poverty, established new programs for community action and created a new agency, the Office of Economic Opportunity, to oversee them. OEO, in turn, delegated responsibility for administering community action to Community Action Agencies (CAAs). By issuing grants directly to public or private nonprofit organizations, OEO transcended the New Deal legacy of local welfare offices and county officials. In many cities local CAAs established neighborhood health centers, emergency food and medical services, job and literacy training, alcoholic counseling, drug rehabilitation, and migrant workers' assistance. But community action also fed resources into local civil rights organizations, who used these resources to pursue the struggle for racial equality. As community action became an agent of equal political opportunity, mayors and city commissions found their authority usurped by upstart civil rights groups with massive federal resources. Not surprisingly, they rebelled against a program that empowered the poor at the expense of those who, after all, formed the backbone of the Democratic party. The Johnson administration could not afford to ignore their complaints, and, in response, retreated from the program that could have done much to improve the quality of life in inner cities.

Defining a Mission

When OEO was established initially its mission was only vaguely defined: to coordinate the antipoverty effort. But Sergeant Shriver, whom President Johnson appointed to run the agency, decided to operate the antipoverty programs within his own agency rather than merely coordinate the actions of other agencies. This decision dramatically altered the antipoverty agenda. It meant that there now existed a new federal agency that had the money to create new programs for the poor, the authority to decide who received grants for these programs, and the ability to totally bypass existing welfare authorities. Not surprisingly, this decision also put OEO at odds with heads of other federal agencies, who resented Shriver's independence and sought to run the programs themselves. Secretary of Labor Willard Wirtz, in particular, had proposed his own antipoverty agenda centered around a job-creation strategy. Hostile to the new agency from the start, Wirtz refused to supply OEO with any data on overlapping programs.[1]

To ease conflicts that made OEO a target of resentment even before it spent its first dollar, Shriver agreed to turn over the administration of the job-training programs to the Department of Labor, although OEO technically retained authority over them. An old-line agency, the Department of Labor had institutional linkages to state and local governments through its Employment Service offices. Shriver also promised the Department of Health, Education and Welfare that it could run all education programs for older children. OEO kept the Job Corps, literacy training for adults, Headstart, and community action, always looking over its shoulder for fear "that the Labor Department would try to co-opt the program, or that Defense would take it over."[2] The decision to share some operations with existing agencies, while politically practical, compromised OEO's ability to circumvent the New Deal administrative state.

Once administrative lines of authority were clarified, OEO had to define the objectives of community action. Created to serve a constituency of the poor, OEO could never have ended poverty in

America. The agency only received $800 million from Congress for its first year of operation, less than New York's education budget. Further, from the start any suggestions that poverty might best be ended by redistributing wealth from rich to poor or by fundamentally restructuring the economy were rejected.[3]

If OEO could not eliminate poverty, what, then, could its mission be? Policymakers planning community action had several visions of what it could accomplish. The most conservative among them hoped to improve coordination among the melange of public and private agencies delivering services to the poor. In their view, community action had three key elements: (1) it would operate at ground level in the sense that community action agencies would be located in poor neighborhoods, not in downtown offices; (2) it would coordinate a variety of services so that poor people wouldn't have to spend half their lives shuffling from one welfare office to another; and (3) it would base its activities on what poor people thought they wanted, not on what government bureaucrats thought they needed.[4]

These objectives could be achieved through "maximum feasible participation" of the "poor . . . in the development and operations of the separate programs . . . intended to help them."[5] But as the cities dutifully prepared their programs, mayors had their own ideas about who should run community action. Instead of appointing the poor, they filled the poverty boards with prominent locals. Immediately, the complaints began pouring in. Civil rights organizations charged that they had not been consulted. Mayors, in turn, responded that the term "maximum feasible participation" was vague and thus difficult to implement. In an attempt to clarify the concept, OEO now specified it meant that the poor were to participate "either on the governing body or on a policy advisory committee" or have "at least one representative selected from each of the neighborhoods" involved. By the spring of 1965, maximum feasible participation meant that at least one-third of the representatives on local boards had to be poor people elected by the poor.[6]

What was still unclear was what the participation of the poor would accomplish. The most conservative interpretation derived from a "culture of poverty" thesis. The term "culture of poverty" was coined by the anthropologist Oscar Lewis, whose research in

Mexico, Puerto Rico, and New York convinced him that the cultural environment of the poor fostered self-defeating attitudes and behaviors. These included a strong present time orientation, a sense of fatalism and resignation, the belief in male superiority, improper speech patterns, incompetence in patterns of middle-class interpersonal communication, and low aspirations.[7] Such traits imbued the poor with a sense of inferiority and conditioned them to accept their position in society, to feel they deserved no better. Politically, these attitudes were displayed through a passive acceptance of the status quo. As Richard Zweigenhaft and G. William Domhoff explain: "When everyday people conclude that they are unfit to govern and that they in some sense deserve their subordinate position in the power structure, in effect a hidden social–psychological dialectic operates between the dominant upper class and the subordinate underclasses."[8] Only by overcoming these social–psychological barriers could those sufficiently motivated move up the class ladder of the equal-opportunity society.

When linked to community action, this vision of how poverty is perpetuated implied the state should become an agent of socialization. If the poor cannot properly prepare their children for school, the government should prepare them; if the poor have bad work habits, the government should teach them how to dress properly and get to work on time; if the poor lack basic skills needed in the job market—the ability to read or to add numbers— the government should provide basic skills.

Lewis's thesis also contained a more radical vision of what political participation meant: the idea that poverty resulted from "the lack of effective participation and integration of the poor in the major institutions of the larger society" and from the inability of the poor to form organizations of their own.[9] Only when the poor joined social movements or trade unions could they overcome apathy, for "any movement . . . which organizes and gives hope to the poor and effectively promotes solidarity and a sense of identification with larger groups, destroys the psychological and social core of the culture of poverty."[10] Empowerment in this version comes not from social–psychological transformation but rather from the raising of class consciousness.[11] In this more radical vision social policy does not change the character of the poor so that they can move into the middle class but rather alters the distribution of political resources.

As community action programs began operating, they vacillated between these interpretations of the "culture of poverty." Community action originated during a period when public consensus regarding the legitimacy of racial integration was emerging. When community action programs fostered what most people saw as legitimate goals, such as forcing southerners to abandon practices that contradicted fundamental democratic principles, they were applauded. This occurred in Mississippi where civil rights activists confronted an intransigent white power structure. Community action there meant helping the poor overcome the social–psychological barriers that engendered defeatism and granting them the opportunity to participate in a segregated society.

In other programs "maximum feasible participation" became more than a bootstrap up; it became a vehicle for organizing the poor so they could become a part of the power structure and challenge the status quo.[12] In Newark, radical activists seized control of the community action programs. They demanded that local authorities give the black community its fair share of resources and turn political control of local government structures over to the black majority. There community action became entwined in the complex issues of the urban ghetto. As a program able to bypass entrenched local interests, it became a force for extending political rights.

Extending Political Rights: Mississippi

OEO operated community action programs in all southern states, but it focused its activities most intensely on Mississippi. Mississippi held both pragmatic and symbolic significance for the idealistic staff at OEO. OEO's official mission was to end poverty in America, and nowhere were the lives of the poor more hopeless nor their political poverty greater than in Mississippi where rates of poverty and illiteracy were the highest in the nation, especially among African Americans. In 1960 median annual family income for the entire state was $2,884. Black family income averaged less than $2,000 in all but six counties. Whites on average completed ten years of school; African Americans completed five.[13]

Mississippi was also most unwilling to let African Americans participate in politics and to share in the admittedly meager resources. As late as 1963, Mississippi stood alone among southern states in having no public school desegregation, and its black voter registration was the lowest in the country.[14] In 1955 there were only ninety registered black voters in three black-belt Mississippi counties.[15] To deter black voter registration the state constitution was amended in 1960 to require that a potential voter be "of good moral character" and to grant local registrars the right to decide who qualified as morally upright. When the Voting Rights Act of 1965 was passed, Mississippi still had the lowest percent of the black voting-age population registered to vote (6.7 percent).

African Americans were kept subservient by the "local racial state," the institutionalized discriminatory features of the South, "where racial criteria [were] used to assign unequal rights to different races."[16] The local racial state hinged on a sharecropping system, which guaranteed planters control over a subservient, black labor force. Although sharecropping declined significantly throughout the South after World War II, it remained deeply embedded in the Mississippi Delta until well into the 1960s.[17]

The local racial state consisted of several layers of government, beginning with local sheriff and police departments, welfare authorities, and county Boards of Supervisors and extending to the governor and congressional representatives.[18] Operating through a one-party political system that depended on low voter turnout by blacks and poor whites, the local racial state was reinforced by the patronage politics of the southern wing of the Democratic party, which rewarded personal alignments with jobs and political favors. In 1960 the governor of Mississippi, Ross Barnett, the handpicked candidate of the Citizen's Councils, campaigned on the slogan "He's for segregation one hundred percent." Barnett's failure to exercise responsible leadership led to a full-scale riot on the campus of the University of Mississippi when a black student, James Meredith, attempted to enroll.[19] Barnett's successor, his lieutenant governor Paul Johnson, continued his policies of defiance. Nationally, Mississippi's senators included John Stennis, a bedrock segregationist and powerful senior member of the Senate Appropriations Committee, and James Eastland, his even more segregationist colleague.[20]

The noninstitutional authority of the local racial state resided in two organizations. The Ku Klux Klan, whose members were largely poor whites, relied on terrorism and secrecy to keep African Americans in their place. Wearing white hoods they beat and murdered "uppity" blacks and burned crosses as a fiery warning to those who stepped across the color line. The other arm of the local racial state was the White Citizen's Council. Composed of a business elite fiercely opposed to civil rights, the Council expanded immensely during the 1950s. In Mississippi just months after the 1954 Supreme Court decision that school segregation must end, the White Citizen's Council could boast of 25,000 members.[21] While the one-party system provided the institutional structure that maintained white domination over African Americans, "during the 1960s the Citizen's Council became the most powerful force in Mississippi politics."[22]

By the early 1960s, the civil rights movement was pushing the federal government toward direct confrontation with the segregationist South and especially Mississippi over that most basic democratic right—the right to vote. Between 1960 and 1964 almost half the Justice Department's lawsuits alleging racial discrimination in voter registration were filed in Mississippi.[23] Further, the federally sponsored Voter Education Project spent more money in Mississippi than any other southern state.[24] As the local racial state began to crumble, the Civil Rights Act of 1964 and the Voting Rights Act of 1965 strengthened the hand of federal officials.

Initially, civil rights activities in Mississippi were coordinated by the Council of Federated Organizations (COFO). COFO members included the Student Nonviolent Coordinating Committee (SNCC), CORE, the SCLC, and the NAACP.[25] In 1964 COFO organized the Mississippi Freedom Democratic Party (MFDP) to let the nation know that the regular Democratic party excluded African Americans. MFDP elected its own delegates who challenged the seating of the regular delegates to the Democratic national convention. As a compromise to the official all-white Mississippi delegation, the Democrats offered the status of delegate at-large to COFO president Aaron Henry and his running mate and granted *de facto* recognition to other MFDP delegates. Henry accepted the compromise, but activists from SNCC and CORE rejected it. This incident created a schism within the MFDP that was to widen over tactics such as nonviolent protest and the black power slogan.[26] In 1965 Henry joined with other moderate African Americans, white liberals, and organized labor to develop a broad-based coalition, whereas SNCC and CORE pursued an increasingly separatist course.

Attacking Political Poverty Through Community Action

As antipoverty funds became available, powerful whites throughout Mississippi unsuccessfully sought to control them. Consistently, OEO bypassed local politicos, siding with local black activists who seized upon the mandate of maximum feasible participation to demand that they participate in the community action agencies and help decide how to spend the funds.

OEO rejected a proposal in Meridian for a community action program, because it was "a political animal spawned by the white county political machine and the Mississippi Governor's office . . . for the purpose of maintaining control of the War on Poverty program and funds." Instead, OEO staff argued, "a new CAP should be organized that will by-pass the County Board of Supervisors and this should be done quickly."[27] In Columbia local African Americans charged that the CAP board included three Klansmen and no poor people. OEO held back funds until the existing board resigned and a new, integrated, democratically elected membership took its place.[28] The Winona CAP, which was controlled by the governor and the Board of Supervisors, tried submitting its application through the Rural Task Force, bypassing OEO, "so that less checking would be done." But local African Americans charged that eight of the twenty white board members were "Johnson colonels," men who supported Johnson's campaign and who were known to be his "men" in the county. The executive director was active in local and state chambers of commerce and in the Mississippi Manufacturers Association, "organizations not known for their liberal attitudes nor for their desire to buck the local power structure for the benefit of the Negro population." Of the fifteen black members eight "depended on the white power structure for their jobs or welfare-pension payments." The proposal also contained no guarantees that African Americans would help staff the program. OEO staff, fearing that this CAP would merely perpetuate "all things that are bad in county control in Mississippi," refused to fund it.[29] The poor now had a powerful ally in their quest for political equality.

Empowering African Americans politically meant more than including them on community action boards. It also meant using federal funds to circumvent local politicians, local educational institutions, and local welfare authorities. Systematic Training and Redevelopment, or Operation Star, a demonstration project initiated by two Catholic priests, established an alternative social welfare system in the state. As one of only two states without a mandatory education law, Mississippi's high illiteracy rates prevented most of the poor from participating in vocational training; no adult basic education programs existed. Aimed at the hardcore unemployed and functionally illiterate, Star planned to use literacy training followed by vocational training and job referral to make the illiterate employable.[30] If it succeeded, Star's founders believed the program could fundamentally restructure class relations in the Delta, not by overturning the system but by educating African Americans and giving them a place in it.

This model of empowerment was clearly based on a vision of a class system that could be changed by changing the poor. However, by funding Operation Star, OEO also placed resources into the hands of individuals who had been powerless. In a cash-poor state like Mississippi, such resources generated their own power.

Star appealed to OEO staff because it was run by the Catholic church, an organization with sufficient resources to completely bypass the local power structure. With such facilities as offices, staff, access to a nationwide news media, and an established bureaucratic hierarchy, the church could circumvent the segregated Mississippi educational system. Further, the diocese, in OEO's view, was "the only capable private institution in the state *willing* to conduct such a program—in *full* agreement and compliance with recent progressive legislation."[31] OEO awarded the diocese $5,307,200, enormous economic leverage in so poor a state.

Star began operating quickly, establishing eighteen centers—primarily in remote rural areas—to train the poor in literacy, arithmetic, and social skills. Star also opened a vocational training center in Greenwood that offered secretarial training, skilled-trades training in basic wood and metal machines, farm equipment maintenance and repair, and auto engine repair and maintenance. Programs devised around a "culture of poverty" model were oriented toward changing the poor and enhancing their self-esteem. Star staff pointed proudly to the accomplishments of people like Jemiah Jones, a heavyset, dignified sharecropper, who explained what Star meant to him:

> I was hired out at the age of 9 to help with family finances. . . . Having to work, I attended school at least two days out of a week, and sometimes did not attend at all. I lived about five miles from school and when I got there it was 9 or 10 o'clock. I was promoted to the third grade. But I did not learn to read and write. I have ten children and a man in my shape feels pretty bad when his child asks a question about his school books and you cannot tell him anything. Star has meant more to me than I can express to you. I can now write my name and I will be able to help my younger children when they start school.[32]

Star sought more than individual self-improvement, however; it also sought to change the South. The core issue for the civil rights movement was segregation, and Star confronted this southern institution head-on by integrating its programs. Statewide, 13 percent of Star trainees were white, while 55 percent of the staff was black.[33] In many communities Star Advisory Boards held the first racially-integrated meetings ever. In the Carthage Center Star Basic Adult Education program, for example, "Negro and white supervisors work side by side in providing training and counseling services for 78 Negroes, ten whites and three Indians."[34] As the site of the 1964 murders of civil rights workers James Chaney, Michael Schwerner, and Andrew Goodman, Carthage was a deep southern town with a violent history, and local Klan members "bitterly resent[ed] the fact that [the black center director was] supervising all white employees."[35] A cross burning on the lawn of a Star recruiter on March 19 was the first in a series of violent incidents, culminating on May 4, when the home of a social worker was burned to the ground and the Catholic church, site of the school for Star trainees, dynamited.[36] Still, students continued attending classes; the night after the cross burning only one student out of eighty-seven was absent. By confronting segregated institutions, Star not only helped increase the students' self-esteem but also provided the knowledge that they could defy the system and win.

By implementing programs in the South, OEO promoted black moderates at the expense of more militant civil rights activists. Star's board of directors consisted of white and black moderates, including Aaron Henry and other "members of the older generation of Negro leaders." But its founders shunned individuals associated with SNCC and CORE.[37] When local African Americans accused Star of appointing only "Uncle Toms," OEO responded that if radicals were appointed, then "even the most interested members of the white community" would shun it.[38] OEO also feared the disruption militants might cause. In supporting a Headstart program for Bolivar county, an OEO report concluded:

It is likely that further postponement will raise the level of emotional discontent of the Negro/poor from one of frustration, channeled into constructive effort, to one of frustration resulting in overt demonstration. In other words, there had better be a Headstart quick *before* the lid blows.[39]

Empowerment could only go so far. It could increase the self-esteem of the poor and it could reduce their political poverty, but it could not foment revolution.

Indigenous organizations provided a natural coalition for an agency still in the process of defining its mission, and the goals of moderate civil rights activists became the goals of community action in Mississippi. Throughout Mississippi, where the franchise and integration were the issues, OEO insisted community action agencies be integrated, distributed resources in a way that undermined the existing political system of patronage and created new networks that included African Americans. Through such activities, Star and other community action agencies built racially integrated community institutions and helped extend political rights to African Americans.

Maintaining the Status Quo

Two important jobs programs, the Concentrated Employment Program (CEP) for adults and the Neighborhood Youth Corps (NYC) for young men, were run by the Department of Labor. Unlike OEO, a new agency unconstrained by long-standing institutional relationships, the Department of Labor obtained data on employment patterns through the state Employment Services, established during the New Deal. Employment Service offices ran many of the department's programs. Historically, the Employment Services had served as a conduit for low-wage, menial employment for African Americans. These prior institutional relationships made it impossible for the Department of Labor to bypass patronage networks in Mississippi. Instead the programs it ran fed them.

The nationwide CEP was designed "to combine . . . the diverse Department of Labor manpower programs into a single flexible system for delivery of services."[40] Its goals were to provide training and supportive services to disadvantaged persons so that they could obtain steady, decently paid employment. By law a single sponsor had to contract to coordinate CEPs, which, like other manpower programs, were given to the state Employment Services.[41] The first CEP was funded in mid-1967 in Cleveland, Ohio, and by late 1968 seventy-six were operating, thirteen of these in rural areas.

The Mississippi Delta CEP received funding in June 1967. The totally segregated Mississippi Employment Service (MES) became its prime sponsor. Charges against the MES of racial bias in conducting other programs made it difficult for the Department of Labor to justify selecting MES as prime sponsor. Instead OEO and the Department of Labor compromised, granting MES control over most CEP programs, with adult education under OEO control.

OEO subcontracted the adult education program to Star and hired an outside contractor, Afro-American Associates, to supervise the CEP. MES and Star agreed to hold a joint training session in the presence of the outside evaluator to help job developers understand the product they were selling to employers: black labor. All MES job developers, recruited through the state merit system roster, were white. Four were recent college graduates, two from "Ole Miss." According to Afro-American Associates, the latter

> had very negative attitudes . . . one said that he had spent one summer forming groups to counteract the efforts of the Civil Rights groups in the Delta, the other displayed nothing but contempt for the Negro in poverty and seemed to think that they were that way because they were lazy and shiftless. Another one from this group of young men has spent considerable time as a "deputy" putting Negroes in jail who "step out of line . . ." and it's hard to believe that he will really be interested in developing meaningful jobs for Negroes.[42]

The negative report triggered complaints about OEO's unnecessary scrutiny of the Mississippi CEP. William Norwood, the Department of Labor's Regional Manpower Administrator, charged:

> We have attempted to work cooperatively with OEO at the Regional Office level and we do not intend to ignore any legitimate questions concerning discrimination or the whole Civil Rights issue to go unanswered. I am concerned that the OEO National Office staff apparently regards Mississippi as their own preserve, by-passes the OEO Regional Office, deals directly with interest groups in Mississippi, and appears to be dedicated to the proposition of creating discord, not reaching solutions.[43]

Unlike OEO, which had no institutional ties in Mississippi, the Department of Labor reinforced elite control over manpower programs and discouraged the participation of African Americans in these programs. A policy legacy, created during the New Deal, had established linkages that blocked innovation.

The NYC was also administered through the Department of Labor, which issued contracts in Mississippi granting the MES sole control. Like the CEP, the NYC maintained the status quo. Not only were the young men selected for NYC jobs all white, but the program itself became merely an extension of the patronage-based political system—one more favor to dispense to local authorities, particularly boards of supervisors who issued contracts for road construction and maintenance.

An evaluation of the Corinth NYC revealed it as "merely a conduit from the Mississippi Employment Service to the municipal officers. When a County Supervisor asks for three boys, he gets three." [44] Further, the president of the local Amalgamated Clothing Workers Union complained that "the Street Department is working some of the boys under the Youth Program along with their regular crews. The story is that the boys are working 10 hours and being paid for 8 hours as the crews normally work 10 hours." Labor unionists, excluded from the all-white Advisory Committee, bitterly claimed that it was "set up only to serve and line the pockets" of the power structure. [45]

Under what conditions can social policy restructure societal institutions and reorganize patterns of stratification? The evidence from Mississippi suggests that at a minimum the agency charged with implementation must be autonomous from those with a stake in maintaining the status quo. As a newly-created agency, OEO had no connections to other federal agencies and was ideologically committed to increasing the political participation of the poor. It had two powerful tools at its disposal: federal funds and the ability to decide who received them. In selecting which programs to fund, OEO staff supported those favoring civil rights objectives and denied funding to those linked to the white power structure. Bypassing the local racial state, OEO grants undermined the patronage-based system of party politics, empowered racially integrated community organizations, and created new distributive networks.

Unlike OEO, the Department of Labor had institutional ties to the white power structure through its Employment Service offices. Linked to a constituency dominated by the old agricultural leadership, these agencies constituted part of the local racial state. The programs run by the Department of Labor fed local patronage networks and sustained traditional power relationships. Because the Department of Labor embodied elite interests, it resisted fundamental social change.

Fomenting Race Rebellion

By the mid-1960s the civil rights movement had changed course. With such issues as segregation of public facilities and voting rights settled, at least in terms of law, the movement turned to other, more complex, issues like economic injustice. Accompanying this shift in goals was a shift in tactics from nonviolence to black power. Black power articulated a mood rather than a program—disillusionment and alienation from white America and race pride and self-respect. In politics black power meant independent action—black control of the ghettos and its conscious use to improve the living conditions of slum dwellers. This agenda took the form of organizing a black political party to control the political machinery within the ghetto without the guidance of white politicians.[46]

Among the civil rights groups, SNCC and CORE most fiercely espoused the black power ideology. The more radical of the two, SNCC called for totally independent action outside the established political parties, applauded the idea of guerilla warfare, and regarded riots as rebellions; CORE, while approving the SNCC strategy, was willing to work within the Democratic party and, while justifying riots as the natural explosion of an oppressed people against intolerable conditions, advocated violence only in self-defense.[47]

In a few cities community action went beyond increasing the political participation of the poor to incorporating this more radical vision of social change. One such city was Newark, New Jersey. Here the civil rights movement captured the community action program and used the leverage created by its autonomous structure to challenge city hall.

Newark experienced a rapid influx of southern migrants; by the early 1960s nearly 200,000 resided there. In response the white middle class fled to the suburbs. Between 1960 and 1967 Newark lost more than 70,000 white residents; in that period the city moved from 65 percent white to 52 percent African American and 10 percent Puerto Rican and Cuban.[48]

Newark was run by a Democratic political machine which controlled the city even though the white population had fled. Newark's mayor Hugh Addonizio, a liberal seven-term congressman, counted on the black vote to win elections. In 1962 he forged an African American–Italian coalition to overthrow the Irish who had controlled city hall for decades. As mayor, Addonizio proclaimed that his door was open to African Americans, who the Irish had shut out. He also began integrating the police department, a point of contention since most police officers were Italian and most persons arrested were African American. Still, both the City Council and the Board of Education had only two black members, and, according to an OEO evaluation, it was an administration that had "lost sight of the growing needs of the lower income Negro residents in the ghettos."[49] Segregated neighborhoods could provide no sanctuary. If local politicos made concessions to African Americans, who were in the majority, they could take over city politics.

The Capture of Community Action

Newark's community action program, the United Community Corporation (UCC), was divided into nine Area Boards, which became pawns in the political struggle between the Democratic party and the African American community. The Area Boards had no apparent relationship to economic or social features of the city but rather, an OEO report noted, were "obviously designed to structurally compete with the existing political wards." In the program's first year in operation, Addonizio used the community action agency to "buy off all potential insurgency. . . . The slightest sign of influence used against the regime will put a Negro into a patronage job, an effective gag." Instead of using federal funds to solve problems, they were used "to get people to shut up about them."[50]

Immediately, complaints began surfacing that in areas controlled by the mayor the machine-dominated boards were misusing antipoverty funds. One summer camp for poor youth received equipment that was not only inadequate but also more appropriate for kindergartners than for older children. The only activities were field trips where "no refreshments or food was furnished and usually the youths returned from the trips hungry, disappointed and at times in tears." The poor were also denied jobs in the program, with most of the community action funds instead paying the salaries of school teachers on summer vacation, off-duty policemen and firemen, and "people favored by City Hall." The only African Americans who benefitted from the program were civil rights leaders who were "given jobs . . . as insurance that demonstrations and pickets will not be used against UCC."[51] At first, then, community action fueled local patronage coffers while buying off militant activism.

Although the mayor controlled six of the boards, they "were up for grabs in a number of political power struggles." One of the power struggles surrounded the Newark Community Union Project (NCUP), a coalition of three civil rights groups—Students for a Democratic Society (SDS), CORE, and SNCC—dedicated to improving the ghetto. Recognizing the antipoverty program as a potential resource, the NCUP decided to take over the UCC. Mobilizing quickly, NCUP seized Area 2 and Area 3, which almost completely absorbed the local civil rights groups, and began competing with the city's central ward for power.[52]

The first issue NCUP tackled was urban renewal. The Demonstration Cities and Metropolitan Development Act of 1966, or Model Cities as it became known, authorized the federal government to make grants to city agencies to develop programs to improve their physical environments, increase the housing supply to low- and moderate-income people, and provide educational and social services.[53] In 1967 Newark received Model City funds. The City Council voted to use them to clear 150 acres of ghetto housing for a medical and dental college.

At hearings of the Planning Board, UCC staff from Areas 2 and 3 vehemently denounced the medical school complex.[54] The proposed clearing, they argued, contained no procedure for relocating the displaced residents and, indeed, no guarantee that they would be resettled within the city limits. Further, they feared the plan was designed to break up an area that could elect a black mayor.[55] The controversy came to a head at a tumultuous Planning Board meeting in June when speaker after speaker denounced the city's plan to raze the ghetto.[56]

Instead of responding to the issue, city authorities charged that black nationalists controlled the antipoverty program. Police Director Dominick Spina complained that the UCC was using "resources and manpower . . . for the purpose of fomenting and agitating against the organized and democratic government and agencies of the city of Newark." According to Spina UCC was using rented vehicles to agitate against the planning board and coercing staff members into picketing and demonstrating.[57] A disgruntled former UCC board member also charged that forty-five members of a black liberation movement (unnamed) had chartered a bus with OEO funds, held covert meetings in a motel in East Orange, and used OEO funds to incite racial violence by distributing black nationalist literature.[58]

As OEO considered these charges, its investigation team warned that although two incendiary incidents in 1966 had been minimized by the collective action of the police, the UCC, and local groups, "things have changed." There had been a resurgence of black Muslims and other black nationalist groups, and everyone believed that Newark was next. Further, they feared the opposition to the medical school location could trigger violence. The memo closed by warning that "the major concentration of these various groups will be centered around the community action agency."[59]

As civil rights activists seized the community action program, social policy became a weapon in the battle for racial equality. What made it possible in a city where the local power structure had tried to keep control of the antipoverty effort was the numerical dominance of the African American community plus the presence of civil rights activists organized for radical action.

The Response to Rebellion

On a hot summer night, July 12, cabby John Smith was arrested for driving with a revoked license. From the high-rise towers of the Reverend William P. Hayes Housing Project, residents watched as Smith was dragged out of the police car and into the red brick building of the Fourth Precinct Police Station. As taxi drivers all over the city began broadcasting reports of his arrest on their radios, a UCC board meeting was interrupted by a phone call reporting that the police were beating a cab driver. The UCC leaders immediately headed for the Fourth Precinct and demanded to see the prisoner. By this time a crowd had gathered outside the precinct station, and as the prisoner was moved to the hospital "the crowd remained curious and alert." [60]

Within an hour the crowd had grown to 150. Civil rights leaders urged them to "keep cool." "They commenced singing and chanting civil rights songs, believing it to be an escape valve, to keep the crowd cool." Three civil rights leaders tried to calm the crowd, urging the on-lookers to form a line to march toward city hall. Some joined the line while others milled about the narrow street. A rock was thrown from the crowd. A minute later a young man threw a fire bomb. When a fire truck arrived on the scene, the now unruly crowd bombarded it with rocks. Minutes later a liquor store was looted, a car was set on fire, and a full-scale riot ensued. [61]

The next day anonymous leaflets were distributed in the streets calling for a protest rally at the Fourth Precinct that night. One of the mayor's men accused Area Boards 2 and 3 of producing the leaflets. At 7:00 PM Jesse Allen, Area Board 3 organizer, led a march toward the police station. What began as a protest over unfair treatment of African Americans on the police promotion list became unruly as a rapidly growing crowd began throwing rocks at the station. As the police attempted to clear the streets, violence and looting initiated another night of rioting. The following day the National Guard was placed on alert. That afternoon police shot and killed a black man. As darkness rolled in, massive looting and vandalism increased. Gunshots were heard throughout the night. On Saturday the National Guard moved in with automatic weapons and quelled the riot. [62]

Following the riot Police Director Spina "made sweeping charges about the role of militants and subversives in the operation of UCC." [63] UCC reputedly had used sound trucks to agitate, had printed flyers, and had promoted activities that increased tensions. Spina produced 500 copies of "provocative material" found in UCC offices, "capable of both creating and stimulating racial hatred." In response to these charges OEO sent a site visit team to Newark, theoretically to evaluate the program but actually to determine whether or not to shut down UCC. Although the investigators found "no evidence to support charges that UCC or any of its employees participated in or planned the riot" and in fact had attempted "to calm the atmosphere in several riot areas," still they concluded that "central program planning and development activities [were] nonexistent," and that the result could only be defined "as a perversion of the original design."[64]

Sensitive to public criticism that the antipoverty programs were causing riots and unwilling to support what was widely perceived as revolutionary activity, OEO recommended "that the present agency be abandoned, that a high level OEO task force be sent to Newark to quickly organize a new CAP, and that the delegate agency programs and funds be transferred to the new agency." Although OEO investigators agreed that people in target areas should be able to run their own programs, the Newark neighborhood group "ain't ready yet."[65]

Improving Service Coordination

As the sharecropper system faded away, defeated by machine cultivation and civil rights laws that made black labor more costly, the displaced sharecroppers migrated north in search of new opportunities and a less hostile environment. These migrants created a dilemma for the political machines in the northern cities where they landed—how to incorporate them politically without losing the white vote. A number of critics of community action suggest that it would have worked better if it had operated through rather than around local government authorities.[66] The answer as played out in Chicago suggests yet another irony of American welfare politics. Here the local party machine ran the community action program, and services to the poor were administered efficiently. Yet the overall impact of the program was to maintain a pattern of racial stratification that kept African Americans at the bottom of the patronage system.

While in Newark the white middle class fled to the suburbs, Chicago's machine worked to keep whites (and thus white machine voters) inside the city limits by rigidly maintaining neighborhood segregation. In Chicago the political establishment was represented by the powerful Democratic party machine, ruled by the iron-fisted Mayor Richard Daley. A pudgy, squat man who looked more like a butcher than a powermonger, Daley had built his organization by distributing patronage and favors to individuals, ethnic groups, and neighborhoods. No reform-minded organization could operate without cooperating with the mayor, whose machine penetrated every component of city politics.[67] People who moved into the wards would be visited by a precinct captain who would inquire into their needs. Those who served the machine well would receive jobs: "jobs with the city, with the county, with the state, with the Post Office, and even with the many private companies that used the machine as an employment agency in return for favorable treatment from City Hall." The payoff was absolute loyalty on election day. As one Daley protégé put it, "When you're born, a politician signs your birth certificate; and when you die, a politician signs your death certificate, and everything in between is government."[68]

Chicago faced its own racial crisis, brought about by the black migration. During the 1950s the city's south side experienced a steady influx of southern African Americans. By 1960 some neighborhoods were more than 90 percent African American, while the traditional ethnic neighborhoods remained primarily white. The dilemma for Daley's machine was to keep the loyalty of black voters, who provided a plurality in the 1955 election, while maintaining neighborhood segregation. Neighborhood racial transition posed a threat to the machine, for if a ward went from white to black, white voters would be lost to the suburbs. Efforts to maintain the color line meant that African Americans went to inferior schools on double shifts, lived in crowded and crime-ridden public housing, and were excluded from the city contracting jobs controlled by all-white unions.[69]

Until 1960, except for the appointment of three black judges, African Americans were excluded almost entirely from patronage appointments. In the 1963 election for mayor, however, the seven wards headed by black aldermen delivered 70 percent of Daley's winning margin. Daley responded by providing the black ward organizations their first real rewards.[70]

Community action, as OEO defined it, was absent in Chicago. Daley's machine kept tight control of the city's antipoverty programs, run through the Chicago Committee on Urban Opportunity (CCUO) with Daley serving as its ex-officio chairman. CCUO was administered by Deton Brooks, a Daley appointee and local black bureaucrat who delegated little authority. All the neighborhood antipoverty centers displayed 2 × 2 foot pictures of Daley and Brooks along with signs identifying the centers as part of city government.

CCUO's version of community organization was from the top down. Ostensibly, the poor were represented by the chairmen of the Advisory Councils in each district. Yet with only seven districts, including one that had no Advisory Council, these representatives constituted only six of the seventy-four Steering Committee members. The rest, appointees of the mayor, included members of the Mayor's cabinet, officials of state and local public agencies, and persons "whose future economic interests and social status would be adversely affected by any display of recalcitrance against the wishes of the City Hall machine." [71] At the bottom were Daley's block captains, PTA officers, and other patronage appointees, who carried out orders and policies determined by Daley's henchmen. [72]

Supposedly, nominations of Advisory Council members came from neighborhood groups, but in fact nearly all were appointed by Brooks. As a result, the Councils operated as a rubber stamp for the CCUO downtown. Meetings were run in an authoritarian manner and controlled by the chairman, who in turn was controlled and constantly advised by CCUO staff people who were present, visible, and very vocal. Rather than developing policy, determining priorities, and initiating action programs, the representatives of the poor merely lent an aura of respectability to the authoritarian decision-making. As an OEO evaluation team caustically noted, the Chicago CCUO was "the same old story of *noblesse oblige* with the trappings of grassroots democracy added." [73]

Instead of empowering the poor, the antipoverty program usurped resources for political purposes. Local community representatives canvassed neighborhoods before a primary election, passing out political propaganda for a bond issue local civil rights leaders denounced as a blank check to the Daley organization. CCUO officials were also hostile to programs involving indigenous community action and to individuals involved in civil rights activities. Marillac House, a settlement with an excellent reputation but outspoken on civil rights, asked to be included in CCUO, but its application was rejected. So was that of Lawndale for Better Jobs, a program designed to match the unemployed to jobs and which was hostile to city hall on civil rights matters.

Local civil rights groups did launch some challenges, which were quickly quelled. When local antipoverty workers participated in a "March on Cops," a protest against the Welfare Department sponsored by the militant JOIN (Jobs Or Income Now), CCUO held hearings on the issue of poverty monies being used to sponsor demonstrations. Although the hearings showed that demonstrators were recruited from the Neighborhood Youth Corps, they received no pay during the march. Nonetheless, within a month Kathleen Morris, target of the investigation, was terminated from the NYC "due to income above government standards."[74] Thus, Daley used the antipoverty programs to augment his own political power and to crush spontaneous community action.

When the poor did participate, they did so on Daley's terms. Chicago's community action served mainly as a conduit for jobs, with the poor being hired as outreach workers in the antipoverty programs. Rather than playing the broader role in community organizing that OEO had envisioned, they became social workers engaged in specialized tasks, a tendency "which must be fought."[75] Yet even the most antagonistic OEO staffers conceded grudgingly that services ran smoothly in Chicago.

OEO's view of community action conflicted with Mayor Daley's, who saw the program as an opportunity to extend his patronage network and who operated the program as it was envisioned by program planners—improved coordination of services and increased participation of the poor in providing those services. Instead of changing the status quo, community action in Chicago helped maintain it.

In summing up the Chicago program, an OEO evaluation team concluded that Chicago had failed to provide for maximum feasible participation. Rather, "in many respects, the present CCUO philosophy is even worse than the 'old order' it is supposed to replace. At least the 'old order' made no claims to democratic decision-making."[76] Further, the *sine qua non* of aiding the poor in Chicago, "producing fundamental changes in the structure of the city and community" was not realized through the program.[77]

But OEO was a poor match for Daley, for his influence

extended beyond the Chicago city limits. As head of the local Democratic party, he could count on the nine Chicago Democrats in the House of Representatives to act cohesively. He also was elected to chair the antipoverty committee of the U.S. Conference of Mayors. A call to the president could squash any interference by an upstart federal agency.

Faced with confronting Daley directly and cutting off funds to Chicago, a politically risky move for the Democrats, OEO struggled with a compromise. The compromise involved increasing representatives of the poor on the CCUO Steering Committee, eliminating the proviso that "members of the Advisory Committee serve at the discretion of the director of the center," prohibiting an individual from serving on more than one Neighborhood Advisory Board, and requiring advance notice of meetings.[78] Such minor tinkering did little to increase African American participation in the poverty program.

In Chicago OEO was unable to move community action from service provision to political empowerment. The local power structure was firmly entrenched and institutionally linked through all levels of government. Local government officials readily resisted federal intervention. By contrast, OEO lacked those institutional linkages with other agencies that might have supported it efforts to relax the machine's hold on local programs. Daley was also able to co-opt civil rights groups, isolating the agency from indigenous organizations that might have supported it.

The Legacy of Community Action

Black migration to northern cities posed a dilemma for urban political machines. The presence of large numbers of African Americans made for a significant electoral presence. But allowing them to participate fully in local politics risked white flight and the potential demise of the machine. In Chicago Mayor Daley solved the problem by providing patronage to African Americans while maintaining rigid neighborhood segregation, a tactic that retained white voters in the city. This strategy of co-optation kept the machine alive and allowed Daley free rein over the antipoverty program.

In Newark, by contrast, the pattern of white flight made the machine totally dependent on the black vote and thus more unstable. Local civil rights activists captured the antipoverty program and used it to demand a redistribution of resources and political power. The rage unleashed by peaceful demonstrations and unfilled promises defined the boundaries of liberal government intervention. Fostering equal opportunity in politics was an acceptable goal; fostering revolution was not.

Early in 1965 OEO withheld funds from New York, Los Angeles, Philadelphia, and San Francisco as well as Chicago on the grounds that their community action plans did not provide the poor with maximum feasible participation. By that fall the mayors had openly revolted. As budget director Charles Schultze, a fierce opponent of community action, wrote President Johnson, "Many mayors assert that the CAP is setting up a competing political organization in their own backyards."[79]

That September Congress passed a series of amendments, removing the words "maximum feasible participation" from OEO's operating agenda and establishing new procedures for creating poverty boards. In addition to the one-third poor, the boards were to include one-third elected officials and one-third local community groups. State or local governments had to design or approve antipoverty agencies operating in their jurisdictions, and large amounts of funds were earmarked for "safe" programs such as Headstart, an early education program for children from culturally deprived homes. By 1967 nearly two-thirds of OEO's budget was so designated.

In 1973 Nixon unceremoniously abolished OEO. No one challenged his action. The demise of OEO wiped the inner cities off the legislative agenda for the next twenty years.

Yet community action succeeded, at least at an elementary level, in extending political rights to African Americans. The community action agencies introduced a profusion of resources into the ghettos, including such basics as telephones, office staff, stationery, newsletters, meeting places, and access to legal advice. They also brought organization by founding a network of affiliated agencies which provided the first patronage jobs open to African Americans.

Community action also produced opportunities for black men and women to enter politics. When Johnson declared the War on

Poverty, there were no black mayors and only seventy elected black officials at any level of government. Five years later there were 1,500; by 1981 5,014 including 170 mayors. Many of the new leaders gained experience and visibility in community action programs where they campaigned for the poverty boards, chaired meetings, lobbied, litigated, and delivered speeches.[80]

The creation of a cadre of black political leaders remains a permanent legacy of community action. These leaders have been unable to capitalize on their newly won power, however, because the ascendance of black politicians occurred in concert with the decline of the cities. Before a war was waged on poverty, local party organization was concentrated in the urban machines. Since the 1970s, changes in the procedures for nominating candidates and the racial transition in city government undermined the local political party. Mayors became less important to candidates for national office, who began assembling their own electoral machines and depending upon political-action committees for funding. These developments have weakened the influence of cities on national politics and thus the influence of black leaders.[81] At the same time, increasing racial concentration in urban ghettos has undermined possibilities for political coalitions between the city and the larger community. As a result, black political leaders have been unable to keep federal funds flowing to the cities both because persistent racial segregation has isolated them and because they lack leverage in national politics.

Could community action have worked better if it had been run by existing agencies or through local governments? The evidence suggests it could not. In Chicago Daley's machine used community action to fuel its coffers. In Mississippi programs run by the Department of Labor used job-training programs to perpetuate segregation and keep African Americans subservient.

Margaret Weir argues that a full-employment policy would have incorporated African Americans into the Democratic party through unions instead of through community action agencies.[82] Could full employment have drawn African Americans into unions and into union party politics at the local level? Of course, some labor unions, mainly the unions of mass-production workers, were already bringing African Americans into local political networks. But as I show in Chapter 3, the skilled trade unions were among the most formidable opponents of equal employment opportunity. Further, working-class politics generally operated on the basis of membership in the local community rather than membership in a union. And most communities were racially segregated. Thus, even with full employment residential segregation would have obstructed the formation of class solidarity across racial boundaries. As I show in Chapter 4, no issue elicited greater opposition than housing integration.

THREE

Extending Equal
Employment Opportunity

In the South, African Americans clearly lacked the most basic
civil right—the right to freely pursue an occupation without
constraint. Less obvious were the constraints on free labor in the
North. Here discrimination by the skilled trade unions prevented
black men from pursuing work in these coveted jobs, a practice
that the federal government had tacitly allowed since the New
Deal. As poor, black men moved out of the job-training programs
established by the Economic Opportunity Act and into the labor
market, their inability to obtain employment highlighted the barriers to equal opportunity erected by the unions. Federal officials
could no longer ignore practices that threatened the success of the
antipoverty effort. Yet in banning discrimination by trade unions
on projects using federal funds, the government provided an easy
and highly visible target for civil rights protestors. Federal job sites
became the locus of the struggle for equal opportunity, mandating
government intervention in union prerogatives to make the recalci-
trant unions admit black men. The conflict between these two
Democratic party constituents—trade unionists and African
Americans—triggered a backlash among resentful skilled tradesmen. That resentment was translated into political support for
George Wallace in the 1968 presidential election, undermining the

party's power base and creating a constituency of Reagan Democrats in the 1980s. It also resulted in declining support for federally funded job training but, ironically, gave rise to an affirmative action policy mandating equal employment opportunities for minorities and women. Thus, in a period when European trade unions worked for full-employment policies and more comprehensive welfare packages, American trade unions were caught up in internecine warfare and racial conflict.

Who Defines Economic Justice?

At first glance the objective of ending racial discrimination in the skilled trades seems so inherently just and the goal of equality of opportunity—a goal which polls show most Americans support—so clearly defined that no challenge to it holds legitimacy. Yet the idea that equality of opportunity is a moral right threatened established traditions within trade unions, traditions that had been won in confrontations with employers. As federal policy sought to balance competing visions of economic justice, it became engulfed by the battle between African Americans who claimed that an open labor market was an essential civil right and skilled trade unionists who believed that the right to select their own members was a fundamental perquisite of democratic governance.

For years civil rights activists had accumulated a litany of grievances against the skilled trade unions for preventing African Americans from learning and practicing a trade. In 1958 the NAACP released a report charging the railroad and construction industries with racial discrimination and criticizing the AFL-CIO's Civil Rights Committee for being more concerned with creating a liberal image than with pursuing discrimination within its own ranks. When the AFL-CIO ignored the charges, the NAACP and a delegation of black trade unionists planned a showdown at the 1959 AFL-CIO convention. The United Auto Workers union was the sole supporter of the black delegates. The convention voted down all their resolutions.

In 1960 black trade union leaders formed the Negro American Labor Council to increase the influence of African Americans within the union movement and to provide a public forum for their grievances.[1] In his presidential address at the Council's second annual convention, A. Philip Randolph attacked the AFL-CIO leadership for ignoring union racism and blamed the unions for generating black poverty. Randolph singled out the construction unions for denying black men apprenticeships.[2] That same year the U.S. Commission on Civil Rights issued a *Report on Employment*. The report documented persistent and undeniable union discrimination and criticized the AFL-CIO for failing to curb it. It also echoed Randolph's charge that by excluding black men from apprenticeships the skilled trades contributed to black poverty.[3]

In 1960 the national Democratic party was more worried about retaining the loyalty of the southern Democrats than civil rights. But the Democrats won because John Kennedy received 70 percent of the black vote. Most political analysts agree that winning Illinois, New Jersey, and Michigan, as well as South Carolina and Delaware, where he took the black wards and precincts, was the key to his election victory.[4]

President Kennedy refused to aggressively pursue civil rights issues for fear of wrecking his entire legislative agenda. Instead, he took a piecemeal approach. The following year he issued a toothless executive order requiring unions engaged in work under government contract to eliminate discrimination. Although the order also created a Committee on Equal Employment Opportunity (CEEO) to enforce it, the CEEO could only hold hearings and make recommendations. Ninety percent of the AFL-CIO membership signed voluntary pledges to comply with the order but not the building trade unions.[5] The government was still unwilling to fight the skilled trades over who controlled union membership.

In 1962 Kennedy issued a second executive order prohibiting racial discrimination by federal contractors. Since federal contracts represented a large and lucrative share of construction jobs, this order had greater leverage than the first. Administered by the Office of Contract Compliance, the order established compliance offices, created a machinery for victims of discrimination to pursue complaints, and allowed the government to withdraw a contract if the order was violated.[6]

One could readily interpret the two executive orders as merely "symbolic politics"—a sop to civil rights activists—since neither initiated tangible action. But they did create a political opportunity for civil rights leaders, who began organizing protests at federal job sites where discrimination was highly visible. In 1963 in New York, Newark, and Philadelphia, civil rights groups blocked tax-supported construction projects on which few or no African Americans were employed.[7] Was it justice, they asked, for some taxpayers to be denied the right to jobs created in part by their tax contributions?

As civil rights demonstrators seized the opportunity created by the executive orders to demonstrate against union policies, federal authorities increasingly came to fear that this issue alone could trigger rioting. A task force of mayors from large cities, meeting to consider how to reduce racial tensions, blamed the construction unions for creating a climate that increased the likelihood of a riot.[8] The NAACP concurred but held the government equally responsible: "We maintain that the government's continuing failure to take adequate steps on a national basis to insure equal job opportunities for Negroes in federally aided construction has materially contributed to high rates of Negro unemployment and consequent demoralization and unrest in Negro communities throughout the nation."[9]

Promises of change now came fast and furious from the unions. That year more than 300 union leaders signed an antidiscrimination pledge; the presidents of eighteen building trades agreed to eliminate discrimination in apprenticeship training, membership, and referrals. But making promises was easier than keeping them, and when then-Vice President Johnson met with the leaders of forty building trade unions, he came away convinced that "Nobody can move these people. They simply don't mean to do it."[10]

Civil rights leaders, who also knew the unions didn't mean to do it, honed their protests, not only challenging what they defined as the core issue—union discrimination—but also targeting practices that made it possible. In St. Louis, for example, the head of CORE charged that unions working on a government-financed construction project had added a "grandfather clause" to their apprenticeship regulations, giving applicants whose fathers were journeymen construction workers a ten-point bonus on exams.[11] The clause—a sort of affirmative action in reverse—clearly disadvantaged black men, who automatically lost ten points. In Philadelphia, six construction unions—plumbers, steamfitters, sheet metal workers, composition roofers, and electricians—had kept black men out by verbally administering admission tests. Like the tests given by southern clerks to blacks who tried to register to vote, no outsider could judge the fairness of these oral exams.

Civil rights leaders demanded that the unions halt secret admission exams and eliminate rules that automatically excluded black men. They scored a minor victory in Philadelphia where, after much hedging, the Building Trades Committee signed an agreement with the Pennsylvania Human Rights Commission to admit African Americans. In 1963 one local of the electrical workers union admitted five black men.[12]

More often, however, demands for change ran into a stone wall of union resistance. In November, 1964, the NAACP asked the government to halt construction on a federal office building in Cleveland, Ohio. Of 7,000 construction union members in Cleveland, only 13 were African American.[13] Although the Department of Labor forced the unions to disclose their plans for selecting apprentices, it allowed them to retain a personal interview that counted for one-fourth of the total score. Items such as physical health, appearance, neatness, interest, attitude, and suitability were left to the discretion of the interviewer.

The right of unions to select their own members was a property right of the working class. This was a most compelling argument for nepotism—the tradition of passing on the craft from fathers to sons. Among Philadelphia plumbers, for example, 40 percent of apprentices were sons of members who wanted their sons to be trained as plumbers and eventually carry on their businesses for them.[14] As one construction worker plaintively explained:

Some men leave their sons money, some large investments, some business connections and some a profession. I have none of these to bequeath to my sons. I have only one worthwhile thing to give: my trade. . . . For this simple father's wish it is said that I discriminate against Negroes. Don't all of us discriminate? Which of us when it comes to choice will not choose a son over all others?[15]

Civil rights leaders didn't see it that way. The NAACP urged the AFL-CIO to outlaw father–son unionism as official policy for all construction unions. Although the AFL-CIO ignored the request, in 1963 the New York State Supreme Court ruled against the Sheet Metal Workers union, forcing it to abandon nepotism.[16]

From the trade unionists' perspective, union prerogatives were under attack from all directions; their most cherished privileges, privileges that protected *unions'* civil rights, were being gradually and insidiously eroded, and the fault lay with the civil rights movement. Instead of creating solidarity, the job-training programs became engulfed in a struggle that intensified racial cleavages.

Jobs or Job Training?

When Johnson took office, his task was to unify the party's two key constituents—trade unionists and African Americans. At first that task posed no problem. Organized labor could demonstrate its good will toward African Americans by serving in their president's noble war against poverty. Two AFL-CIO vice presidents served on the National Advisory Council on Economic Opportunity, OEO's top policymaking body; eighteen other prominent labor leaders served on OEO's Labor Advisory Board; and locally more than 2,000 AFL-CIO leaders served on community action agency boards.[17] The AFL-CIO also established its own Anti-Poverty Office to "train union members for active service in the war against poverty." Union men and women attended specially created centers where they learned how to write grant applications for local projects to help the poor and how to encourage the participation of the poor in community organizations.[18] Throughout the nation union locals ran Neighborhood Youth Corps, Headstart and VISTA programs.[19] In California, for example, the Alameda County Central Labor Council operated a Neighborhood Youth Corps (NYC) to teach poor youths good work habits and marketable skills and to help them find jobs. Another NYC program brought urban youth into a carpentry apprenticeship program. In Jacobs Creek, Tennessee, the International Union of Operating Engineers sponsored a Job Corps Center to teach young men to maintain and operate heavy equipment.

In the summer of 1965, just six days after Congress passed the Voting Rights Act, Watts, a poor, black neighborhood in Los Angeles, erupted with a fury so intense it seemed nothing could stop the waste and destruction. As a stunned nation watched five nights of televised disorder, the message that the progress toward black equality could not assuage black anger over more deeply ingrained racial inequities became embedded in the national conscience. At the heart of that message was a demand for the right to work. As Attorney General Ramsey Clark, whose Justice Department became the eye of the storm, explained:

> Back into the summer of '64 . . . we were so consumed with the South and there was so much to be done there . . . and when we thought of the North, we didn't think of civil rights then really . . . It was August 11, 1965, before we—that was the beginning of Watts—really focused on the problem of the riot in the big cities . . . But we saw from Watts very clearly employment as a major element. The people said, "Jobs first. Give us jobs, and the rest will take care of itself." [20]

How could the government meet this demand? Secretary of Labor Willard Wirtz believed that job creation was the only solution: "The Poverty Program must start out with immediate, priority emphasis on employment. . . . The single immediate change which the poverty program could bring about in the lives of most of the poor would be to provide the family head with a regular, decently paid job." [21] But the poverty warriors had already considered direct job creation and rejected it. As Adam Yarmolinsky, the first candidate considered to head OEO, explained, "You ask yourself, do you concentrate on finding jobs for people or preparing people for jobs. There our tactical decision was, let's concentrate first on preparing people for jobs." In deciding to change the characteristics of the individual rather than the structure of the economy, federal officials initially ignored barriers impeding the *right* to work, emphasizing instead barriers impeding the *ability* to work.[22] This seemingly noncontroversial decision was relatively easy to implement. Some job-training programs were already operating. Others were in the planning stages. All the government had to do was expand them. Between 1964 and 1970 federal expenditures on job training increased from $200 million to $1.4 billion.[23] The Job Corps, the Neighborhood Youth Corps, the Manpower Development and Training Act (MDTA), Jobs in the

Business Sector (JOBS), and WIN all sought to make the poor more employable.

Federally run job training meant increased federal intervention in labor–employer relations. At first federal officials appeased union concerns over government intervention in job training. At the Excelsior Spring Women's Job Corps Center the American Federation of Teachers organized the teaching staff and struck for more than a week over bargaining rights. And at the Albuquerque Women's Center the Hotel and Restaurant Workers Union picketed when the contractor refused to recognize the union as the bargaining agent.[24]

What stance should the federal government take when its own employees and its own programs created labor unrest? Since no single federal policy governed union–employer relations, the Office of Economic Opportunity, which ran the Job Corps, was forced to develop its own. Some federal agencies were decidedly pro-labor, others neutral or even antagonistic.[25] The Department of Defense, for example, considered labor relations irrelevant in deciding who received defense contracts. It issued no guidelines to contractors regarding the kind of relationship they should establish with labor organizations, did not intervene in collective bargaining agreements, and limited its review of such agreements to considering whether the costs they generated were reimbursable. On the other hand, when the Atomic Energy Commission awarded contracts, it not only actively monitored labor relations policies but insisted that agreements favor trade unions. AEC required contractors to maintain "constructive relations with labor organizations and to strive towards the peaceful resolution of disputes." AEC also reviewed collective bargaining agreements to insure that they were "calculated to promote industrial peace and to provide mediation and conciliation if normal collective bargaining failed to resolve disputes."[26]

Over the heated objections of its Jobs Corps contractors, OEO took a strongly pro-union stance, affirming "the right of employees in the Job Corps program to organize and to bargain collectively." OEO also went beyond the National Labor Relations Act ruling that an employer must negotiate with a union if it had the support of the majority of employees in the bargaining unit. Instead, OEO asked Job Corps contractors to abandon their "traditional . . . refusal to deal with representatives of organized labor except when absolutely required by the National Labor Relations Act" and to follow the spirit as well as the letter of the Act. OEO made employers "give labor representatives reasonable access to employees, permit the union to post its meeting notices on center bulletin boards and make meeting facilities available at the center during non-duty hours." OEO also prohibited contractors from obstructing unionization by "delaying the time when center management must bargain with labor unions" and forced employers "to coordinate the development of on-the-job training programs with concerned labor unions." [27]

Initially, then, organized labor had no reason to oppose job-training programs. Although the programs did nothing to alleviate organized labor's concern about unemployment, trade unionists gained political capital by demonstrating their commitment to the antipoverty effort. More importantly, the training programs became the impetus for a pro-labor shift in federal policies. Supporting labor in its battles with employers while training black workers might suffice to keep both constituents satisfied with the government's efforts and loyal to the Democratic party.

But racial targeting of job-training programs put the federal government on a collision course with the skilled trade unions. By 1968 African Americans constituted 47 percent of the Neighborhood Youth Corps, 81 percent of the Concentrated Employment Programs, and 59 percent of the Job Corps.[28] Trainees were recruited from urban ghettos, and job training not only included job skills but also basic skills such as reading, arithmetic, and getting to work on time. What made job-training programs unpalatable to the skilled trades was their role in the pursuit of civil rights. Initiated to enhance the ability of poor, black men to work, job-training programs rapidly became agents of equal opportunity. The skilled trade unions, which already feared that job-training programs would increase the skilled labor pool and thus threaten wage rates, soon learned that job training also threatened their most sacred prerogatives—the right to run training programs and to select apprentices.

The Right to Work

In the mass-production industries like automaking, tasks require little skill, training requirements are minimal, and workers have little discretion in organizing the flow of production. In the skilled crafts, by contrast, workers rely on apprenticeship programs to monopolize entry to the trade and so maintain a tight labor supply. As Michael Piore and Charles Sabel note: "Limitations of the number of apprentices and of what is taught to outsiders is the craft community's best long-term defense against scarcity of work . . . and also facilitates the craft's control over wages."[29] In periods of prosperity a shortage of skilled labor enhances the bargaining power of workers; in slack periods the unions divide the available jobs among their members with less loss of employment. Only by restricting membership can skilled workers control the supply of labor and maintain their wage rates.[30]

In 1964 only 160,000 registered apprentices existed, and these were concentrated in three industries—construction, metal trades, and printing—with the bulk (103,000) being in construction. The 3.5–million-member Building and Construction Trades Department formed the most powerful block in the AFL-CIO, a power that stemmed not only from its size but also from its monopoly of craft labor.[31] Construction unions limited entry to the trade, and thus the labor supply, by tightly controlling entry to apprenticeships. No issue generated more intense opposition among construction workers than challenges to their control of apprenticeships.

Even before the War on Poverty expanded federal job training, the unions had resisted MDTA, which gave employers subsidies for apprentices receiving on-the-job training. When the construction unions adamantly refused to participate in MDTA, federal officials made numerous concessions to the union. They agreed to establish MDTA-funded apprenticeships solely in nonunionized occupations and to approve no training projects without first consulting the unions. By creating training programs that didn't compete with union apprenticeships and by allowing unions some veto power over projects, federal officials hoped to placate workers in the construction trades and thus retain their loyalty to the Democratic party.[32]

Despite these efforts, the work and training programs, which operated outside of the union apprenticeship system, invariably confronted the rights unions believed were theirs and theirs alone. In each confrontation the government gave in to union demands to keep hands off. In one instance, OEO officials also enthusiastically endorsed a Job Corps training program for floor mechanics proposed by the nonunionized Armstrong Cork Company, a program they believed would provide trainees with "an excellent opportunity for steady, year-round, well-paid employment on an entry level basis." The Carpenters and Painters International immediately protested that there was no shortage of skilled labor in these areas. They said that the proposed program did not meet the standards of existing labor-run apprenticeship programs and that "the injection of poorly trained workers into the contemplated field [would] destroy training standards, wages and working conditions." [33] Although the program promised to open doors in the skilled trades to poor youth—an objective that OEO heartily endorsed—union concerns took priority. OEO officials hesitated to challenge the unions directly: "should the unions still oppose the program after knowing all the details, then the Job Corps must decide whether to go ahead or not." [34] In the end, OEO persuaded Armstrong Cork to run its training programs through the union.

But the strategy of gentle persuasion was doomed. When the civil rights movement declared war on the skilled trade unions, the government could no longer ignore union practices that fostered racial injustice and worsened black poverty. The conflict seemed unavoidable. Federal officials could not simultaneously meet union demands to steer clear of apprenticeship training and civil rights leaders' demands to implement laws against discrimination.

Nearly all skilled craft unions discriminated, but none had a worse record than the building trade unions where less than 1 percent of the membership was black. What the civil rights movement demanded was nothing less than the right guaranteed the white working class since the New Deal—the right to organize and compete without impediments in the labor market. On what grounds could the skilled trades deny to African Americans this fundamental democratic right, so central to all labor struggles?

Taking Affirmative Action

Even before Johnson became president it was apparent that the job-training programs had put the Democratic party on a collision course with the skilled trade unions. Seeking some compromise that would placate the unions without alienating African Americans, Johnson tried to entice the skilled trades with a voluntary agreement. In February of 1964 he asked the Construction Industry Joint Conference to devise a program to provide at least 5,000 apprenticeships for disadvantaged youths. The program the Conference endorsed offered remedial education and closely supervised on-the-job experience. It also used funds from MDTA to reimburse contractors for 20 percent of wage costs. All who completed the program—and 70 percent of the first group of trainees were African Americans—were guaranteed a union card and entry into an apprenticeship. By funding a program that was "union-initiated, union-sponsored and union-conducted," Johnson hoped that the "unions might well think a long time before refusing this chance to cooperate. . . ."[35]

Secretary of Labor Willard Wirtz praised the program as a "Model of what can be done to break this cycle of employability." It would preserve apprenticeship standards while "opening the doors to new opportunities for youngsters who otherwise would be facing the blind alley of the unskilled."[36] As Wirtz declared:

> I suggest no slacking in our enforcement of 64–7 [Kennedy's executive order] but believe that a program such as this might provide a very attractive alternate compliance route to many program sponsors. . . . It should have tremendous impact on those civil rights leaders who are disillusioned with pledges and distrustful of procedures, and who will not be satisfied until there are actual placements . . . it will also permit the President and the construction industry to show that results can be obtained without demonstrations.[37]

Although some union locals objected that the programs competed with bona fide apprenticeship training and subsidized nonunion competition for the jobs of union men, overall, union leaders agreed, "there is now generally a warmer climate toward MDTA programs than there was last year among apprenticeable trades."[38]

The warm climate turned quickly chilly when Title VII of the Civil Rights Act of 1964 put additional weight behind the federal government's right to intervene in union affairs. Title VII banned discrimination in employment on the basis of race, religion, national origin, or sex by private employers with fifteen or more employees, employment agencies, and local, state, and federal governments.[39] A clause specifically directed at unions prohibited discrimination in the admission of members, in admitting persons to apprenticeship programs, and in referring workers to jobs.[40] As the pressure increased on the building trades, labor organizations protested that Title VII "will allow a new federal bureaucracy to run roughshod over business and labor."[41] Trade unionists had reason to fear intervention by the federal government, for while Title VII initially had little clout, it provided a vehicle for circumventing organized labor's stranglehold on apprenticeships.

To administer Title VII the Act established a five-member Equal Employment Opportunity Commission (EEOC). The EEOC was authorized to investigate charges of discrimination and decide whether they had merit. If "reasonable cause" was found, it could attempt to eliminate the unlawful practice through informal conciliation and persuasion. If the charging party and the union failed to agree, the union could be sued in federal court. The U.S. attorney general could also institute proceedings, but this was likely only if the case had some national import. In practice, the right to sue had little significance, since few people with employment grievances could afford a lawsuit and such grievances were difficult to prove.[42]

Although the EEOC could agitate, the unions easily circumvented the law, an outcome expedited by the influence they wielded within the Department of Labor. The Bureau of Apprenticeship and Training (BAT), located within the Department of Labor, was responsible for establishing apprenticeship and training standards. Staffed primarily by former trade unionists, BAT persistently dragged its heels in making unions comply. BAT officials ignored most complaints filed against unions under the Equal Opportunity Act and took no action when its investigations revealed violations. Three years after passage of Title VII, BAT was still compiling a list of programs that had been warned. Further, unions listed as complying merely had to supply a statement of intent but did not have to demonstrate that they had put their intentions into action.[43]

I argued in Chapter 1 that policy legacies may thwart innovation, an outcome that is facilitated when state offices and agencies are linked to entrenched interests. All important BAT officials were former trade unionists, and BAT was run like a union department. Because the Department of Labor was linked to organized labor it frustrated federal efforts to pursue equal employment opportunity.

Despite linkages to the Department of Labor that allowed the skilled trades to defy the law, the pressure intensified. In 1964 the National Labor Relations Board ruled that discrimination by labor unions constituted an unfair labor practice. This ruling put unions that discriminated at risk of losing their certification. Decertification could pull the rug out from under the apprentice programs of at least 200 unions which relied heavily on federal funds. But decertification posed little threat to the building trade unions, which seldom depended on NLRB services and which often did not register for certification under the Taft-Hartley law.[44] For unions like the plumbers decertification merely meant losing the right to use apprentices on federal jobs.

Not surprisingly, a year after passage of the Civil Rights Act little progress had been made. Loopholes in the regulations made it possible for an apprenticeship program to comply with federal standards but still bar African Americans from membership.[45] In fact, as pressure to integrate increased, unions accelerated their use of tests, oral interviews, and education standards under the guise of maintaining standards.[46]

In 1965 the Department of Labor contracted with Professor Ray Marshall to study opportunities for African Americans in the building trades. Marshall's report in 1967 demonstrated that the building trades still refused to admit African Americans despite all federal efforts and all promises to do so. In fact, by 1967 the Department of Labor had yet to withdraw a contract for noncompliance. Following the report, the Department of Labor pushed BAT to take a harder line against unions that discriminated. It also made a special effort to increase participation of African Americans in construction. A landmark court decision in Ohio lent weight to these efforts, specifying that where African Americans were denied equal opportunity in apprenticeships, the Department of Labor had to withdraw federal contracts.

In 1968 the Department of Labor ruled that contractors could not receive federal contracts unless they took "affirmative action." Taking affirmative action meant proving that minorities would be represented in all trades on the job and in all phases of the work. Although the regulations did not establish quotas, they did state that hiring had to be related to the supply of minority workers in the area. Still, unions could get around the rules by issuing work permits to minorities without making them union members.

Under the new regulations the EEOC could now require all unions to report on whether they were complying with affirmative action and then decide if a particular union was discriminating. If it was, EEOC could then turn the case over to the attorney general to bring a civil suit against the offenders. While the process was time consuming, the Justice Department was filled with liberal, young, reform-minded lawyers eager to pursue such suits and to press for quotas in hiring.[47] They shaped the nature of affirmative action, establishing a framework that would become the basis for measuring racial, and later gender, equality. Whereas the Department of Labor had allowed unions to select the *most qualified applicants* as apprentices, the Justice Department insisted they accept for apprenticeship any African American who possessed qualifications equal to or higher than those of the *least qualified white person*. In subsequent court challenges, Justice Department lawyers won recognition of affirmative action principles. Affirmative action thus became a vehicle for bypassing union apprenticeship standards and pushing resistant unions to grant African Americans the right to work at jobs in the skilled trades.

As the federal government responded to demands from the civil rights movement for jobs in the building trades, it created programs that undermined trade union autonomy. BAT lost clout, the Department of Labor and the Department of Justice gained new weapons to pursue antidiscrimination policies, a new commission whose sole purpose was to enforce the law was created, and a new program of affirmative action was adopted. The state, which had virtually no power to touch internal union politics at the beginning of the decade, could now dig deeply into its core privileges.

Racial Cleavages in the Working Class

Discrimination in the skilled trades highlighted a wider concern of the labor movement: by excluding low-wage workers in general and black workers in particular, they were eroding their own power and vitality. As one OEO staff member noted:

> The manifestation of the change—which seems to me to be most profound—took the form of frank recognition by the union leaders [in private discussions] that subtle bars have heretofore limited the opportunities of ethnic minorities to participate widely in union activities, i.e., to get jobs. But just as profound and perhaps more significant, is the union leaders' recognition that the ebb of history is flowing against the role of the labor movement, and the further recognition that the incorporation of the so-called hard-core unemployed into the labor movement may be the only remedy which will stem the gradual loss of inertia in the trade union movement.[48]

Of course, not all trade unionists agreed that union discrimination hurt the cause. The building trades' members believed they had become the scapegoat of the civil rights movement, taking a "bum rap because of public concern over bigotry." The attack on their apprenticeship programs was motivated not by a moral cause but by an attempt to use "apprenticeship . . . to absorb the displaced persons, particularly youth, of an historic social crisis." In Philadelphia, where the building trade locals still refused to admit African Americans, the AFL and CIO split into warring camps with the CIO unions advocating a more aggressive nondiscrimination policy and the AFL affiliates holding back.[49]

On the national front Walter Reuther, president of the United Auto Workers and a man deeply committed to civil rights and to organizing the unorganized, represented the mass-production workers. The skilled workers' spokesman was the more conservative George Meany, a former plumber who envisioned a narrow role for trade unionism and who ruled the AFL-CIO with an iron fist. In 1968 a disgruntled Reuther withdrew the UAW from the AFL-CIO and formed an Alliance for Labor Action with the Teamsters.[50] Among the estimated two million black trade unionists 750,000 belonged to unions affiliated with the Alliance.[51]

The war over apprenticeships had badly damaged trade unionism, altering the nature of the union movement both structurally and ideologically, and weakening it politically.

In an attempt to salvage some shred of credibility and head off further government intervention, the AFL-CIO finally decided to tackle racism head-on. Working with the A. Philip Randolph Educational Fund, the AFL-CIO's Civil Rights Department designed an Outreach program to recruit minority workers into the skilled trades and to prepare them for the apprenticeship exams. From the unions' standpoint the Outreach program represented the solution to minority exclusion from the skilled trades: "It includes guarantees to the minority-group member of an avenue to higher-paying jobs and to the building trades member of maintaining the standards of his craft."[52] Funded in 1967 by the Department of Labor, Outreach was implemented in sixty-eight cities. By the end of 1969 5,304 minority apprentices were in the program, 2,910 of these in the targeted skilled trades controlled by the segregated unions. Still, the number of apprenticed African Americans in the Outreach program for the whole country was not even one-third of what civil rights leaders had asked for Chicago alone.

In his 1968 State of the Union address, President Johnson made job training a major priority. In addition to Outreach, MDTA received more than $11 million for apprentice-level on-the-job training programs.[53] Hoping to heal the breach between the Democratic party and the skilled trades, the Johnson administration sought to make Outreach a joint union–government effort. In Washington MDTA training funds supported Project Build, a joint project of the Building and Construction Trades Council (a local antipoverty agency), the U.S. Employment Service, and several community groups. Project Build was designed to give disadvantaged youth instruction and practical work experience in the construction industry and to prepare them for apprenticeships. Under the joint sponsorship of the Building and Trades Department and the Department of Civil Rights, similar programs began operating in twenty-three other cities.[54]

Simultaneously, presidents of the eighteen AFL-CIO building trade affiliates adopted their own "affirmative action" plan to bring more minorities into apprentice training. The plan essentially meant cooperating with planned or on-going programs in forty-eight cities jointly run by the unions, the Department of

Labor, and civil rights groups. In return for this gesture of compliance, Labor Secretary Wirtz promised not to impose a quota on minority hiring, an option that the unions vehemently opposed.[55]

In 1968 the AFL-CIO also established the Human Resources Development Institute (HRDI) to develop training programs for unemployed black workers. Operating under a Department of Labor contract, HRDI began training programs through local central labor councils in forty-seven cities. During the 1970s its activities expanded to include job development, placement, and apprenticeship programs.[56]

Despite these cooperative efforts, as Johnson stepped down from the presidency relations between the skilled trade unions and the Democratic party remained strained. Even as the Johnson administration sought compromises that would allow unions to desegregate at their own pace, the government gained considerable leverage in union activities. As one construction union officer complained: "In 1960 there were those who would have scoffed at the idea that federal government coordinates would be overseeing and in a sense steering the apprentice programs."[57]

In the 1968 election the Democratic share of the votes dropped by 19 percent as more than one-quarter of the 1964 Johnson vote shifted to Richard Nixon and George Wallace.[58] While the Vietnam War dominated public concern, voting patterns indicated that the presidential vote was more sharply polarized along racial lines than along lines of class or other social cleavages.[59] This "white backlash" reflected both white fears of the spectacle of urban ghettos in flames as well as growing weariness of the civil rights movement. In both the North and the South, "the occupational center of gravity of Wallace support was clearly among white, skilled workers."[60]

Undermining Union Autonomy

As the decade drew to a tumultuous close, public opinion on civil rights shifted from support for demonstrators with just grievances to resentment and anger against rioters who seemed ungrateful for the benefits bestowed by the Great Society. Attuned to the national mood, Richard Nixon repudiated the Great Society's solutions for ending poverty. During the 1968 campaign, he played on the resentments created by the antipoverty programs: "For the past five years we have been deluged by government programs for the unemployed, programs for the cities, programs for the poor, and we have reaped from these programs an ugly harvest of frustration, violence, and failure across the land." [61]

Though Nixon had won some hard-hat support in 1968, he owed nothing to black voters, 90 percent of whom had voted for Humphrey.[62] His constituents were the business community and the disgruntled middle class. Yet he revived a program called the Philadelphia Plan to force the construction unions to integrate. Why would he pursue a program that was bound to alienate his union converts?

One factor was his desire to temper criticism from the civil rights movement over his opposition to school busing and his conservative Supreme Court nominations. Further, in 1969 job protests in Chicago, Pittsburgh, and Seattle shut down construction projects and led to violent clashes between demonstrators and the white construction workers.[63] When the Department of Labor held hearings in October, construction workers staged angry counterdemonstrations.[64] Nixon might have owed little to African Americans but he could ill afford to ignore the threat of racial violence. Another concern was the inflationary wage–price spiral, which his advisors attributed to union wage increases. Implementing the Philadelphia Plan also represented a political calculus designed to keep the core Democratic constituencies at odds. As aide John Ehrlichman explained:

> Nixon thought that Secretary of Labor George Shultz had shown great style in constructing a political dilemma for the labor leaders and the civil rights groups. The NAACP wanted a tougher requirement; the unions hated the whole thing. . . . Before long, the AFL-CIO and the NAACP were locked in combat over one of the passionate issues of the day, and the Nixon administration was located in the sweet and reasonable middle.[65]

The Philadelphia Plan

On June 27, 1969, Labor Secretary George Shultz announced that government contracts in Philadelphia would fall under the "Philadelphia Plan." The Plan set a target range for minority hiring and timetables for meeting it. On each construction site, contractors were responsible for ensuring that between 22 and 26 percent of plumbers, pipefitters, and steamfitters and between 19 and 23 percent of sheetmetal, electrical, and elevator construction workers were minorities.[66] If the plan succeeded in Philadelphia, it would be instituted in nine other cities.

Not surprisingly, the plan triggered vehement opposition from the AFL-CIO, especially from the building trades department, whose president declared the union "100 percent opposed to a quota system."[67] The plan, in George Meany's estimation, would not increase minority representation in the trades, because contractors could comply by simply transferring African Americans already on the payroll from private to government jobs. Further, since the plan only applied on a job basis, it often would mean only a few months of work. Finally, a "good faith effort" clause in the plan created a loophole that allowed a contractor to comply with the federal order without hiring a single minority worker; simply calling the Urban League, an employment agency, or the union would be considered evidence of good faith. As Meany guessed, using "the Building Trades as a whipping boy could be designed to give the Nixon Administration a few brownie points to off-set their shortcomings in the civil rights area as a whole."[68]

Meany's strident protests reflected the importance of government contracts to the building trades. Over several decades the construction unions had lost the majority of home building to small, nonunion contractors; the bulk of their work came from industrial, commercial, and government construction.[69] The Philadelphia Plan posed a real threat to craft autonomy over hiring. Under the plan if a racial imbalance existed in the union membership, the employer could bypass the hiring hall and look elsewhere for workers. Not only would the union lose control over its most closely guarded prerogative, but the loss of autonomy over hiring in federal contracts could easily set a precedent that private employers would pursue to reduce wage costs.[70]

Yet the Philadelphia Plan worked. Through the early 1970s the Philadelphia Plan was implemented in cities throughout the country. Minority representation in the skilled craft unions increased significantly during this period.[71] In 1967 minorities accounted for less than 6 percent of all apprentices. In March 1971, the Department of Labor expanded the scope of the Philadelphia Plan to cover private construction projects of *all* federal contractors, an estimated one-third to one-half of the U.S. labor force. By 1973 minorities represented 14 percent and by 1979 17.4 percent.[72] Minority males had reached parity with whites in apprenticeship training. Hiring practices among federal contractors also experienced an enormous shift. In 1966 the workforce of federal contractors was disproportionately white; by 1974 their workforce had become disproportionately black.[73]

The Philadelphia Plan represented the first effective use of affirmative action to implement civil rights legislation by directing employers to guarantee equal employment opportunity. This outcome was only possible because the program evaded the entrenched union power structure. Yet the policies needed to implement equal opportunity also instituted a legacy that facilitated further government intervention in union affairs.

Expanding the Skilled Labor Pool

In the minds of skilled tradesmen, federal job training had become a formidable opponent. But the Nixon administration intervened even more directly in union prerogatives when it moved from hiring to wages.

In 1969 the wage–price spiral became an issue of national concern. A factor in creating it was the expansion of federal housing construction, initiated to relieve a housing shortage. In 1969 two commissions recommended a massive infusion of federal dollars into the housing market. The expansion of federal housing was a boon to construction workers, for it meant the job creation strategy, earlier rejected by the Johnson administration, was adopted indirectly. More jobs might alleviate the tensions between African Americans and the unions. But officials in the Nixon administration focused instead on increasing the labor supply to reduce spiraling wages. As Samuel Simmon, Assistant Secretary at the Department of Housing and Urban Development, argued: "It is an established fact that the high cost of skilled construction workers is a contributing factor to the inflationary nature of construction cost. Undoubtedly, the critical shortage of skilled craftsmen in the industry is a major reason for the union's ability to demand large wage increases. . . . It is absolutely essential that the Federal Government do everything possible to increase the supply of skilled craftsmen." [74]

Federal officials agreed that the wage–price spiral could not be controlled without controlling wage settlements in the construction industry. They suggested doubling vocational school training in construction trades, training 50,000 returning Vietnam veterans in construction, and requiring that apprenticeship programs be provided on all federal construction projects. Only by flooding the labor market with skilled workers could wages be reduced. [75]

In 1969 the Department of Labor increased funding for apprenticeship programs, expanding the labor pool in the skilled building trades and arousing the building trades' greatest worry. Defined as a civil rights measure, programs expanding the construction workforce were clearly designed to undermine union control over entry to the trade. Johnson had let the unions control the training programs. Nixon was less accommodating. So what if trade unions were "upset by the fact that in developing our plans for handling construction industry contracts, we . . . left out the AFL-CIO." [76]

Housing added fuel to the anti-union fire. On March 17, 1970, Nixon made a speech on the crises the nation faced. In Nixon's mind, the blame for the housing shortage lay on the shoulders of greedy construction workers. America couldn't provide adequate housing, he argued, because the scarce supply of skilled labor had run up labor costs. Runaway inflation in construction costs resulted "in the urban and rural decay that breeds crime, ill health, joblessness and despair." The solution to problems in the construction industry, and thus to urban unrest, lay in moderating "severe increases in the cost of labor (by) increasing the labor supply to meet the increasing demand." [77] Nixon proposed resolving the crisis by extending the Philadelphia Plan and by encouraging new technologies, such as off-site assembly of housing units, to reduce the need for skilled labor. Thus, in one proposal Nixon held the building trades responsible for urban rioting, proposed a means for reducing their control over entry to the crafts and for de-skilling labor, and addressed minority access to construction jobs. These measures, he declared, would spell "an end to archaic regulation that hampers productivity, more dynamic management, and most of all, more trained workers."[78] Then he went to work.

On March 29, 1971, Nixon asked labor and management to agree on a voluntary arrangement of wage controls. When none was forthcoming, he created a Construction Industry Stabilization Committee consisting of four members each from labor, industry, and the public and granted the Committee final jurisdiction over all wage increases in the industry.[79] In its first six months in operation the Committee disapproved more than 20 percent of collective bargaining agreements in the industry, forcing the unions to reduce wages. In 1970 wages and fringe benefits increased 19 percent; by the following year they had been reduced by 11 percent.[80]

In August, Nixon further pummeled the construction unions. "Our great construction industry," he declared, "accounts directly for almost one-tenth of the entire national output. . . . Yet costs and prices in the construction industry are moving up at an even more rapid rate than the already unsatisfactory performance of the general price level." To control the rapidly escalating prices, costs, and wages in the industry, Nixon directed all federal agencies to immediately reduce new contracts for government construction by 50 percent and to eliminate overtime on projects.[81]

Organized labor's control over wages hinged on maintaining a scarce labor supply. But just how scarce was it? To take a measure, the Department of Labor asked all state Employment Security Agencies to project manpower requirements in the construction industry to 1975.[82] The resulting "Special Survey of Manpower Needs in the Construction Industry" predicted industry expansion of 21.9 percent plus exits of present workers due to retirements or death, resulting in 801,000 new construction jobs by 1975.[83] To build the labor supply for the predicted manpower shortage, Nixon authorized the Construction Industry Collective Bargaining Commission to encourage local school districts to develop vocational education programs and to lobby unions and construction contractors to accept these programs as partial fulfillment of the requirements for entry to apprenticeships. He also commissioned the Department of Health, Education and Welfare to work with the states in developing vocational education programs in construction crafts and "to channel these trained people into productive employment."[84] These programs would offer to ghetto youth and to returning Vietnam veterans, many of whom were African American, the chance to learn a trade.

Nixon also directed the Department of Labor to expand enrollment in construction training programs by 50 percent and to increase this pace over the next five years. Rule after rule, plan after plan, undermined one union privilege after another. Now the Labor Department would study how apprenticeship programs could be improved, removing control over quality evaluation from the unions and placing it under federal jurisdiction. Now all federal construction contracts had to include a clause requiring the employment of apprentices. Now apprentices would be defined as individuals trained through a federal or state training program and certified by the Manpower Administration rather than individuals trained by unions. Now the Department of Labor would establish programs to upgrade skills in states where no formal apprenticeship programs existed—largely nonunion states. As program administrators explained: "About 50 percent of the construction industry is non-unionized. Training to meet the needs for this non-unionized segment should be no barrier in planning and establishing training courses." Now administrators would experiment with the classroom/shop setting for training in construction skills instead of the on-the-job training typical of union apprenticeships.[85] And now a pilot program would track information about jobs in the industry, a task previously under union control. Since tracking jobs involved extensive intervention in union affairs, government officials decided "to bring the International Union on board, and give them a voice in selecting the area where the project will be conducted."[86] But federal officials found union officials unwilling to discuss this project and went ahead without them.[87]

Not surprisingly, the predicted labor shortage never materialized. With new trainees flooding a recession-dampened market, by 1974 unemployment among construction workers had skyrocketed to 12.4 percent.[88] The combined impact of the antiunion activities of the federal government and the building contractors expanded the open shop share of the construction dollar from around 20 percent in 1968 to nearly 40 percent by 1975.[89]

In 1973 the Comprehensive Employment and Training Act (CETA) consolidated all of the major training programs into a single administrative structure. Although CETA began modestly, by 1979 its budget had grown to approximately $2.54 billion and its enrollments to three million annually. But unlike the training programs of the 1960s, CETA no longer directed funds to the most disadvantaged. Rather, job training was open to anyone who had been unemployed at least one week.[90]

The Legacy of Job Training

Rather than addressing practices in the private economy that impeded the right to work, the War on Poverty embarked on an ambitious agenda to train individuals and improve their employability. But as young, black men learned the skills to prepare them for construction jobs, they confronted trade unions that denied them this basic civil right. Discrimination in the skilled trades forced federal officials to find some means of ending the impasse. The strategy of gentle persuasion accomplished little. But civil rights activists seized the opportunity created by the new federal regulations to demonstrate against racist practices and to demand an open job market and the right to belong to a labor union. The outcome was a program of affirmative action that sought to implement equal employment opportunity and thus guarantee the right to work.

Affirmative action has recently come under attack by those who believe that the backlash against it has been too costly politically. The most fully developed argument has been presented by William Julius Wilson whose critique hinges on the distinction between two strategies in the development of affirmative action—equality of opportunity and group rights.

Wilson argues that the concept of equality of individual opportunity dominated the first phase of the civil rights movement when antidiscrimination legislation was designed to eliminate racial bias. In this first phase the important principle was not the percentage of minorities in certain positions but rather that candidates for these positions be judged solely on individual merit.[91] In the second phase, by contrast, government policy focused on the equitable distribution of group rights, which involved formally categorizing people on the basis of race or ethnicity. In this phase, affirmative action not only sought to ensure that minorities were free from discrimination but also to ensure that they were adequately represented.

What's wrong with programs emphasizing group rights, according to Wilson, is that they disproportionately benefit the more advantaged members of minority groups because they generally require a level of skill or of educational attainment that excludes the disadvantaged. Thus, minority individuals from the most advantaged families are most likely to be qualified for special admissions programs to law and medical schools, for high-level government jobs, for the foreign service, and for positions on university faculties. What's also wrong with programs emphasizing group rights is that they offend traditional American values that emphasize democracy and freedom of choice.

The problem with the first argument is that these two phases in the search for racial justice, equality of opportunity and group preference, did not originate as distinct strategies. Rather, they represent two components of a single objective. The concept of equality of opportunity defined an ideological vision of what American society promised its citizens; group rights became the means of achieving that vision.

As federal officials developed job training programs, they had to initiate group preference to enforce equality of opportunity. Instituting "targets" or quotas was the *only* way federal officials could make the skilled trades comply with the laws preventing discrimination in hiring and the *only* way they could measure whether they had succeeded. The concept of equality of opportunity is not inherently more in tune with traditional American values than the concept of group rights. What rankled skilled tradesmen was when federal officials tried to make equal opportunity a reality. Implementation, not ideology, was what was politically unacceptable.

The historical record also challenges the assertion that affirmative action favors the more privileged minorities. Affirmative action evolved out of federal efforts to open the skilled trades to poor, ghetto youths, not the more privileged middle class. The jobs they sought—as carpenters, bricklayers, plumbers—had few formal educational requirements. Rather, the only route of entry was through the union-controlled apprenticeship system, and the only formal preference was for relatives of union men. If more recently affirmative action has come to favor more advantaged, better-educated persons, the flaw lies not in the concept but in its implementation.

Finally, the argument that equality of opportunity fits with traditional American values whereas group preference offends them oversimplifies the trade-offs occurring. What was at stake in the battle between the skilled trade unions and the civil rights movement was not merely the skin color of apprentices but arduously constructed mechanisms that protected wages and working conditions in a volatile industry in which the demand for labor fluctuated seasonally and yearly.

Could any policy have created working-class solidarity instead of racial cleavages? Margaret Weir argues that a full-employment policy could have united African Americans and trade unions, since both felt the pressure of high unemployment. Instead, it created "narrow, constituency-targeted programs . . . that helped undercut the potential for an effective coalition."[92] Yet it seems unlikely that a full-employment policy would have been sufficient to encourage unions to willingly admit African Americans.

In the late 1960s a natural experiment occurred that can help determine whether a full-employment policy would have been sufficient to eliminate the racial divide in the working class. Beginning in 1969, before Nixon introduced the first quotas in the Philadelphia Plan, the federal government made a massive commitment to expand the supply of low-income housing. The construction unions had more work than they could handle. Instead of opening their doors to African Americans, despite enormous pressure to do so, they took advantage of the high labor demand to push up wages. The union response suggests that fears of job loss were not the only reasons the skilled trades discriminated against African Americans. Union racism mandated affirmative action. I explore these issues more fully in Chapter 4.

FOUR

Abandoning the American Dream

The right to choose one's place of residence is a basic civil right that is inextricably linked to the right to work without coercion. This concept was established in a British judgment in 1705 when a chief justice proclaimed: "All people are at liberty to live in Winchester, and how can they be restrained from using the lawful means of living there."[1] Decades of forced residential segregation had denied that right to African Americans and thus also the right to freely choose employment, obtain an education, and achieve a standard of living compatible with the prevailing living standard for white Americans.

From the New Deal to the 1960s, federal housing policy encouraged private home ownership for white families but not black families. Instead, federal policy reinforced barriers to residential choice erected by builders, money lenders, and realtors. Housing barriers not only relegated minorities to racially segregated housing but also virtually ensured that the quality of housing open to them was inferior. With the damage wrought by barriers to residential choice only too painfully apparent in the teeming urban ghettos, the civil rights movement demanded that the nation confront this impediment to democracy.

In response, the Johnson administration enacted the Fair Housing Act which banned discrimination in housing and the Model Cities program which promised to improve the quality of life in inner cities. Johnson also created a new Department of Housing and Urban Development (HUD) to provide more and better housing for the poor and put local housing authorities under HUD's jurisdiction. As it became apparent that improving housing quality for African Americans meant integrating white neighborhoods, these old-line agencies geared up to hold the color line. Hampered by this unwieldy conglomeration of New Deal programs, HUD was unable to realize its goals. Thus, the racial dynamic of the American welfare state was again set in motion. Social policy driven by racial inequality provoked a backlash that reduced the federal commitment to housing support except in the form of tax breaks on mortgages for the middle class. Urban ghettos were left to decay.

Building the Urban Ghetto

In the post-World War II era, black families migrated from rural areas to towns and cities in the South and from the South to the North. Private builders, lenders, and real estate brokers conspired with local officials to keep them confined to black neighborhoods. Zoning ordinances specifying where people could live and restrictive covenants—private agreements to exclude designated minority groups—created separate black and white neighborhoods. Any attempt by African Americans to cross the color line triggered sustained and often violent resistance from whites. In Detroit alone between 1945 and 1965 more than 200 violent incidents occurred in racially transitional neighborhoods.[2]

The victorious veterans returning from the war created a large and politically powerful lobby. In 1944 Congress established the Veteran's Administration (VA) to provide home loans for veterans. The VA operated like FHA, insuring low-interest, long-term loans for the purchase of single-family homes.[3]

In the years following the war, FHA-insured and VA-insured mortgages became the engines driving the housing markets. Expressways stretching across the countryside carried commuters to the ever-more-distant jobs, spurring the development of apartments and houses at the fringes of central cities or in their suburban rings. Combined with conventional loans, government-subsidized loans expanded housing construction to unprecedented levels in a frenzy of borrowing and building. Farms and orchards disappeared, leveled by developments with names like Sunnyside, Lakeshore, and, the pioneer of suburbia, Levittown. By 1962 the VA and FHA had financed more than $120 billion in new housing. Less than 2 percent was available to nonwhite families and most of that on a segregated basis.[4] Two powerful government agencies dominated the U.S. housing market, and their loan policies ensured that neighborhoods remained racially segregated.

Public housing, the ugly stepsister of federal housing policy, got a boost with the Housing Act of 1949, which promised "a decent home in a suitable living environment for every American family."[5] The Act authorized the construction of 810,000 public-housing units over the next six years and provided funds for massive urban redevelopment, ostensibly to clear slums and make way for new developments. Five years later the Housing Act of 1954 provided additional funds for "urban renewal."[6] Devised by a powerful lobby of realtors, banks, and downtown merchants, urban renewal allowed local authorities to assemble large parcels of land, bulldoze them to the ground, and then sell the land to private developers.[7] In city after city, local authorities used urban-renewal funds to demolish the homes of the poor. Instead of building public housing in their place, they developed "enterprise" zones of office buildings, hotels, and shops.[8] By 1960 more than 400,000 homes had been destroyed but only 10,760 low-rent units built. Much of the destroyed housing was owned or rented by black families. Critics of federal housing policy caustically noted that urban renewal was a synonym for Negro removal.

The public housing that *was* built was racially segregated and confined almost entirely to central cities. And every city had its projects.[9] In San Francisco six nearly all-black public-housing projects were grouped in the Hunter's Point area. In Chicago two FHA projects, one in a virtually all-white neighborhood, the other all-black, resulted in totally segregated public housing. In Cincinnati two projects were 99.7 percent African American, as were those in Boston.[10]

Indirectly, other government agencies reinforced housing segregation, in the process locking African Americans out of opportunities for good jobs. In choosing where to locate military installations, the Department of Defense ignored local housing policies in its off-base housing program. As a result, African Americans could not work at many installations because they couldn't find housing. The General Services Administration awarded the enormous rental and leasing business of the government to realtors whose housing operations were racially restricted. The Atomic Energy Commission located the world's largest atom smasher, an enormous jobs-generating facility, in an area notorious for housing barriers.[11] No one seemed to care about the plight of black families, least of all the federal government.

The civil rights movement was gathering steam, however, and housing segregation was among its grievances. During his 1960 presidential campaign, John Kennedy promised to sign an executive order eliminating discrimination in housing. But eliminating housing segregation meant enforcing housing integration, a political hot potato that Kennedy was unwilling to touch. Postponing action on housing until after the 1962 congressional elections, Kennedy then issued a limited order prohibiting federally supported housing projects from selecting tenants by race.[12] The Public Housing Authority narrowly interpreted the order as referring only to housing built after 1962 and as applying only to the selection of tenants, not to the selection of sites. As a result, public housing—massive, ugly, concrete-slab buildings that squeezed hundreds of families into a few city blocks—was still built in the inner cities.

Title VI of the Civil Rights Act of 1964 banned discrimination in housing receiving federal assistance and established an open housing policy for all newly constructed housing in urban-renewal areas. These new policies did little to end housing segregation, however, because the era of FHA and VA domination of housing finance had drawn to a close. By 1963 FHA and VA financed less than 20 percent of new housing; the executive order and Title VI combined covered less than 4 percent of the existing housing supply and only 15 percent of anticipated new development.[13] Further, provisions for enforcing the law were so weak that local officials who wanted to keep black families out could easily circumvent them.[14]

Planning the Nation's Housing Agenda

In 1964 Johnson established a Task Force on Metropolitan and Urban Problems. Chaired by Robert Wood, head of the Department of Political Science at the Massachusetts Institute of Technology, and comprised mostly of intellectuals from elite eastern universities, the task force first had to decide what the key issues confronting the cities were. As Wood recalls, at that time "a number of the intellectuals still doubted that there was an urban crisis."[15] They finally proposed a rent-supplement program to help bridge the gap between the very poor who resided in public housing and the working poor, who were ineligible for any support from Uncle Sam.[16] Rent supplements had several attractive features, the biggest being that they would disperse the poor throughout all neighborhoods. By mixing rent-supplement families in buildings with families paying full rents, the stigma associated with public housing would be avoided.

A seemingly innocent idea, rent supplements provoked heated arguments from opponents. Since black families could use them in any neighborhood, the supplements could become a backdoor mechanism for integration. Southern congressmen eliminated that risk by guaranteeing localities the right to approve rent supplements before they were put into effect.[17] The agreement replicated the New Deal compromise that had relegated African Americans to the inferior social assistance programs: keep direct benefits to individuals under local control.

Johnson threw his weight behind the rent-supplement program, which he lauded as "the most crucial new instrument in our effort to improve the American city." Families eligible for rent supplements would pay 25 percent of their income toward rent; the government would pay the difference up to full-market rent. Older people, people who lost homes to the urban-renewal bulldozer, *and* anyone living in substandard housing could have help with housing costs. That last category, so vague and thus so troublesome, was attacked by fiscally conservative Republicans, who charged that the income limits were too high, and by southerners, who feared so open a program.[18] That year Congress appropriated funds for planning rent supplements but refused to fund them.[19]

The Housing Act of 1965 made rent supplements a reality but only for the very poor. Section 23 authorized local housing authorities to sublet private housing units to low-income families who were poor enough to qualify for regular public housing. The tight income limits meant the working poor were excluded. *If* rent supplements had supported working families and *if* they had had no loopholes that communities could use to exclude African Americans, they could have helped to integrate the entire housing market and thus have given upwardly-mobile black families a boost out of the ghetto. They did neither. Rather, they reinforced the view that federal housing support was only for the poor, especially the black poor.

In addition to rent supplements, Wood's task force recommended that Johnson gather the nation's housing programs under an umbrella agency. The new agency could subsume the functions of the Housing and Home Finance Agency (HHFA), the Federal Home Loan Bank Board, and such programs as urban highway construction and waste treatment that affected the quality of housing in the nation.[20] Such a plan would allow the government to achieve more ambitious goals than merely constructing (or demolishing) housing for the poor.

Southern congressmen, ever vigilant, opposed the merger, denouncing it as creeping socialism. They feared not only what a powerful federal housing agency might do but also that Robert Weaver, a black man in charge of the HHFA, might become its new head. Their opposition put the proposal on hold.[21] Despite the momentum generated by the Civil Rights Act and the War on Poverty, the southern racial agenda still exerted a negative influence on federal policy.

Committed to rebuilding the cities, Johnson was not so easily dissuaded. In his 1965 State of the Union message, he proposed a new Department of Housing and Urban Development that would become the center of urban policy. Instead of merely encouraging new construction, the new agency would develop entire metropolitan areas and become a focal point "for thoughtful innovation and solutions about the problems of our cities."[22] That July Johnson asked Robert Wood to put together a new Task Force on Urban Problems to plan the cabinet-level housing agency.[23] Brought on board were Ben Heineman, president of the North-western Railroad, civil rights leader Whitney Young, and Walter Reuther, president of the United Auto Workers. Midway through an elegant White House dinner, the president joined the men and made a few remarks. As Wood recalls, Johnson was "superbly at home on the domestic issues for August [the Watts riot] had not occurred." [24]

When Watts erupted a month later, it altered the meaning of the "urban problem," infusing it with a new urgency. Johnson was now eager to mount an assault on the slums. He ordered the Task Force to plan the new department so it could better integrate physical housing needs with the more complex social issues that any discussion of housing policy invariably generated. The new department would not only coordinate federal programs but seek ways to apply them between the cities, where the black migrants were concentrated, and the lily-white suburbs. Though the Task Force rejected a proposal to also transfer OEO's community action programs to the new agency, it clearly envisioned an ambitious agenda for housing policy, one that might resolve the "urban problem" by integrating the suburbs.

Without a new federal agency, housing policy would remain mired in precedents established during the New Deal, precedents that maintained housing segregation. But numerous housing programs were already operating, and the federal government couldn't simply start over. Further, even a new agency could do little as long as housing segregation was legal. The dilemma was thus twofold: the nation needed a federal agency that could merge existing housing programs into a single unit and it also needed a fair-housing policy.

Pursuing Equal Opportunity in Housing

In 1960 only four states and two cities had fair-housing laws banning racial discrimination in private housing. And housing segregation was at the heart of racial inequality. Between 1954 and 1965 more than half of the new industrial buildings, stores, hospitals and schools were built outside the central city. During the same period costs of public transportation rose faster than costs of automobiles. The new jobs developed where African Americans could not live and where transportation was time consuming, expensive, and often unavailable.[25] By 1965 housing integration had moved to the top of the civil rights agenda.

That year Martin Luther King launched a civil rights campaign in Chicago. He staged a series of marches in white neighborhoods to protest housing segregation. Housing segregation mobilized the flagging movement as no other issue had been able to do, but it also mobilized white opposition as entrenched as that of any backwater Mississippi town. A violent confrontation between civil rights demonstrators and white protestors terminated one march. Two days after a rally at Soldier Field, when police turned off a fire hydrant where children had been cooling off, a four-day riot erupted.

When King threatened to march in Cicero, a notoriously racist white suburb, Mayor Daley agreed to convene a summit meeting between the city's establishment and the civil rights leaders. At the second meeting, King promised to stop marching if Chicago would open its suburbs. But open housing never materialized in Chicago. Instead, King suffered the worst defeat of his career as he learned the hard lesson that white resistance here was far more effective than in the South.[26]

Elsewhere other civil rights groups picked up the torch. For more than a decade the National Committee Against Discrimination in Housing (NCHD), a conglomeration of labor and civil rights groups, had been agitating for open housing.[27] A relatively weak organization initially, the committee's annual budget grew from $18,000 in 1956 to $120,000 in 1964 and its member organizations from twenty-four to sixty-three. The NCHD focused its attack on federal housing policy: "The federal government is primarily responsible for building a ghetto system that has created racial alienation and tensions so explosive that the crisis in our cities now borders on catastrophe."[28]

Other organizations focused on local issues. In Akron a coalition led by the NAACP and CORE carried out a door-to-door campaign against the city's failure to pass fair housing legislation.[29] In New York the Urban League began an "Open City" campaign to encourage African Americans to seek housing in white neighborhoods. In the District of Columbia CORE lodged a complaint against a real estate agency for quoting higher prices to black buyers than to whites.[30]

Civil rights leaders found an unexpected ally among some business leaders who recognized that fair housing could be good for business. Employers who depended on government contracts had to hire minorities to comply with equal opportunity initiatives. A labor shortage also made employers aware that segregated housing patterns put most skilled and unskilled minority workers out of reach. The Caterpillar Tractor Company, for example, studied the residential patterns of its 584 black employees and found that none lived in the county where they worked. Eleven offers the company had made to black college graduates the previous year had been rejected because there was no integrated housing in commuting distance. As the *Sun Times* explained: "Skilled Negro workers are refusing jobs in the suburbs because they can't find homes there, and the situation is giving labor-short white industrialists a pain in the pocketbook." [31]

Some business executives undertook activities to open white neighborhoods and communities to African Americans. In Portland, Oregon, the prestigious City Club, an organization of doctors, lawyers, and businessmen, forced the city council to approve a public housing site in a prosperous white, middle-class neighborhood. In Hartford, Connecticut, the Senior Vice President of Traveler's Insurance Company headed a local housing committee that provided a business-backed revolving fund for integrated housing. And in Illinois, Indiana, and Maryland, individual business leaders testified in favor of open-housing laws, often in the face of strong local opposition. [32]

By 1966 twenty states had enacted fair-housing laws, and legislation was pending in ten others. These laws varied greatly in scope, with some limited to publicly-assisted housing while others included privately financed housing as well. In addition to the state legislation, more than thirty municipalities had adopted fair-housing ordinances. [33]

As the fair-housing movement made headway, a backlash against it began gathering steam. Detroit approved an ordinance preventing anyone from interfering with the rights of property owners. In Akron, Ohio, the people approved an amendment to the city charter requiring the electorate's approval of any ordinance regulating the lease or sale of property on the basis of race. The Ohio Association of Real Estate Boards petitioned for a referendum to nullify the Ohio fair-housing law. The Kansas state legislature rejected a fair-housing bill. And voters in Berkeley, California, and in Seattle and Tacoma, Washington, voted down fair-housing ordinances.[34]

The scattered resistance to housing integration coalesced in California, where voters passed Proposition 14 repealing the state's fair-housing laws. Fair housing brought down Governor Pat Brown, whose opponent, Ronald Reagan, campaigned against fair-housing legislation as "an infringement of one of our basic individual rights."[35] The defeated Brown later ruefully recalled the price he paid for being out of touch with the average voter:

> I supported a bill called the Rumford bill, which was a fair housing bill. . . . It had real teeth. . . . I fought very hard for it. . . . It was only at the last day we got it through. This, however, was a very pyrrhic victory because the real estate people and the great majority of people in California were very offended by the housing bill. They knew that I led the fight for it, and they put on the ballot an initiative measure that prohibited a legislature from ever compelling a person to sell his home for any reason whatsoever. . . . In other words, I was completely out of tune with the white citizens of the state who felt that the right to sell their property to whomever they wanted was a privileged right, a right of ownership, a constitutional right. I just went down to defeat and it played a great part in my subsequent fall.[36]

Following the California victory, thirteen other states introduced similar legislation.[37] For many white Americans, property rights superseded civil rights.

Fair-housing legislation also faced resistance from the real estate lobby, comprised of 17 national trade associations—including the National Association of Home Builders, the United States Savings and Loan League, and the Mortgage Bankers of America—and the Chamber of Commerce.[38] The lobby had geared up when Title IV of the 1964 Civil Rights Act loomed on the horizon. But this time key groups within the lobby took no position on fair housing, and some organizations even supported the proposed legislation. Supporters were found among those who developed federally assisted housing and who believed that private developers had a competitive edge in not having to abide by existing regulations. Thus, splits within the lobby itself as well as the national momentum toward civil rights issues neutralized the realtors' opposition.

Despite the opposition, in 1966 Johnson first tried to push a national fair-housing bill through Congress. The road ahead seemed long and hard. As staff assistant Joseph Califano recalls, the bill "prompted some of the most vicious mail LBJ received on any subject (and the only death threats I ever received as a White House assistant)."[39] The bill that emerged from the House contained such limited fair-housing provisions and so many anti-civil rights amendments that Martin Luther King said it wasn't worth passing. It recognized the right of individual families to discriminate in selling their homes and to require their realtors to do so. Fair housing faced an ever greater battle in the Senate, where Everett Dirksen branded it a threat to the country and insisted that the real problem was the behavior of African Americans who moved into white areas. A filibuster by opponents ended the fair-housing debate that year.[40]

In 1968 Congress passed a fair-housing bill with little debate. What intervened were two years of riots and the assassination of Martin Luther King.

At 7:30 on a balmy spring evening in April, an assassin's bullet ended the career of Martin Luther King. It also ended the civil rights movement's commitment to passive resistance. Within hours the cry "Burn, Baby, Burn" swept through Memphis; New York; Boston; Jackson, Mississippi; and Raleigh, North Carolina with the worst devastation visited upon Washington, D.C. As the riots intensified, it seemed nothing could assuage the fury. Determined to avoid the bloodshed of Watts, Johnson at first refused to use the Marines guarding the capitol. But after four days the riots had spread to more than 100 cities. Fed up with restraint, Congress demanded that looters be shot at will.

Even before the last riot ended, Johnson, flanked by black leaders and members of Congress, called for "constructive action instead of destructive action in the hour of national need."[41] What might better rekindle hope than fair housing? Just a month earlier, on March 11, 1968, the Senate had approved a fair-housing bill, but chances of getting it through the House were slim. On

April 10, less than a week after King's assassination, it passed in the House. Title VIII of the Civil Rights Act of 1968 banned discrimination in the sale, rental, or financing of most housing units and brought millions of single-family homes owned by private individuals under federal fair-housing law. The Act authorized the new Department of Housing and Urban Development to handle specific cases of housing discrimination as well as a broad range of affirmative action activities.[42]

Confronting the New Deal Legacy

HUD had begun operating in 1966. It subsumed under one roof all the federal housing agencies, except FHA.[43] Each agency had its own lobby in Congress and its own source of congressional support. HUD's new head, Robert Weaver, saw his first task as pulling the whole thing together by scrambling it up. He decided to reorganize by areas of specialization: the inner city would be placed under one assistant secretary, the metropolitan area under another, urban renewal under yet a third, and so forth. Only the Federal National Mortgage Association, Fannie Mae, remained intact.[44] By erasing clear lines of authority between agencies, Weaver's decisions allowed the former New Deal agencies to continue operating independently at the local level. Local agencies were staffed by employees committed to maintaining the status quo and vulnerable to pressures from local communities. Prime culprits in creating patterns of racial segregation and in shutting African Americans out of the housing market, most continued business as usual.

At the top, however, Weaver's new staff consisted of idealistic liberals who optimistically believed they had the tools to resolve the ghetto's ills. As one staffer wrote, "Many of the conditions . . . can be substantially corrected with a minimum of organized, well directed effort." Still, the central office had to convince local staff to adopt HUD's new agenda: "If there are staff members who suffer a misconception of HUD's purpose, they must be convinced . . . that HUD's very existence is based on the broader motives . . . of human revitalization. . . ."[45] But convincing the regional offices to restructure housing policy proved a formidable task.

HUD's Civil Rights Agenda

HUD was responsible for both the executive order issued by Kennedy prohibiting racial discrimination in public housing projects and Title IV of the Civil Rights Act requiring open housing in all newly constructed housing financed by the federal government. Administering both pieces of legislation was in itself a complex task, for some HUD projects were subject to the executive order alone, some solely to Title IV, and some to both. The executive order exempted one- and two-family, owner-occupied homes from antidiscrimination regulations; Title IV did not. The executive order applied only to low-rent public housing built after the date of the order; Title IV was retroactive to all low-rent public housing.[46] Separate regulations covered government-subsidized housing and the private market; within the private housing market, similar housing was governed by different rules depending on when it was built. The lack of a single national fair-housing policy, still more than two years down the road, made enforcing any regulations onerous.

Integrating public housing meant changing rules for selecting tenants and for selecting sites. In principle, policies for selecting tenants could be easily revised. Prior policy allowed prospective tenants to choose among housing projects when an opening became available. As a result, housing projects dominated by African Americans had numerous vacancies, despite long waiting lists for public housing. White families simply waited for openings in sites in white projects. HUD's new policy limited free choice. When an opening became available in any project—regardless of its racial composition—the next eligible applicant would be offered a unit in that project. If the applicant declined that offer, he or she would be eligible for three more choices and then dropped back to the bottom of the waiting list.

Local housing officials, who felt community antagonism most directly, strenuously resisted the new policies. When local officials in Portland, Oregon, were told of HUD's new policy for selecting and assigning tenants, "the mood was one of anger and opposition to the tightened policy requirements."[47] The Seattle Housing Authority ominously told HUD officials, it would be "heard from" in Portland.[48]

As controversial as tenant selection was, site selection drew even greater opposition. HUD policy prohibited building new projects in segregated neighborhoods, which in practice meant black neighborhoods, unless no other acceptable sites were available. However, when sites in white neighborhoods were available, local residents fiercely fought locating public housing there, and local housing authorities backed them up. So HUD continued building new housing in black neighborhoods. In Atlanta, for example, the NAACP complained that the local housing authority built new public housing in the primarily black northwest area, where 83 percent of the low-rent housing was already located. HUD officials then insisted that two of four new public housing proposals originally proposed for the northwest area be shifted to the southeast, one to a mixed neighborhood, the other to an all-white neighborhood.[49] Immediately local whites complained. Thus, instead of integrating public housing, the new regulations drew whites out of public housing.

HUD was also responsible for ensuring that families displaced by urban renewal found adequate and affordable new housing. When local housing authorities relocated the victims of urban renewal, they often moved them to racially segregated neighborhoods, thereby increasing racial concentration.[50] In Louisville, Kentucky, for example, the local housing authority relocated all black families displaced by a development project into the West End even though "employment opportunities, good schools, recreational facilities, stores, etc [were] located in the city's East and South End."[51] Similarly, in Cleveland 1100 of 1300 families displaced by urban renewal were black; 88 percent of the black families were then relocated to already segregated neighborhoods.[52]

Civil rights organizations complained bitterly that HUD was moving too slowly, that by 1967 the Department of Justice had yet to initiate litigation to enforce either the executive order or Title IV, and that Weaver continued to grant funds to townships operating in violation of Title IV.[53] Yet HUD's hands were tied, not only by the lack of cooperation at the local level but also by lack of funds. In 1967 Congress cut its requested appropriations for enforcement from 15 million to less than 2 million.[54]

As HUD came under fire for delaying integration, Johnson established yet another task force to evaluate HUD's civil rights efforts. The Aggressive Action Task Force of Intergroup Relations Staff was convened in March 1966 to develop comprehensive affirmative action measures for all existing HUD programs and to achieve "equal opportunity in housing, maximum participation by minorities and maximum desegregation and racially inclusive use patterns." [55] Housing policy had become fully absorbed by the struggle for racial equality. And it had still to address an equally complex issue, that of improving the quality of housing.

HUD's Social Rights Agenda

The idea of rebuilding the cities had been brewing in Johnson's mind since Walter Reuther had first proposed an ambitious plan for converting unused bomber plants to factories for mass producing low-cost housing components. [56] A task force suggested initiating a demonstration project to see if the government could transform the slums. "Demonstration Cities" would build new homes, parks, and community centers and provide health care, transportation, and police protection. Johnson agreed to try a modest project. [57] But by the time his Demonstration Cities and Metropolitan Development Act went to Congress, it had expanded to include six large cities, ten medium-sized cities, and fifty small cities. It also included a plan to promote racial integration of housing. The latter was more than Congress was willing to swallow, especially its southern contingent. Southerners raged against the plan for promoting racial integration and complained that there were already enough "demonstrations," meaning riots, in the cities. To pacify the opposition, the name was changed to "Model Cities" and the requirement that new housing be integrated was dropped. On November 3, 1966, Johnson signed the Model Cities bill, minus any provisions against discrimination. [58]

Model Cities authorized HUD to provide grants and technical assistance to communities to rebuild neighborhoods. It also required that residents of the neighborhood be employed in planning activities and executing the program, a watered-down version of community action. [59] But final authority rested in the hands of the mayors, a strategy designed to avoid the controversy surrounding the community action programs. As Weaver explained, "The CAP organizations are outside of city government. I take the position that in Model Cities we've got to work *through* city governments."[60]

The only problem was that working through city governments made undoing the New Deal legacy difficult, if not impossible. As Model Cities began operating, it perpetuated racial discrimination in housing policy. In Atlanta, according to the NAACP, the Model City proposal excluded African Americans from the executive board and advisory committees: it "was weak in the area of citizen participation and had no Negro representatives from the target neighborhood."[61] In Louisville, Kentucky, both CORE and the NAACP protested that the city's Model Cities application was "actively vindictive against Negroes" and would increase segregation patterns.[62]

Housing Policy and Urban Disorder

Every project HUD launched fueled the struggle for racial equality and created a white backlash. The National Urban League, the NAACP, and the National Committee Against Discrimination in Housing now focused the civil rights effort against HUD. They sought to halt urban-renewal projects, they challenged the location of low and moderate income housing, and they threatened to sue over tenant assignments in public housing that perpetuated racial segregation.[63] HUD became an agency under siege, a focal point for the anger and discontent over the intransigent civil rights issues that plagued the nation's cities.

Stung by charges that HUD was fomenting disorder, in August 1967 Weaver created an Urban Tensions Response Network to evaluate HUD's role in the riots. The Network would develop a tension data plan, create a central information file, and develop a system for gathering information from the regional administrators, all centered in HUD's "war room." In the war room, staff tracked urban racial tension and calculated HUD's contribution to it.[64]

As regional administrators circulated reports of unrest, it seemed that HUD policies were, indeed, at the center of urban disorder. In Pittsburgh HUD's tenant selection policy inflamed black and white residents of public housing. In New York conflict over the distribution of Model City funds set African Americans and Puerto Ricans at odds. In Nashville local civil rights groups complained that the Nashville Housing Authority employed few African Americans, that less than 15 percent of the public housing units were integrated, and that the Housing Authority had failed to adopt a satisfactory plan for assigning tenants to housing.

Urban tensions were exacerbated by a housing shortage. The housing shortage was created by the massive black migration to the cities and the lack of outlets outside the urban centers. By 1967 it had reached crisis proportions. Two government commissions investigating the problem, the National Commission on Urban Problems and the President's Committee on Urban Housing, agreed that 26 million new and rehabilitated housing units needed to be produced within 10 years.[65] Yet with the Vietnam War absorbing an ever-increasing share of the federal budget, the government could little afford to finance so ambitious an objective. Instead, Johnson turned to the private sector. The proposal that emerged was written by the banking lobby. The lobby opposed direct government subsidies to the poor, because new money pouring into the housing market would increase the money supply and lower interest rates. Instead, the bankers proposed an interest subsidy program, which would drive interest rates up. The proposal looked like this: If interest on mortgages was running at 7 percent, the Treasury would pay 6 percent to the mortgage bankers, who would immediately put $5 billion into financing new construction. Since 6 percent of $5 billion was only $300 million, the nation would get $5 billion in new housing for only $300 million.

The proposal became the Housing and Urban Development Act of 1968. Hailed as a solution to riots and housing shortages, the sweeping but hastily conceived measure promised twenty-six million new low-income housing units within 10 years. Among the new programs aimed at achieving that objective was Section 235, a program of subsidies to encourage home ownership among the poor. Section 235 allowed HUD to make monthly subsidy payments to lenders, thereby reducing rates to borrowers to as low as 1 percent. The loans were made at the market rate with the government paying the difference between the market rate and the 1 percent. Section 235 made possible riskier loans in areas that had been redlined by substituting an "acceptable risk" requirement for the "economic soundness" requirement in previous FHA loan policies. A Special Risk Insurance Fund that would pay losses to lenders also opened FHA mortgage insurance to older, declining urban areas.

The new legislation encouraged FHA to pay moneylenders to make loans to the poor. But by eliminating the standards that had locked African Americans out of the housing market, the legislation also eliminated the regulations that had stabilized property values. Because the subsidy provided under Section 235 was attached to the house rather than to the family, it encouraged builders to sell poor families expensive homes. Families were only responsible for mortgage payments of 20 percent of their adjusted gross incomes. It didn't matter whether a higher priced house represented more "house" since they did not pay the extra cost themselves.[66] HUD appraisers and inspectors were the only means of holding down costs and preventing fraud. The 1968 Housing Act thus allowed private capital to transfer the risk of financing inner city housing to FHA, in the process creating a lucrative new market that was almost totally unregulated.[67]

The FHA now had a national mission to house the poor, and the word from Weaver and the FHA commissioner to cautious bureaucrats was: deliver housing. However, inner cities lacked sufficient space on which to build six million new units of assisted housing, and the government could not increase existing patterns of racial segregation by building there. The production goals of the Housing Act combined with the integration goals of the Civil Rights Act could *only* be met by building the new low-income housing in suburbia. Although both the mandate and the funds were available to undo the damage of the New Deal legacy—to eliminate ghettos and to provide decent housing for poor people of all races—the suburbs, the primary constituents of Richard Nixon's new right agenda, remained lily-white. At first, Nixon pursued fair housing more aggressively than his predecessor, but as he realized the political costs of pressing housing integration, he reneged on his promise and turned his back on low-income housing.

Lowering the Curtain on Low-Income Housing

In assuming the presidency, Nixon made two fateful changes in HUD operations. First, he merged FHA with HUD, placing an old-line conservative agency under the management of a new, liberal one. Then he further decentralized responsibility on the grounds that district offices were better able to monitor their own needs and problems. In practice, decentralization meant that those at the top had no way of knowing what was going on in the field. It allowed the policy legacy of the New Deal to continue to frustrate efforts to alter the course of federal housing policy.

Creating Open Communities

In forming his cabinet, Nixon appointed his former opponent for the Republican nomination, Michigan governor George Romney, to head HUD. Immediately, Romney tackled the fair-housing mandate he had inherited from the Johnson administration. His ambitious "open communities" policy promised to provide African Americans access to housing and thus to job opportunities in the suburbs. The push for fair housing was a joint effort between HUD and the Justice Department. Within months after the 1968 Civil Rights Act was passed, the attorney general began pursuing violators of fair-housing codes. In *U.S. v. Elaine Mintzes and Allen S. Mintzes*, the Supreme Court upheld the constitutionality of the prescription against blockbusting. In *U.S. v. M. E. Rockhill Inc.*, the attorney general asked that covenants in any deed forbidding the sale of lots to African Americans or other noncaucasians be declared void and unenforceable. In *U.S. v. Lake Lucerne Land Co.*, the attorney general asked that the private club associated with the Lake Lucerne subdivision be enjoined from using a covenant forbidding the sale of lots to African Americans and Jews. In addition to such direct discriminatory acts, the attorney general also took action against the more subtle tricks used to discourage African Americans. Suit was brought against the Charnita Vacation Estates for failing to solicit African Americans to attend dinners for potential customers and for failing to provide African Americans information about the availability of property on the same basis as it was provided to whites. The Lake Caroline

Property Owners Association was charged with instructing their employees "to use special racial designations regarding prospective purchasers to assure that Negro purchasers would not be solicited." [68]

HUD's most powerful weapon was its ability to hold back funds from communities that refused to comply with open-communities priorities. Because HUD programs were so diffused across different departments, however, staff had difficulty identifying which communities weren't complying. Not only were data lacking that separated HUD outlays from total federal expenditures, there was no way to even know how much HUD funds most cities received. And even if a community could be identified, withholding such incentives as FHA mortgage insurance was unlikely to have much impact. Less than 14 percent of new housing received FHA financing.

HUD could also use its grant program to reward communities that came up with concrete proposals for reducing segregation. But most established middle- and upper-class suburbs were constructed primarily through private, not public, loans and found HUD programs were of marginal interest. [69] Still, with few alternatives HUD officials decided upon a "radical reorganization and coordination of our grant decisions" that would emphasize the carrot, not the stick. Reorganization would "expand suburban housing opportunities for low-income families and particularly members of minority groups and make the core cities more attractive to middle- and upper-income groups." [70]

By September, open communities was on the move. Rochester, Boston, several Long Island counties, and Newark, where both housing and labor were in short supply, became the first prongs of the attack. As open communities advanced, the latent backlash began to boil to the surface. Yes, people were sympathetic to the plight of the inner-city residents at whom the 1968 legislation was aimed. But white, working-class, urban residents were already feeling threatened by racial integration and ignored by federal policies that seemed solely devoted to bettering housing for African Americans; suburbanites remained uninterested in ghetto problems and increasingly fearful of what open housing might do to their communities. Low-income families would place more of a burden on sewers, roads, and the water supply than they contributed in taxes, would flood the school systems and reduce the quality of education, and would bring in unwanted high-density developments. And though Romney stressed economic integration, this term was quickly translated by suburban residents into racial integration, which might also reduce property values. As one Chicago planner explained:

> A mayor would have to be nuts to want to do what the Government says he ought to. Can't you just see him telling his constituents, "Now it may hurt your property values, and overcrowd your schools, and mix you with people you came here to get away from, but don't fret. It will also cost you money." [71]

Suburban communities had already devised a number of strategies to protect themselves from such unwelcome invasions. By failing to adopt workable programs or by local resolutions, they excluded housing that received rent supplements. By zoning only large lots, they increased the cost of housing beyond that which low-income families could afford. They used zoning and building codes to deter developers. They refused to install water and sewage facilities that would be sufficient for high-density development. Though these tactics could be overcome through federal legislation, HUD staff recognized that "the more frontal the assault on cherished principles of home rule, the less likely the legislation is to be enacted." [72]

As Romney attempted to pursue his open communities policies, both urban and suburban communities dug in their heels. When HUD decided to fund a six million-dollar public-housing project in an all-white section of south Atlanta, congressman Fletcher Thompson reported that his office was swamped with calls from angry residents. At Thompson's request Romney agreed to hold up funds pending a review of the project's suitability. But though Romney backed down in Atlanta, in cities like Toledo, Ohio, and Warren, Michigan, he held firm, refusing to release federal funds where racial discrimination in housing existed.

The Blackjack case was a turning point for the Nixon administration. To exclude a low- and middle-income-integrated housing project, Blackjack, Missouri, a suburb of St. Louis, reincorporated itself and then changed its zoning laws. In response, Romney then

asked the Justice Department to file suit, a move supported by a
Federal Court of Appeals ruling that HUD had an affirmative action responsibility to consider what impact site selection would
have on integration.[73] In September 1970, Attorney General John
Mitchell called Romney to the White House and told him to back
off. Instead, the White House decided to study discrimination in
housing, putting all policy decisions on hold until the study was
completed. For nearly a year the civil rights laws regarding housing were suspended, though hundreds of grants were approved in
the interim.[74]

The political calculus was plain. Nixon could not afford to
alienate the suburbs, the middle-American heartland, the core of
his political support. On June 11, 1971, he declared that while his
administration would support the law of the land, "open housing,
open cities, open suburbs, open neighborhoods," it would not go
beyond the law by using federal money to force *economic integration*. "The law," he declared, "does not allow the federal government to use its monetary and other power, coercive power for the
purpose of changing the economic pattern of a neighborhood."[75]
Surely, it was wrong to deny housing to a person because of race
but neither should "a municipality that does not want federally
assisted housing have it imposed from Washington by bureaucratic fiat."[76]

Nixon's decision to support a civil rights measure in principle
while failing to implement it in practice was consistent with his
strategy on all civil rights issues. By establishing a gulf between
abstract principles and the reality of enforcement, he was able to
"stake out a position lending comfort to racial conservatives while
remaining publicly committed to racial equality."[77] Although
Romney continued to define actual housing market areas—the inner city and the suburbs—as the proper measure for project site
selection, fair housing existed solely on paper.

No social issue was more volatile, nor more likely to incite racial conflict, than fair housing. The battle over enforcement of fair
housing only revealed how deeply embedded resistance to it was.

The Destruction of the Cities

It was not only racial integration that deterred the development of
a satisfactory national housing policy but also the contradictions

in the legislation mandating more housing. When Romney took over the reins at HUD, he inherited the mandate to increase mortgage production. As Romney explained:

> When I took over the department in 1969, the concern of Congress was that we had never been able to get volume housing production for low income families. . . . The pressure was on me to get some results, to get some housing. . . . I went ahead to get the volume production that the nation had been seeking for many years.[78]

The laxity of the regulations in Section 235, the program of interest subsidies to lenders, provided built-in incentives for abuse among private moneylenders and realtors while HUD's decentralized structure made the abuses invisible to top officials until long after the program had made a mockery of federal housing policy. As the operating standard became mortgage production, acceptable risk came to mean "anything goes."

In part abuses occurred because Congress mandated the use of these new programs just as the more conservative private lenders and experienced builders—their property threatened by riots—began pulling out of the cities and locating their investments in the safer suburbs. They left a vacuum that was filled by speculators and the "suede shoe" artists, hustlers who used the new programs to sell shoddy property to the unsophisticated poor.

In the scramble to provide housing for the poor, the program was ripe for abuse. The typical scenario went something like this: A realtor would buy a house in the ghetto at a low price, secure FHA financing under, at best, a cursory appraisal and, at worst, no appraisal, then with the FHA guarantee inflating its value sell it at double or triple the original price. The result was inflated housing prices for shoddy homes in shocking stages of disrepair. Robert Lindsay, a professional house buyer who told his story to a Detroit newspaper reporter, explains how the FHA program operated in Detroit:

> The FHA came into the inner city in 1968, after the riot. The FHA was just a sitting duck. . . . They loosened the requirement for FHA and would insure houses by expressways, airports, in front of a factory entrance or in an area considered commercial. . . . Before then, we wouldn't get (FHA) insurance on the East Side. It was all redlined. . . . I started buying these properties, cash. . . . We'd buy

them for cash and sell to other investors or mortgage companies. . . . A lot of these houses were bought "subject to," that is, subject to FHA appraisal. Because without the appraisal, these houses were no good, no matter what you bought them for. . . . This house on East Forest, I bought for Paan Investment Company. The house had building code violations on it at the time. I purchased it for $2,500 from a widow. The house was flipped to a mortgage company, sold under FHA and defaulted. . . . Before they started the easy FHA money, we really had to fix a house up to sell it. Afterwards, all we did was cosmetic repairs. Sometimes we didn't do anything at all— just sold them FHA. The buyers, those welfare mothers and poor people, didn't know nothing about houses.[79]

Poor people defaulted on housing loans by the thousands, leaving the government with worthless, dispossessed homes in the inner cities. In St. Louis, for example, Birdie Lee Perry, mother of eleven, left the Pruitt-Igoe housing project to buy an FHA-certified house for $10,000. Under the fresh paint and wallpaper she found major defects, including rats and a faulty furnace. During her second winter in the house, the furnace didn't work at all. Just before Christmas her 6-month-old granddaughter died of pneumonia in a bone-chilling, second-floor bedroom.[80] As people abandoned their homes, often stealing away in the middle of the night, looters and vandals scavenged among the skeletal remains. Then the leaking, filthy, ravaged remnants were either burned to the ground or bulldozed down.

Unscrupulous realtors also took advantage of the FHA-guaranteed loans by operating as panic peddlers, using the threat of racial change to make a profit. The speculators would buy a house from a white family for a low price, secure an FHA guarantee, and then resell it, often riddled with code violations, to a black family at double the price. Rapidly, the term "FHA" came to be synonymous with "blacks only," hastening the process of white flight.[81]

On January 6, 1971, the House Committee on Banking and Currency issued its first report on the FHA scandal, and as the abuses became public, Romney shut down the Section 235 program. Yet the problems were centered in the inner cities; more than 90 percent of the subsidized housing for the poor did not have the problems of defaults and bilking that were found there.

By 1972 HUD had once again redlined the inner cities, the result of directives from Romney aimed at stopping the avalanche of foreclosures. Redlining the inner cities destroyed the housing market there. It meant that even homeowners who faithfully made their mortgage payments would not be able to resell their homes if they bought them through FHA loans. As a result of price fixing and the inflation built in to the sale–resale market, inner-city housing prices increased 200 to 300 percent from 1968 to 1972 while FHA foreclosures ruined neighborhoods and destroyed the value of houses so they were worth less than in 1968. When FHA stopped making inner-city loans, prospective buyers simply disappeared.

On January 7, 1973, Nixon dropped a bombshell on the housing industry by imposing a moratorium on all subsidized housing programs, pending a reevaluation. In September he recommended that the bulk of the government's subsidized housing activity be shifted to a leased housing program under which private owners would lease new or existing units to low-income tenants who would pay 25 percent of their income for rent.[82]

The 1974 Housing and Community Development Act attempted to reduce racial concentration in the inner city by revitalizing deteriorating neighborhoods and attracting the middle class back to the central cities. To implement these objectives, the act required each local jurisdiction applying for HUD funding to submit a housing assistance plan specifying how it would reduce the concentration of low-income people. The act provided important tools to further fair-housing goals of the Civil Rights Act of 1968. It required all-white suburbs receiving federal housing and community development funds to provide housing for low-income minorities. At the same time central cities had to provide integrated community developments to attract higher-income whites closer to the core city financial and corporate centers. HUD failed to employ the programs in this coordinated fashion, however, instead allowing local communities and housing authorities to subvert linkages between individual housing projects and actual area-wide housing needs. Although HUD had the authority to bypass unwilling local communities if they supported private developers who refused to develop low-income and integrated housing, the agency rarely invoked its bypass power. Instead, it allowed local developers to manipulate their land-use authority.

Though the 1974 act promised that federal housing would now be used to overcome rather than finance racial and economic ghettoization, it never lived up to that promise. Most of the new housing went to whites and to the elderly. Thus, federal funds continued to finance segregated housing and communities.[83]

The Legacy of Housing Policy

Between 1974 and 1983 the supply of affordable housing contracted sharply, while the ratio of rent to income increased significantly. As a result, in many cities waiting lists for public housing grew to more than double the number of units.[84] The decline in affordable housing is neither solely nor even primarily a product of random market forces. Rather, it reflects the government's retreat from its commitment to housing the poor, a commitment that peaked in 1968 when federally subsidized housing accounted for 29 percent of annual housing production, declined significantly in 1972 when subsidized housing dropped to 14 percent of new production, and then was nearly eliminated between 1981 and 1985 when federal funds for subsidized housing were slashed from $26.1 billion to $2.1 billion.[85]

Notably, of all the federal benefit programs, including both cash assistance and in-kind benefits, subsidized housing has the highest proportion of African American recipients. In 1979 38.5 percent of those receiving it were black.[86] Its high minority ratio has made the program especially vulnerable to budget cuts. In 1982 President Ronald Reagan almost completely terminated all funding for new construction of subsidized housing and asked that housing recipients pay 30 percent of their income rather than 25 percent. These cuts passed through Congress with little dissent.[87]

The decline in housing subsidies provides a powerful argument against targeted benefits. Because the benefits are narrowly distributed by race and by class, no majority coalition can be mobilized to protect them. Housing subsidies pose an easy target for budget cutters. Targeting is only part of the problem, however, for what has also made housing support unpopular is its association with efforts to achieve racial integration. This, coupled with the image of public housing as a repository of all the social ills that have triggered white flight to the suburbs, has made subsidized housing the pariah of federal social programs.

Although the War on Poverty had grand ambitions for altering the course of housing policy, it failed to extend either social or civil rights. It neither increased the supply of housing for poor people nor opened the housing market to minorities. The exception has been the middle- and upper-income nonwhite families, who have moved without incident into solid middle-class neighborhoods and who now routinely share in these privileged communities, largely isolated from the problems of the ghetto.[88] For the minority poor, however, the quality of the housing supply has continued to deteriorate while levels of housing segregation remain high. Why? Because housing as a welfare state issue cannot be divorced from housing as a racial issue.

FIVE

The Politics of
Welfare Reform

No program better exemplifies the racially divisive character of the American welfare state than Aid to Families with Dependent Children (AFDC). Conservatives attack AFDC for discouraging work and family formation and for rewarding laziness. Such comments are really subtly veiled messages about family structures and employment patterns among African Americans. However, often the attacks are neither veiled nor subtle.[1]

But it's not only conservatives who revile AFDC. Liberals also despise it for stigmatizing and humiliating those who receive it, for coercing women into taking menial jobs, and for providing benefits that are below the poverty line. And feminists denounce it for trading off dominance by a man for dominance by the state.[2] AFDC has few of the qualities inherent in the concept of a social right. In the words of T. H. Marshall, it has failed to provide poor women with "a modicum of security" and it has alienated them from "the social heritage of the nation."[3]

Only once, when the nation almost replaced this miserly and means-tested program with a guaranteed annual income for all of the working and nonworking poor, was revolutionary welfare reform considered. Surprisingly, the proposal took shape during the administration of conservative president Richard Nixon. On

August 8, 1969, Nixon proposed a guaranteed annual income for the working and nonworking poor. His Family Assistance Plan (FAP) promised "a totally new approach to welfare designed to assist those left far behind the national norm and provide all with the motivation to work and a fair share of the opportunity to train."[4] The FAP would provide $500 each for the first two members of a family and $300 for each additional member. Whereas AFDC penalized work, the FAP would encourage work. A household head could earn up to $720 annually and still receive the full FAP benefits. Those who earned more than $720 would pay a 50 percent marginal tax. As family earnings rose, benefits would be reduced fifty cents for each dollar until they reached zero and the family was supported entirely by earnings. Thus, a family of four with an employed household head would be considerably better off than a welfare family, since benefits combined with earnings could reach $3,810.[5] By contrast, a family of four with no working members, that is, a welfare family, would receive $1,600 a year.

On April 16, 1970, the FAP (H.R. 16311) passed the House by a margin of 243 to 155. Passage in the more liberal Senate seemed guaranteed. Yet the bill was never reported out of the Senate Finance Committee, and two years later, by a vote of 52 to 34, the Senate defeated a substantially revised proposal. Why would so conservative a president endorse so radical a measure?

The answer resides in the racial dynamic that propelled all social policy issues in the 1960s. One factor was Nixon's desire to forge a conservative political base by eliminating equal opportunity from the agenda of the welfare state. By providing a minimum income for *all* of the working poor, not just African Americans, the FAP could have accomplished this goal. The second was the intense pressure for welfare reform that originated in the urban riots and the rising welfare rolls. Policymakers believed that AFDC contributed to social unrest and that welfare reform could cool things down. Racial issues also led to the FAP's defeat. Black women on welfare feared that the FAP might reduce their welfare benefits. White, southern congressmen feared that the FAP might undermine wages in the South. Their objections scuttled a proposal that could have put a floor under the income of the working poor.

Social Rights for Welfare Mothers

Whereas the struggle of men for social rights has taken place in the market and in the state, women's rights have been shaped in the context of the state, the market, and the household. Debates about economic security have been entwined with cultural notions of motherhood and family responsibility.[6]

AFDC originated during the Progressive era as a remnant of the "Mother's Pensions," which were designed to support "deserving" mothers who had no male breadwinner. Mother's Pension advocates won support by arguing that mothers should be allowed to stay home and care for their children rather than be forced to work outside the home: "Family life in the home is sapped in its foundations when the mothers of young children work for wages."[7] These arguments were remarkably successful. Between 1911 and 1920 forty states legislated Mother's Pensions but only for mothers of worthy character. Although in theory Mother's Pensions privileged mothering over work, in practice they often merely subsidized low-wage jobs.[8]

When the Social Security Act of 1935 incorporated Mother's Pensions into Aid to Dependent Children, it created a racial division in the distribution of benefits to women. Southern congressmen, who chaired the key committees, insisted that states retain the right to establish eligibility criteria and to decide who received benefits.[9] Only if local welfare authorities retained control over the distribution of benefits would the southerners support the measure. As a result, most of the initial ADC beneficiaries were white, widowed women with young children.[10]

In 1939 Congress allowed the widows and children of retired workers to receive benefits from the old-age insurance program. As the white widows of the industrial workers shifted from ADC to old-age insurance, ADC became the last resort for divorced, single, and deserted women. Many of these women were African American. To keep them from receiving benefits, southern states, as well as some northern states, tightened their eligibility criteria. During the 1940s and 1950s states created additional restrictions: seasonal employment policies cut ADC recipients off the welfare rolls during cotton-picking season; "man in the house" rules allowed social workers to make unannounced visits and eliminate from the rolls any woman found living with a man.[11]

After decades of increasingly restrictive rules, during the 1960s Congress began loosening eligibility requirements. One reason was rising rates of single parenthood, especially among black women, which convinced some legislators that the perverse regulations in ADC were to blame. In 1961 Congress allowed states to include families with unemployed fathers in the programs, though few states took advantage of the opportunity.[12] Another reason was the pressure from organized groups of welfare mothers. The welfare rights movement began in the mid-1960s as a loosely knit social movement.[13] On August 8, 1966, welfare rights groups around the country formed a National Coordinating Committee of Welfare Groups, which began planning tactics for a three-month organizing drive. That organization produced the National Welfare Rights Organization (NWRO). NWRO members staged sit-ins and engaged in confrontations at welfare offices. They demanded increased benefits, jobs, and the removal of a host of odious statutes that prevented women from receiving benefits.[14] In Detroit demonstrating welfare mothers caused such a commotion that relief offices were closed for four days.[15] In Boston the beating of demonstrators by police led to three days of rioting.[16] One after another the courts struck down the despised regulations.

As a result of the more liberal rules, in just one year—from 1966 to 1967—the number of welfare recipients increased from 7.8 to 8.4 million.[17] The costs of the skyrocketing welfare rolls were primarily borne by working- and middle-class taxpayers, whose tempers rose in tempo with welfare costs. Why, they wondered, should families struggling to make ends meet pay for loafers who lived off the government's largesse?[18] With increasing numbers of women entering the labor force, arguments for paying poor women to stay home were less compelling.

In 1967 Congress enacted a Work Incentive Program (WIN). WIN allowed clients to keep the first $30 in monthly earnings plus one-third of the rest, making it more profitable for welfare mothers to work.[19] WIN also provided employment, on-the-job training, and work-experience training. Even mothers with young children had to participate in job training *if* day care was available.[20]

Despite these efforts to increase the labor-force participation of poor women, WIN did little to stem the rising welfare tide. Most job training for women never got off the ground, and funds for day care were minimal. By 1970 12.4 million people were on welfare, with one-fourth of the total increase occurring in just two states, New York and California.[21] The increase inflamed the anti-welfare backlash, forcing governors in the hard-pressed states to seek other ways to cut the welfare rolls. In New York, in a brawling, marathon session, the legislature rammed through a series of welfare cuts, chopped family allowances by 8 percent, and slashed the Medicaid program. In Illinois the governor sent out 3,000 caseworkers to "redetermine" the eligibility of 75,000 welfare mothers and cut $12 million from the budget.[22]

Building an Income Strategy

Out of the turmoil emerged a seemingly illogical response: eliminate AFDC and replace it with a guaranteed annual income for the working and nonworking poor. The idea for a guaranteed annual income emerged during the Johnson administration in 1967 when riots occurred in sixty-four cities.[23] As a worried nation pondered ways to calm the ghettos, policymakers converged around the seemingly simple solution of a guaranteed income. Its earliest proponent was conservative economist Milton Friedman. Appalled by what he saw as a bureaucratic excess in the "present rag-bag of measures," Friedman proposed replacing all existing welfare programs as well as the cumbersome welfare bureaucracy with a negative income tax administered by the Internal Revenue Service.[24] Liberal economist John Kenneth Galbraith hailed the proposal as "one of the two or three new ideas in economics in twenty-five years." In 1968, 1,300 of the nation's leading economists signed a petition urging Congress to adopt a national system of income guarantees.[25]

Johnson's entire domestic agenda was wrapped up in a service strategy, and the idea of replacing his programs, however tattered, with an income-based approach was inconceivable. Instead, he appointed a national commission on income-maintenance to contemplate welfare reform.[26] Headed by Ben W. Heineman, chairman of Northwest Industries, the Heineman Commission included other influential corporate executives as well as professional economists, politicians, and union officials. The Commission first considered then rejected a jobs strategy, which its members felt would not only have been too costly but also worthless to the more than 10 million workers who earned less than the minimum wage. The Commission finally agreed on a universal income supplement for the working poor.[27] Although a wage supplement represented a radical departure from existing measures, it rested on premises compatible with business interests. It accepted the spread of low-wage labor as inevitable and provided an alternative to a minimum wage. Unlike in-kind benefits such as food stamps and housing, which the commission wanted abolished, it worked on market principles. And unlike the inefficient social-insurance programs, which paid regardless of need, income supplements only paid benefits to the poor or near-poor.[28]

When the Heineman Commission concluded its evaluation in 1969, Johnson was no longer president. Its recommendation to President Richard Nixon supported escalating sentiment for some form of a guaranteed income.[29] It wasn't until the National Advisory Commission on Civil Disorders linked the riots to economic inequality and "the deprivation of ghetto life," however, that the proposal for a guaranteed income moved forward.[30]

If a guaranteed annual income was out of synchrony with Johnson's priorities, it was more compatible with Nixon's philosophy. The historical record depicts Johnson as the big spender, yet his antipoverty programs gave few direct cash benefits to the poor. Nixon was the genuine big spender. He expanded the food stamps program, supported large increases in Social Security benefits, and added a new program of payments to disabled people. During his administration, spending on all human resource programs exceeded spending for defense for the first time since World War II.[31] Why did a conservative president put butter before guns?

Nixon's income strategy was linked to his political goal of building a Republican coalition among the forgotten middle class. The unraveling of the New Deal alliance meant that formerly loyal Democrats were now a volatile force, surging through the electoral system without the restraint of party attachment. They were available for courting. As a presidential candidate, Nixon had promised that he would not rob the working class of the fruits of its labors:

> In a time when the national focus is concentrated upon the unemployed, the impoverished and the dispossessed, the working Americans have become the forgotten Americans. In a time when the national rostrums and forums are given over to shouters and protestors and demonstrators, they have become the silent Americans. Yet they have a legitimate grievance that should be rectified and a just cause that should prevail.[32]

As the silent majority swung in line behind Nixon, he began building a political strategy designed to reward them for their support. The welfare issue represented one answer. Nixon would not only reform the despised welfare system but also reward the deserving working poor.[33]

Nixon's Family Assistance Plan, his guaranteed income proposal, could help build a constituency among the newly enfranchised, white working poor in the South, where low wages kept the bulk of the population below poverty level. It would also help him please working-class homeowners concerned with rising property taxes, which resulted from soaring welfare costs. Urban mayors would love him, for they believed that higher benefits in some states encouraged the black migration to the cities. And best of all, the FAP resoundingly reaffirmed the Protestant ethic by promising to force those welfare loafers to get a job.[34] As Nixon proudly confided to a liberal friend, "Tory men with liberal principles are what has enlarged democracy in this world."[35] Government spending had political uses, and in a period when the electorate was equally divided between the Democratic and Republican parties, Nixon, the consummate politician, recognized that broad-based social spending programs could woo voters to the Republicans.

Reconstructing the Black Family

What initially propelled the FAP on to the national agenda was the threat of further riots. The report of the National Advisory

Commission on Civil Disorders found that the rioters were primarily young, black males. In Detroit, for example, 61.3 percent of those who admitted to participating in a riot were between the ages of 15 and 24; 86.3 percent were under 35. Nearly 90 percent of those arrested for rioting in Detroit were male, more than half single. But those eligible for the new FAP benefit would not be single, young men but working heads of households with children. How could a benefit targeted to employed, married men stop single, unemployed youths from rioting? The answer was that it would encourage young men to marry and form stable, male-headed households.

While policymakers had plenty of evidence tying social unrest to high unemployment, the underlying cause, they believed, was the disintegration of the black family. This thesis first appeared in a 1965 report by Daniel Patrick Moynihan, Nixon's advisor on policy issues. According to Moynihan, "the breakdown of the Negro family led to a startling increase in welfare dependency." [36] The problem stemmed from the inability of black men to earn enough to support a family. Because black men could not be breadwinners, there was a "tendency for black women to fare better interpersonally and economically than men and thereby to dominate family life." [37] In "a society which presumes male leadership in private and public affairs, the dependence on the mother's income undermines the position of the father." [38] To restore male dominance, Moynihan called for "a national effort to strengthen the Negro family," an unobtainable objective unless the government guaranteed that "every able-bodied Negro man was working, even if this meant that some jobs had to be redesigned to enable men to fulfill them." [39] In other words, federal policy should reinstate black men as household heads by reducing the labor-force participation of black women. In Moynihan's view, establishing male dominance in the black family was a prerequisite for social stability.

The National Advisory Commission on Civil Disorders reached a similar conclusion: "The condition of Negroes in the central city [was] in a state of crisis because of chronic unemployment among males and because of the concentration of black males at the lowest end of the occupational scale." High unemployment among black males made them "unable or unwilling to remain with their families." The instability of male employment forced mothers to work to support their families. Black family structure was directly related to the riots, as "children growing up under such conditions [were] likely participants in civil disorder."[40]

The Commission also concluded that the welfare system "contributed materially to the tensions and social disorganization that [has] led to civil disorders."[41] To get black women off welfare and back in the home, the Commission advocated income supplements to subsidize those who worked at low-paying jobs and "to provide for mothers who decide to remain with their children."[42] An ingenious solution to the AFDC mess, the FAP would indirectly resolve the turmoil in urban ghettos by providing incentives for black males to become family breadwinners and for black women to stay home with their children.

Yet the FAP also contained an internal contradiction. Not only did it promise to restore the traditional patriarchal family, it also promised to encourage women on welfare to work more. How could the same program increase the work efforts of single welfare mothers while encouraging married women to stay home? These conflicting expectations about women's roles were reflected in plans to implement the FAP. Supposedly a plan to increase work among welfare mothers, the FAP contained few programs to help poor women improve their job skills or find jobs and provided little support for child care. Rather, the employment component of the bill was directed at men.

The original version of the FAP called for 150,000 new training slots "to train people for jobs at decent wages whenever we find that they cannot get good jobs with their present skills."[43] In discussing the training programs, Frank Carlucci, Director of the Office of Economic Opportunity (OEO), suggested ranking those eligible for job training. Welfare mothers came last:

> We believe that priorities for manpower services should be explicitly structured to provide for the maximum improvement in employability and earning potential, at minimum federal cost. We have already suggested that a high priority be assigned to AFDC-UI fathers. In general, we would support giving higher priority to the training and employment of men than women. Given the greater employment opportunities for men generally available, they are more likely to

achieve self-sufficiency. Moreover, training and employment will often be much more expensive for women, if child care must be provided.[44]

To program bureaucrats, the working poor were male. Their challenge was to train unemployed men so they could join the ranks of the working poor and, with the FAP subsidy, earn a sufficient income to support a family.

In planning how to administer the FAP, Department of Health, Education, and Welfare (HEW) staff agreed that the manpower services were "clearly the responsibility of the Department of Labor alone."[45] The problem, however, was which agency, HEW or the Department of Labor, should administer benefits to those registering for training or seeking work. HEW decided to take responsibility "for female headed families in which no member is required to register for work or training" but agreed to transfer jurisdiction to the Department of Labor when "a family member actually enters a training program or public service job."[46] Since training and employment would be oriented toward male household heads, this arrangement placed men in training or in employment under the jurisdiction of the Department of Labor and welfare mothers under the jurisdiction of HEW. But HEW officials had no interest in ensuring jobs for welfare mothers. That issue, HEW Secretary Robert Finch told the Senate Finance Committee, "more appropriately comes under Labor."[47] HEW had neither studied the potential job market for welfare mothers nor assessed how these women might find jobs.[48]

If welfare mothers were to work more, they would also need child care. Day-care planning was minimal, however, and regulations about who was eligible and what agency was responsible for day care were "unclear."[49] Further, the FAP left provision of day care to a market that wasn't meeting the existing demand, let alone the new demand the program would generate from low-income families. HEW estimates placed the costs of adequate day care at $2,000 per child per year, yet the FAP budgeted only $858 per child per year. Could quality child care be provided at less than half of what the government's own estimates considered adequate?

The FAP would help "the proudest poor, the people who are

On August 20, 1964, Lyndon Baines Johnson signed into law his War on Poverty bill. *(UPI-Bettman)*

Peaceful civil rights demonstrators confront a southern sheriff. *(Florida State Historical Society)*

The civil rights movement activated the Ku Klux Klan. *(Florida State Historical Society)*

Operation Star Inc., a community action program in Mississippi, operated the first integrated educational programs in the state. *(National Archives)*

Throughout the South literacy training programs provided adults an opportunity to learn to read. *(National Archives)*

In northern cities like Chicago poor people subsisted under appalling living conditions. *(UPI-Bettman)*

The Watts Labor Community Action Committee was one of the anti-poverty programs supported by the AFL-CIO. *(UPI-Bettman)*

In Job Corps training centers, young men learned skilled trades designed to help them escape poverty *(UPI-Bettman)*

An advertisement for a segregated housing development. *(Florida State Historical Society)*

Above Right: More than 50,000 mourners attended the funeral of Martin Luther King. *(UPI-Bettman)*
Below Right: The assassination of Martin Luther King Jr. triggered rioting across the nation. Less than a week after his death, the Fair Housing Act was passed. *(UPI-Bettman)*

The rise of the welfare rolls created a backlash that led to cuts in welfare benefits. *(UPI-Bettman)*

The Headstart programs provided enriching educational experiences for pre-school children. *(UPI-Bettman)*

struggling in the best American tradition" but "who cannot make it." [50] The proudest poor were men. As Finch explained: "In no state is any federally-assisted welfare available to families headed by full-time working men who earn poverty wages—the working poor. . . . We have backed ourselves into a situation in which we will help men who don't work [under AFDC-UI], but we cannot help those who do work." [51] The following year his replacement at HEW, Elliot Richardson, repeated: "taken together these proposals do assure that the family of a working man will always be better off than a family of the same size headed by a man who is not working." [52]

The FAP would have done nothing for welfare mothers, for they were not the working poor. Less than 25 percent had some earnings.[53] Nixon's only guarantee to AFDC mothers (a promise he could not keep) was that "in no case would anyone's present level of benefits be lowered." [54] The implicit solution for increasing the income of poor women was to find them a breadwinner husband.

Although the FAP promised to create a Republican base among traditional working-class Democrats, the idea of a guaranteed annual income generated opposition among those the Nixon administration sought most to woo—southern conservatives. During the 1968 presidential campaign, the Republican party's southern strategy first emerged as a calculated political ploy. It began as a bargain with South Carolina Senator Strom Thurmond. Thurmond would campaign in the deep South for Nixon if Nixon would ease up on federal pressures to force school segregation. After Nixon's narrow electoral victory, the southern strategy evolved into a long-range plan "to woo southern support so ardently that there might once again develop a solid political South—but this time as committed to the Republican party as it once had been to the Democratic party." [55]

This cynical strategy catered in both subtle and not-so-subtle ways to segregationist, white southern voters. Slowing down school desegregation, recommending conservative judges for Supreme Court appointments, and reorganizing HEW to eliminate bureaucrats southerners resented were all tactics to solidify southern support. The FAP played into this agenda. Reducing inequity between the working poor and the welfare poor became a euphemism for reducing what whites perceived as racial inequity in the tax/benefit ratio. What Nixon failed to take into account was the impact the FAP would have on the political and economic structure of the South.

The Political Economy of the South

According to HEW estimates, more than 30 percent of all FAP funds would go to California, another 38 percent to five northeastern states, with the other forty-four states receiving the remaining 32 percent.[56] Southern states would receive little or no fiscal relief because their benefit levels were so low. Yet because per capita income in the South was only 66 percent of that of the North or West, the FAP would still have an enormous impact on the southern economy.[57] The FAP funds would raise the entire southern wage base and provide southern workers, especially black workers, an opportunity to refuse demeaning, low-wage work. Economic emancipation would undermine the political institutions that reproduced racial inequality in the South.

FAP's Impact on Political Rights in the South

For more than a century, the southern welfare system had reinforced the racial caste system.[58] Fifty-five percent of Mississippi residents had incomes below the poverty level but only 14 percent received assistance; less than 10 percent of Mississippians participated in the free federal lunch program.[59] In 1970 929,000 Alabamians lacked the income necessary for a marginal diet, yet only 277,000 benefited from the Department of Agriculture's (USDA) food-assistance programs.[60] Welfare officials supported field hands at federal expense during the winter and cut them off the rolls in the spring and summer.[61] Under the Work Incentive Program, "welfare recipients are made to serve as maids or to do day yard work in white homes to keep their checks. During the cotton-picking season no one is accepted on welfare because plantations need cheap labor to do cotton-picking behind the cotton-picking machines."[62] As Robert Clark, the first African American elected to the Mississippi legislature in almost 100 years, explained:

"Should you be able to walk or crawl, then you do not qualify for such programs." [63]

Although the Voting Rights Act of 1965 eliminated political barriers to voting, economic barriers remained. By 1970 few African Americans held political office. Between 1965 and 1970 fewer than 50 percent of eligible black voters voted in county-wide elections in all but twenty-nine Mississippi black-majority counties. [64] The key to black voter turnout was not the amount of income but the source -- counties with high black voter turnouts were those in which African Americans depended least on whites for their livelihood. No other variables were "as strongly or as consistently related to the differences between black and white voter registration rates as were the combined effects of the concentration of white farm owners and the black farm tenants and laborers who typically worked for white farm owners." [65] African Americans who engaged in civil rights activities or who tried to register to vote were systematically excluded from welfare. During voter registration campaigns, county officials cut African Americans off the welfare rolls, suspended commodity distributions, and warned they would only restore benefits when blacks "surrendered their uppity ideas about changing the local balance of power." [66] In a 1968 report, the U.S. Commission on Civil Rights concluded that voting barriers in the South could be torn down only "by eliminating the economic dependence of southern Negroes upon white landlords, white employers, and white sources of credit-dependence, which deters Negroes from voting freely and seeking political office." [67] The FAP threatened to emancipate the southern labor force.

FAP's Impact on the Southern Economy

In 1971 approximately 10 million persons were AFDC recipients. The FAP would make 28 million persons eligible for assistance. [68] Instead of being distributed evenly across the nation, however, the new beneficiaries would be concentrated in the South. By HEW estimates, the number of welfare recipients in high-benefit states like New York would increase by 30 to 50 percent, but in the low-benefit states of the South the increase would be 250 to 400 percent.[69] One reason was that southern wages were so low. Any family of four earning less than $3,000 would qualify for a FAP supplement.[70] In 1970 in the southern states 53 percent of black male household heads, 82.5 percent of black female household heads with children under 18, and 37.7 percent of white female household heads with children under 18 had incomes below $3,000.[71] Further, none of the southern states had AFDC-UI, so the FAP would make working-age males eligible for welfare. Overall, 52 percent of those covered by the FAP would be southerners and two-thirds of poor blacks in the South would receive some payment.[72]

Despite the work incentives in the FAP, most southerners would be able to receive the FAP income supplement without working. This was because the FAP exempted from the work registration requirement any woman who had a preschool child, any woman who was over the age of 65, or any woman who had an unemployed husband. In Mississippi alone, the FAP would put more than 35 percent of the population on welfare.[73] According to an estimate of one Mississippi town, only two out of eighteen domestics would have to register to work in order to receive the full FAP payments.[74] As Georgia Representative Phillip Landrum, who cast one of the three negative votes in the House Ways and Means Committee, declared: "There's not going to be anybody left to roll these wheelbarrows and press these shirts."[75]

Since family size determined benefit levels, the FAP would double or triple household incomes. The FAP plus food stamps would provide a family of four a minimum of $2,350. In rural areas where average household size was large, the impact on black families would be enormous. Take Furse Quarter, Alabama, where Mrs. Adie Powell lived with her nine children, her parents, her sister, and her sister's six children. Combined annual income from Mrs. Powell's job at a local wood-processing plant, her sister's welfare check, and her parents' Social Security pension came to $6,052. Under the FAP the Powell's annual household income would almost double to $12,008.[76]

The FAP could also increase wage levels. What kept wage levels low in southern cities was the steady stream of migrants from farms. In 1969 the median wage for a southern farm laborer was

$1,034. The FAP would triple a farm laborer's income. Because urban living was more expensive, the FAP would discourage workers from leaving a farm job for a minimum-wage job in a city. Then, as scarce labor drove wage rates up, urban wages would increase, too.

By raising wages in the South, the FAP could totally undermine local labor markets. For a black male head of a family of four working at minimum wage in a southern factory, the FAP would provide a $296 yearly increase plus $360 in food stamps, a modest improvement. But most black men in southern cities—the cooks, the gas station attendants, the bus boys—earned less than the minimum wage. So did most black women. Two out of three black women in the South worked in service jobs, mostly as domestics, earning on average $40 per week. Under the FAP, a gas station attendant or a domestic earning $40 a week who headed a family of four would receive $3,408 a year, almost as much as a minimum-wage factory worker ($3,984).[77] Thus, the FAP would equalize earnings at the bottom of the wage scale between men and women, African Americans and whites, and minimum and better-paid workers.[78]

Not surprisingly, the most determined opponents of the FAP were southern Democrats. In the House Ways and Means Committee, five of the six southern Congressmen opposed the FAP.[79] Although the House passed the bill by an overwhelming majority, 79 of the 155 negative votes came from the eleven deep South states. Only seventeen southern Congressmen voted for the FAP.[80]

The Fate of the Family Assistance Plan

The South alone could not defeat the bill. The Chamber of Commerce also vehemently opposed the FAP and lobbied heavily against it.[81] With 3,800 trade associations and local chambers and a direct membership of more than 35,000 business firms, the Chamber wielded a mighty club.

Historically, the Chamber of Commerce had opposed all welfare-state programs, which its members believed undermined productivity and created chronic budget deficits. Because the FAP would expand the welfare rolls enormously, it would exacerbate the ills social welfare always produced. Although Chamber analysts approved of the idea of work incentives, they didn't believe the FAP would really encourage work. In fact, the FAP contained no real work requirement. If the household head refused work or training, other family members could still receive benefits. The Chamber pounced on the lack of a work requirement and denounced the FAP as a guaranteed income that would put 50 percent of the population on welfare.[82] The Chamber of Commerce had loyally supported the Republican party. Could the Nixon administration afford to alienate this long-standing ally?

Neither friend nor foe, organized labor remained on the sidelines. When the FAP was first unveiled, the major trade unions charged that it violated "principles the labor movement had long espoused, including opposition to wage subsidies and minimum reliance on means-tested programs."[83] The bill's quick passage in the House caught the labor movement off guard, but by the time the FAP reached the Senate, labor was prepared to extract two major changes in exchange for support of the bill.

The AFL-CIO most bitterly opposed a provision specifying that a family head receiving FAP benefits be required to work at a job not covered by the minimum wage so long as the job paid the prevailing wage for that work. Above all, labor wanted to protect the minimum wage so that wages would not be frozen at poverty levels and union wage levels undermined.[84]

Organized labor also feared the FAP would flood the market with low-wage workers. The work incentives would induce welfare recipients to work and encourage the working poor to increase their work efforts. Competition would intensify for a fixed number of jobs, and low-wage work would proliferate. In the long run, low-wage rates in the subsidized sector would reduce wage rates in the nonsubsidized sector. Burt Seidman, Director of the AFL-CIO Social Security Department, explained: "there is no reason why the government through wage subsidies or tax credits, should 'buy' low-level jobs for welfare recipients."[85] Ever vigilant, the skilled trade unions also feared the proposed job-training programs would undermine the unions' control over hiring and apprenticeships.

Trade unionists agreed to support the FAP if the government would finance a separate tier of public-sector jobs and protect the minimum wage. Recognizing that the FAP could not pass the Senate over AFL-CIO opposition, Nixon incorporated labor's demands, and the unions withdrew their opposition.

Although welfare mothers wanted a guaranteed annual income, they disliked the FAP because they felt the benefit levels were too low and the work incentives too punitive. In the eyes of the NWRO, the FAP was "anti-poor, and anti-black . . . a flagrant example of institutional racism," leading to slavery.[86] Although the media depicted their demands as excessive, the demands reflected a realistic appraisal of what poor women needed to be able to work and care for their children. They wanted the right to keep earnings up to 30 percent above AFDC levels, they wanted day care, and they wanted meaningful job training that led to real jobs.[87] Poor women would willingly get off welfare when there were jobs with adequate wages and decent child care. All they asked was the right to make the same choices middle class white women had—the right to work or the right to stay home and care for their children if work didn't pay.

At the urging of the NWRO, in November of 1970 Senator Eugene McCarthy (D-MN) scheduled an unofficial hearing on the FAP in the Senate office building. At these hearings, NWRO members testified against the FAP and demanded that minimum AFDC benefits be raised to $5,500, the average benefit in New York.[88] Their opposition helped coalesce the liberal position. In the Senate Finance Committee, three of the six liberal senators voted against the original proposal while a fourth abstained.

By 1972 the FAP had alienated a number of powerful constituencies whose support was necessary for welfare reform. Southern conservatives and northern liberals, urban welfare mothers, and the Chamber of Commerce all objected to the proposal. Nixon's political calculations convinced him that supporting the FAP would not only win him no friends but, worse, would risk destroying his "New Majority." As he recalled: "I know abandoning FAP was necessary in order to keep the country together and to keep my coalition together. Politically, I wasn't going to pick up by reason of my support of FAP . . . a substantial number of liberal Democrats. . . . I had to at least take positions that the liberals didn't like." [89]

The Legacy of Welfare Reform

Support for the FAP originated in two issues that linked race to social policy, the urban riots and the expansion of welfare. Both issues alienated working-class Americans, who found the urban rage incomprehensible and the welfare expansion inequitable. Yet the program Congress devised to replace the much-reviled AFDC only exacerbated the divisions inherent in welfare policy. It set northern welfare mothers against poor southern workers, unemployed black men against employed black women, and the organized working class against marginalized workers. The FAP would have done much to improve living conditions for both black families in the South and poor whites. But providing a universal income base for southerners would have been politically costly for an administration seeking to create a conservative base for the Republican party in the South.

The FAP's impact on American social policy did not end in 1972, however; its demise determined the fate of two other programs for those with compelling needs, the children and the elderly. Because day care was inextricably linked to the FAP, the collapse of the FAP meant the end of a national day-care plan, a subject I explore in Chapter 6. By contrast, the campaign for the FAP encouraged the expansion of Social Security. It not only lent momentum generally to a spending strategy but also, because it was popular among a broad middle-class base, provided a welcome relief from more controversial spending measures.[90] I examine this topic in Chapter 7.

SIX

The Politics
of Motherhood

During the first half of the turbulent sixties, child-care policy
remained disengaged from the volatile battles raging over
race and rights. Rather, improving child care remained the ob-
scure mission of two federal bureaus, the Women's Bureau and
the Children's Bureau. Before the decade was over, child care, too,
became embroiled in the struggle for racial equality. Child care
provided through the War on Poverty's Headstart program was
designed to provide enriching experiences for poor children, which
in practice meant black children. Day care provided to welfare
mothers to reduce the welfare rolls also disproportionately benefited African Americans.

In seeking to build a right-of-center coalition, Richard Nixon
seized upon child care as a program that might accomplish that
goal. In his first message to Congress, he promised to provide all
young children a "healthful and stimulating development." [1] The
problem was that his welfare reform scheme—the Family Assistance Plan—contained a day-care component. As day-care costs
became entangled in the controversy over the FAP, Nixon abandoned his commitment to children.

It wasn't only the FAP that undermined support for a comprehensive child-care plan. Equally significant was public ambiva-

lence about the escalating numbers of working mothers. If the government embarked on policies that encouraged welfare mothers to work, what implications might such policies have for all families? Federal support for child care was defeated both because of its connection to welfare reform, and thus to one of the most controversial and racially charged issues of the decade, and because of its implied validation of the right of *all* mothers to work.

Children's Rights/Mother's Rights

In 1912 Congress created a Children's Bureau to investigate the welfare of children.[2] Because its constituency was made up of politically powerless children who could neither vote nor lobby, the Children's Bureau had only limited influence on the federal bureaucracy. The Social Security Act of 1935 expanded the national welfare state, but the Children's Bureau received only a few meagerly funded programs to manage—maternal and child health, crippled children's services, and child-welfare services.[3] The important program, Aid to Dependent Children, went first to the Social Security Board and later to the Department of Health, Education and Welfare. By the late 1950s, in terms of both federal funding and public interest, cash assistance to dependent children had completely overshadowed child-welfare services. The Children's Bureau was relegated to the margins of the federal bureaucracy.[4]

The Women's Bureau, created by Congress in 1920, was located within the Department of Labor. Its charge was to improve working conditions for women. The Bureau's first director, Mary Anderson, was a shoemaker who had risen through the ranks of the Women's Trade Union League.[5] She had observed bone-weary women toiling through the night and believed their most pressing needs were limitations on hours and controls on conditions of work. During the 1920s and 1930s, the Women's Bureau played an important role in pressuring the states to enact protective labor legislation.[6]

Because its constituency was working women, the Women's Bureau never accepted the prevailing view that a woman's place was in the home. Bureau staff recognized that working women needed child care. Although far from indifferent to the needs of children, their interest in child care stemmed from their desire to ease the heavy burden on women.

The federal government provided some child care during the New Deal. In 1937 the Works Progress Administration earmarked funds for day care to provide jobs for unemployed teachers, custodians, cooks, and nurses. Then in 1941 when women were needed in the defense plants, Congress passed the Lanham Act, which provided grants for building and operating day-care centers. But when the troops returned home at war's end, the women were sent back to the kitchen. Within months 2,800 day-care centers were closed, and in 1946 federal funds for day care were eliminated.[7]

By the late 1950s, one-third of the nation's labor force was made up of women, and the Department of Labor predicted that by 1970 two out of every five women would be working outside the home. Philosophically, the Children's Bureau believed day care was necessary only when a family was in crisis, when a child was neglected or abused or when a child had special needs.[8] Day care was primarily for "culturally or socially retarded" children who needed more than substitute care or children who had "a family problem which [made] it impossible for their parents to fulfill their parental responsibilities without supplemental help."[9] But the increasing labor-force participation of women convinced the Children's Bureau that working mothers needed help, too:

> More and more women are entering the labor market and many of them are the mothers of young children. Realistically, we cannot expect to reverse this revolutionary tide nor is there any indication that the mother who works, by the simple fact of her employment, neglects or damages her children.

In 1958 the Children's Bureau asked the Bureau of the Census to conduct a survey exploring the nation's day-care needs. The survey showed that little community-based child care was available. Most (80 percent) of young children of working mothers were cared for in an *ad hoc* fashion in unlicensed homes. While some of these homes provided excellent care, others were merely custodial with no storytelling, no reading, no vocabulary development. Fifteen percent of children went to work with their mothers. Sometimes mothers kept their teenagers home from school to care for their younger brothers and sisters. Only 1 to 2 percent of children were in group care.[10] Eight percent spent the day unsupervised.[11] The survey demonstrated pressing needs among lower- and middle-income families.

To publicize these findings demonstrating the nation's desperate need for child care, the Children's Bureau published bulletins and held conferences on the plight of working mothers. Gertrude Hoffman, the Bureau's specialist in Homemaker and Day Care services, developed a comprehensive statement of what day care should be, which became bill S. 1286, introduced by Senator Jacob Javits on January 1, 1960.

The Javits bill sought $25,000,000 for day care for the children of working mothers, with states to provide matching funds.[12] Although Javits only sought support for working mothers, Congress was beginning to feel the pressure of the swelling welfare rolls and favored instead a plan that might help put welfare mothers to work.[13] As the bill moved through Congress, the rights of mothers and children took a back seat to the alarm over the rising costs of welfare. Instead of helping mothers already in the labor force, the child-care bill became oriented toward putting stay-at-home welfare mothers to work.

The Women's Bureau also supported the Javits bill. But its chief, veteran Democratic labor lobbyist Esther Peterson, was uncomfortable with the bill's emphasis on welfare and concerned that only public assistance recipients and other low-income families would be eligible for services.[14] In her view, all working women needed child care. Peterson also believed that day care could be educational and wished to see the legislation reflect this objective.

Support for the legislation came from a loose conglomeration of women's organizations, which formed an informal children's lobby. The lobby included such organizations as Playschools, the National Federal of Settlements, United Community Funds, and the Child Welfare League.[15] Although the day-care lobby was united in its support of *some* legislation, internal conflicts reflected the cultural ambivalence toward working mothers. Elinor Guggenheimer, head of the National Committee for the Day Care of Children, believed that social workers should first "induce mothers, whenever possible, to remain at home with their young children." In fact, "careful welfare intake processes [would] give us the opportunity to convince many mothers that it is better for them to remain at home with their children than to go to work." Day care should "preserve and strengthen family life," not destroy it. Guggenheimer also believed that women should not compete for the jobs of men: "I personally have been working on a project to induce women to enter the shortage fields of nursing, social work, and education." [16]

To attract public support for the pending bill, the day-care lobby joined with the Women's Bureau and Children's Bureau in sponsoring a conference on child care. More than 400 representatives from labor, management, social service agencies, and health and welfare groups attended. The conference recommended that day care become part of the range of child welfare services offered in every community for all children who needed them. [17] A seemingly innocuous idea, the recommendations signified a tacit recognition that mothers worked and an implied promise to provide adequate child care.

As the day-care supporters lobbied for the legislation, they aroused the opposition of conservatives who believed day care was a communist plot to destroy the traditional family. The files of the Children's Bureau are filled with letters from outraged men and women who saw any state support for day care as "creeping socialism," the degradation of fathers, and the beginning of the end of the family. A distraught Margaret Wainwright wrote: "I am very much against day care centers for working mothers. In fact, I feel that the woman's place is in the home. Children should learn about life at their mother's knee—I'm sure this is the best way to fight Communism." G.H. Randles declared: "Put mom and dad back in the home. . . . Where there is no dad left, put mom back in the home anyway." Raymond Stauble argued that the day-care proposal "should be fought because it will help mothers to compete in the labor market against unemployed fathers . . . it will encourage more mothers to go to work, even when unnecessary, from selfish motives, further weakening the moral fibre of our nation . . . [and it would] promote more socialistic activity on the part of the Washington bureaucracy." [18]

Thus, as early as the 1960s, a conservative coalition that supported the contradictory aims of getting poor women off the welfare rolls (rolling back the welfare state) and returning working women to the household (restoring the traditional family) was emerging. These objectives would later become the core agenda of the New Right.

Day Care for Welfare Mothers

On July 17, 1962, a much-revised Javits bill was enacted. Congress amended Title IV of the Social Security Act to allow states to use ADC funds to purchase day care for the children of welfare mothers. The amendments also authorized the Children's Bureau to provide grants-in-aid to the states for child-welfare services including day care. These funds could purchase day care for *low-income* children of working mothers.[19] Thus, the amendments linked day care to welfare but allowed local agencies some flexibility in providing support for families near but not below poverty level.

The 1962 legislation earmarked $10,000,000 of child-welfare funds for day care.[20] As the first appropriation for day care since World War II, the legislation represented a breakthrough. However, total appropriations never exceeded $7,000,000 for the entire country. The meager funding severely limited the program's ability to meet the child care lobby's goal: to provide child care for working mothers.

Before Congress passed the 1962 amendments, only a dozen states had plans for publicly supported child-care centers, and most had developed no standards or licensing requirements. The limited funds appropriated did little to stimulate child-care programs. In 1965 New York passed a bill enabling commissioners of public welfare to either provide day care directly or purchase it from an authorized provider. In 1968 Maryland established eight day-care centers for AFDC children and increased this number to seventeen in 1969.[21] Overall, state funding was scattered and unable to meet the demand for child care. Those states that developed day-care programs found they only had sufficient funds to serve the welfare population, but not low-income working women.[22]

Regulations in the legislation also discouraged states from expanding day care. To qualify for federal grants, the states had to have an approved plan for providing child-welfare services. If the plan included the use of day-care centers, the centers had to be licensed by the state. With funding so limited, welfare agencies were forced to use their grants to develop licensing standards instead of increasing day-care services.[23] Because public welfare departments could serve only the welfare poor, it was difficult to mobilize public support to expand federal programs: "nationally the attitude toward day care services (was) that they (were) for the poor and not the self-sustaining."[24] Like all targeted programs, day care divided rather than unified its key constituents.

Although citizen interest in expanding day care was minimal, proposals to reduce the rising welfare rolls brought day care to the forefront of the national policy agenda. Senator Abraham Ribicoff, a New York Democrat whose state was especially hard hit, proposed authorizing an additional $5,000,000 in federal day-care support to put welfare mothers to work:

> Among the poorest of the poor in our great cities are women who have been left alone with large families. Their plight is an urgent social problem. These mothers must work if they are to move toward independence and useful lives. . . . Day care is an integral part of the web of social services we must provide.[25]

Yet no day-care measures passed in the conservative Senate. The influential members of the Senate Subcommittee on Appropriations (98 percent male with an average age of fifty-eight) dismissed day care as "federalized baby-sitting."[26] When President Johnson asked for $3 million in federal matching funds for state efforts, the Senate slashed three-quarters of the request and in 1966 cut that amount in half. Eager to put welfare mothers to work, Congress was, nonetheless, unwilling to pay for services that would promote work.

Yet a stimulus to federal child care arose from a different source. The War on Poverty established competing child-care programs that sought to provide enriching, educational experiences for poor children and especially for black children. While day care was the most popular of all the antipoverty programs, its orientation toward minorities meant that all federal day-care programs were linked to racial issues.

Day Care in the War on Poverty

Although many psychologists and educators adhered to the nineteenth-century belief that intelligence was fixed and rates of child development predetermined, an alternative line of thought, beginning with John Watson and perpetuated by Dr. Benjamin Spock, suggested that outside influences could shape infant development.[27] Particularly influential was a book by University of Chicago psychologist Benjamin Bloom, indicating that early environmental influences affected intelligence, verbal aptitude, and personality traits. Bloom's findings implied that children from disadvantaged environments might benefit from day care.[28]

The Economic Opportunity Act of 1964 provided day care as a by-product of other programs. For example, the adult-training programs specified that mothers in training receive child care.[29] The most important child-care program, however, was Operation Headstart, an offshoot of the community action programs. Influenced by child development research, Headstart operated on the premise that positive preschool experiences could give poor children skills to compete on an equal footing in elementary school. Throughout the nation, community action agencies ran hundreds of Headstart programs. While children of all races benefited from Headstart, the program disproportionately served black children.[30]

The placement of a major preschool program under OEO was a blow to the Children's Bureau. The Headstart model not only conflicted with its remedial view of early childhood education, it also threatened to undermine its gains in setting licensing standards. In seeking to preserve their domain, Children's Bureau staff articulated more definitively the distinction between custodial and educational day care.

Because of the enthusiasm which the Headstart program has generated in the public mind, the main focus of that program has been confused with broader purposes of day care. A clear distinction of the purposes of the two programs needs to be made. Headstart is designed primarily to provide educational enrichment for preschool children from deprived homes at or below the poverty level. . . . Its programs, however, do not usually operate during a full working day. . . . Day care services within the Child Welfare Services program are designed to protect and care for children usually for a full day because there are no other means to ensure adequate care for them. Such services are a part of community programs intended to help keep children in their own homes who might in the absence of such day care services have to be separated from their families and placed in foster care.[31]

Headstart provided enriching experiences. Day care provided protection. Neither supported working mothers.

Many children entering Headstart were physically underdeveloped and socially unprepared for school. To enhance early development, Johnson's Task Force on Early Childhood Education proposed establishing Parent and Child Centers to provide infant day care for children under three, health and welfare services, and extensive counseling for mothers. The counseling would break the poverty cycle by teaching poor mothers about the educational, health, and nutritional needs of their children.[32]

These centers, too, threatened the Children's Bureau. As Gertrude Hoffman complained: "There is too much emphasis on providing parents jobs and training to break out of poverty. I am not opposed to these purposes except that a parent and child center is to help parents do a better job of parenting and increase their skills in rearing children."[33] Despite such misgivings, the Children's Bureau was given trial day-care programs to run. Although Johnson's Task Force meant for the programs to break the poverty cycle, instead the centers concentrated on putting welfare mothers to work. In Milwaukee, Child Care Centers Inc. trained women on AFDC to care for the children of other AFDC women who were participating in job training. The advantages of the program, according to its director Camille Wade, were threefold: "The children are the obvious ones to gain. . . . But beyond that the women who work as day care mothers have been able to leave welfare, and the children's mothers are learning jobs that will do the same for them."[34] Although pleased to be given jurisdiction over the programs, Children's Bureau staff doubted that AFDC mothers "could realistically provide the kind of environment children need to avoid growing up as non-achievers."[35]

As the Children's Bureau tried to preserve its status as the champion of child welfare, the competing programs of the War on Poverty redefined day care as educational, not custodial. Thus, the federal agency most interested in promoting day care was thrust to the periphery of the national policy agenda. Instead the civil rights movement and the expanding welfare rolls took precedence.

Day Care and Welfare Expansion

After nearly a decade of disinterest, in 1967 eight day-care bills were introduced during the first session of the 90th Congress. Five of the bills were to provide federal assistance to improve educational services in day-care centers; three were to amend the Economic Opportunity Act to provide day care for poor children so their mothers could participate in the antipoverty job training or employment programs.[36] Women's Bureau head Mary Keyserling noted the newly found interest with surprise: "In contrast to previous years in which the subject was either ignored or hostile, this year all of the comments [by members of the Appropriations Committee] were supporting of day care and some members insisted that there was not enough day care research."[37]

The renewed interest in day care reflected both the popularity of Headstart and the continued expansion of the welfare rolls, which increased by 214 percent between 1960 and 1968. With welfare reform more politically pressing, in 1967 Congress amended the Social Security Act to encourage welfare mothers to get off the rolls and into the job market. A new Work Incentive Program (WIN) required the states to establish community work and training programs. Welfare mothers couldn't participate in training and work, however, unless states also established daycare programs.[38] The Children's Bureau was charged with developing guidelines for the WIN day-care program—quickly. The rush to provide day care threatened to erode any sort of national guidelines. And Children's Bureau staff feared that whatever minimal standards were established would not apply to other federal programs: "My concern is that we may end up with different day care programs with different requirements and standards."[39]

The fears were realistic for by 1967 a conglomeration of federal child-care programs was divided among six federal agencies: the Department of Health, Education and Welfare, the Office of Economic Opportunity, the Department of Labor, the Department of Commerce, the Department of Housing and Urban Development, and the Department of Agriculture. To coordinate the diverse day-care programs, Congress instructed OEO, the Women's Bureau, and the Children's Bureau to develop a master plan. The task increased tensions between the three organizations, each of which had its own definition of what day care should do. Children's Bureau staff were most concerned with keeping regulations precise and consistent. Gertrude Hoffman, the staffer in charge of day-care standards, argued that "care of infants and tiny babies is so full of hazards that I believe many of the suggested standards should read 'must' instead of 'should.' For example, a telephone *must* be available."[40] She also charged that:

> the Women's Bureau [was] repeatedly asking for names of people who would wink at standards in cities like Baltimore and Chicago . . . where the project would fail . . . if standards for day care [had] to be met. . . . The projects should fail if it meant lowering fire and safety standards for children. . . . They only want the experience and expertise of us specialists where we agree with whatever they design. The lives of the children in this program are the least important items.[41]

The final guidelines did nothing to ease these fears. They excluded the specific regulations developed by the Children's Bureau, and they allowed the administering agency to waive the guidelines if the waiver would "advance innovation."[42]

Despite the fuss about standards and the pressure to reduce the welfare rolls, in 1968 Congress appropriated few funds for day care and made no increase in 1969. Why not? One reason was that most male Congressmen still didn't recognize that women needed child care to work. Congress also was hampered by fiscal restraints imposed by the Vietnam War. Finally, as the furor of the civil rights movement wound down, there was a widespread backlash against spending on social programs that benefited the poor, especially the black poor.

Day Care for the Liberation of Women

The federal government did not ignore working women entirely. To repay the hundreds of women who had worked in his campaign (and also to delay demands for an Equal Rights Amendment), in 1961 President John Kennedy established the Presidential Commission on the Status of Women, the first presidential body ever created for this purpose. The Commission was charged with "developing recommendations for overcoming discrimination in government and private employment on the basis of sex and for developing recommendations for services which will enable women to continue their role as wives and mothers while making a maximum contribution to the world around them."[43] The Commission gave women a forum for organizing and for making policy recommendations. During the 1960s, similar state organizations created an unobtrusive but extensive women's network.[44]

The Commission's first report, *American Women*, documented widespread sex discrimination in employment and education. It recommended the creation of an Interdepartmental Committee on the Status of Women and a Citizen's Advisory Council on the Status of Women. These commissions sponsored conferences on the status of women and generated a climate more conducive to the discussion of women's goals and needs.

Two laws advanced the status of women. In 1963 Congress passed the Equal Pay Act, the first comprehensive federal bill prohibiting employment discrimination. The Act banned sex discrimination in employment and required employers to provide equal pay for equal work.[45] Operative in 1964 as an amendment to the Federal Fair Labor Standards Act, the Act established an unwieldy and ineffectual mechanism for enforcing equal pay. It authorized the Department of Labor to make regular inspections, investigate complaints, and, if the complaint was valid, take the employer to court.

Title VII of the 1964 Civil Rights Act further advanced women's rights by making sex discrimination in employment illegal.[46] But the EEOC, which was primarily interested in racial discrimination, ignored complaints of sex discrimination.

In 1966 at the third National Conference of Commissions on the Status of Women, women who were frustrated by the government's inertia when it came to equal rights for women formed the National Organization for Women (NOW).[47] Initially, NOW was a top-down organization with no grass roots base. Its members sought to break down legal and economic barriers blocking equal employment opportunities. However, NOW also recognized that women's problems were linked to broader issues of social justice. It established seven task forces to recommend action on such issues as discrimination against women, the family, and the problems of poor women. In 1967 NOW proposed a six-point Bill of Rights that included child-care centers.[48] But child care was never a priority for NOW, and as child-care legislation moved through Congress, no NOW members testified on behalf of the bills.

NOW spoke for a small fraction of the women's movement. The broader women's movement that swept across the nation in the late 1960s consisted of small groups lacking any formal structure, centers, or coordinating committees. No overseeing organization directed the activities of the groups, which shared only a common culture but were politically autonomous. Indeed, they opposed any hierarchical power structure on principle, for hierarchy was the weapon of male domination. Instead, the primary political project of this minimally organized branch of the women's movement was consciousness raising, an activity which took place in small rap groups. Rather than seeking political change, the rap groups sought to instill personal change by attacking the effects of psychological oppression and by developing self-esteem and a sense of solidarity among their members.[49]

A radical arm of the women's liberation movement developed out of some student and antiwar protest groups among women who were alienated by their treatment by male radicals.[50] These feminists argued that women's oppression centered in the family, because families freed men to work by harnessing women to child rearing. This unnecessary, and ultimately destructive, arrangement deprived children of the company of men and women of the company of adults. Families also made possible the exploitation of women by training them to perceive work outside the home as peripheral to their true role as mothers.[51] As one feminist ardently proclaimed:

> One of the worst things that happens to a woman when she announces that she is pregnant is that she is congratulated and praised as if she has accomplished the most difficult task in the world. . . . She is seen as being of great worth, possibly for the first time in her life. Women who have been leading active, working lives are made to feel as if only *now* are they finally settling down to the real business of life.[52]

Radical feminists claimed that women could only be liberated by having no children and by refusing to enter into any family relationships.

Most feminists recognized that such a vision was utopian and unrealistic. Women would continue to marry and have children. Day care was critical to women's liberation because it would free "women from the traditional tasks of child rearing."[53] Day care could also radically transform societal child-rearing practices *if* day-care centers were staffed by both women and men and *if* children were taught nontraditional sex roles. Communal day-care centers founded by feminists became part of an alternative school movement, which was hostile to all public education. However, because parents active in alternative schools rejected public education, most were also uninterested in any form of government child care. Thus, one group of feminists rejected child rearing entirely, while another rejected the idea of public child care.

Despite aspects of the women's movement that made it hostile to or uninterested in day care, some feminists did recognize the importance of public child care for women's liberation. In November 1969, several loosely knit feminist groups gathered in New York to create a national organization. They formed the Congress to Unite Women and established a political agenda that included employment equality for women, free twenty-four-hour child-care centers, and, until such care was available, the right to deduct child-care expenses from taxable income.[54] The right to a tax deduction would have benefitted middle-class women, but it was not an issue that poor women were likely to rally around.

The women's movement played only a minimal role in the de-

bates over child-care policy. NOW filed complaints against corporations receiving federal funds, while the grass roots women's liberation movement sought personal change.[55] The movement's
absence was partly due to disinterest in organized political activity
and partly because federal day-care policy ignored the needs of
the college-educated, white, middle-class women who dominated
both its branches.

Community Action and Family Values

Although middle-class women remained on the sidelines, at the
end of the decade Congress nearly passed a substantial day-care
program. And it seemed that the new Republican administration
was fully behind the measure. In his message to Congress on January 19, 1969, President Richard Nixon promised national action
on day care:

> So crucial is the matter of early growth that we must make a national
> commitment to providing all American children an opportunity for
> healthful and stimulating development during the first five years of
> life. . . . We are pledged to that commitment.[56]

All American children. Proponents of national day-care legislation
heard Nixon promise to expand day-care provision beyond its
welfare base.

The only problem was that seven months later Nixon made a
guaranteed annual income the heart of his domestic agenda. In an
August 11 speech to Congress, where he laid out his Family Assistance Plan, he linked day care to welfare reform. The success of
the FAP in setting welfare recipients "on the road to self-reliance"
depended on expanded day-care facilities. Although Nixon promised that day care would help in the development of the child,
provide health and safety, and "break the poverty cycle," it now
had a firm base in welfare reform.[57]

In the first eight months of the 92nd Congress, ten child-care
proposals were introduced. Two bills became the forerunners of
the Comprehensive Child Development Act (H.R. 6748). The first,
introduced by Representative John Brademas, provided federal
grants to both public and private agencies for educational

preschool and day-care programs to meet the needs of poor children, all children aged three to five, and children of working mothers. The Brademas bill funded states based on a formula of 50 percent of the proportion of poor and 50 percent of the proportion of children aged three to five. Applications for grants could be made by any number of local organizations, including community action agencies and local education agencies. A similar bill proposed by Senator Walter Mondale tacked child care onto a two-year extension of the Economic Opportunity Act. The Mondale bill allowed any city, county, or other unit of government or any public or private nonprofit agency to apply to become a "prime sponsor." [58]

As the Comprehensive Child Development Act moved forward in the House and Senate, it seemed that Nixon would indeed fulfill his promise to all young children. Yet when administration officials testified before Congress, they objected to the provisions allowing local community groups to become prime sponsors. They proposed instead that prime sponsors be limited to state governments or to cities of over 500,000, a condition that would prevent the local community action agencies from sponsoring day-care programs. Civil rights advocates defended the provisions allowing community action groups to be prime sponsors. [59] For Marian Wright Edelman, author of the Mondale bill and prominent civil rights activist, local control was *the* crucial issue. Community organizations could operate like the Child Development Group of Mississippi, a controversial community action program where Headstart had been "perhaps *the* most important social catalyst for change in the state. It helped poor parents understand new ways of having an effect on their children's education." [60] Only through local control could child care circumvent the racially segregated southern public schools:

> The heart of this bill . . . is the delivery mechanism. Those of us who have worked with the poor, the uneducated, the hungry, the disenfranchised, have had long and bitter experience in how legislative intent is thwarted in the process of implementation. . . . We think this [local administration] essential and those concerned with equal opportunity and civil rights will oppose any control of this child legislation to the states. [61]

As Evelyn Moore, Director of the Black Child Development Institute, explained: "It is to the advantage of the entire nation to view the provision of day care/child development services within the context of the need for a readjustment of societal power relationships." Day-care centers could "catalyze development in black and other communities" but only if consumers of child care made up at least two-thirds of the representatives among prime sponsors.[62] Thus, a proposal for day care now became embroiled in the struggle for racial equality.

By September 1971, the FAP had passed in the House and was awaiting Senate action. But day care faced another hurdle—it had become a threat to the FAP. The income limit in the day-care bill was $6,960 for a family of four.[63] The level of eligibility for FAP was only $4,320. If the day-care bill was passed in its present form, it could drive up the costs of welfare reform and kill the FAP.

Advocates of working women responded that the higher limit was necessary if the bill was to provide any support for the working class. Mary Keyserling, now a private consultant, testified against the administration's proposed income limit. Keyserling explained that a lower cutoff would exclude most mothers in two-parent households, who had the most pressing day-care needs: 81 percent of dual-earner families had incomes over $7,000, high enough to make them ineligible for any federal subsidy but too low to pay the cost of quality child care. An income limit of even $5,000, the final compromise, meant that the program would shut out most of the working poor and all of the middle class.[64] Thus, even as Nixon sought to woo the forgotten Americans, he agreed to income limits that would exclude them.

Two years after committing his administration to day care, Nixon vetoed the Comprehensive Child Development Act, the nation's first and only attempt to provide federal support for all young children. Why did he compromise on and then turn against a program that could have provided a base for building political support among the "forgotten Americans?"

In his veto message Nixon denounced the bill as a program that would plunge the federal government "headlong financially into supporting child development [and] would commit the vast moral authority of the national government to the side of communal approaches to child-rearing against the family centered approach."[65] This statement represented a concession to right wing proponents of family values, who saw day care as a Communist conspiracy to destroy the family.[66] In the final hearings on the bill, spokesmen for the fledgling voice of the Moral Majority launched a tirade against the measure. Rep. Durward Hall exclaimed:

> Can anyone realize, believe, or even imagine he is here today hearing and debating the question of taking the children away from families and training them as wards of the state? . . . It is a question of collectivized child raising, and it perverts all the traditional cultures if you now suddenly assume or believe as inherently defective that families of America would insist on raising their own children. I see this as a long step toward socialization of our nation.[67]

Similarly, Rep. John Schmitz protested:

> It is becoming possible for a government to root out the basic unit of society—the family—and replace it with state control. . . . A free people today must, therefore, be constantly on its guard against such unwarranted incursions into the life of the family.[68]

And in the eyes of Rep. John Rarick, "This amendment insults motherhood and, if passed, will destroy the home."[69]

Equally damning was the idea that the bill would revive not only community action but also the controversial Office of Economic Opportunity. Indeed, Mondale explicitly promoted his child-care bill as a mechanism to revive OEO:

> At the local level, through community action and other related programs, OEO has helped poor people to share in the planning and decision-making processes of their communities. They, as well as others, serve on the boards of neighborhood councils, community action agencies, and delegate social agencies, thereby constituting one of the largest voluntary efforts in the country. In helping to determine the use and allocation of significant sums of money, they and their community action agencies have exercised an impressive degree of sound judgment and responsibility. This unique and successful effort in citizen participation is the heart of the OEO anti-poverty program. . . . The lessons of the past should be used to give OEO a new vitality.[70]

But Nixon had already converted OEO's function from social action to research, and he had no intention of allowing the War on Poverty to be revived through the back door.[71] As he explained in his veto message:

> Upon taking office, this administration sought to redesign, to redirect—indeed, to rehabilitate—the Office of Economic Opportunity, which had lost much public acceptance in the five years since its inception. . . . If this congressional action were allowed to stand, OEO would become an operational agency, diluting its role as incubator and tester of ideas and pioneer for social programs.[72]

Finally, day care had became hostage to Nixon's proposal for welfare reform. If the day-care bill had been enacted, it would have increased the cost of the FAP by $20 billion, whereas the administration had allocated only $1.2 billion. Still deeply committed to welfare reform in 1971, Nixon could not let a day-care measure undermine his chances of success.

The Legacy of Child Care

Child care represented a social right for children, care that would grant them a modicum of security and the opportunity to develop in a healthy and enriching environment and thus share in the nation's full heritage. Child care also represented a civil right for women, a right to work without constraints imposed on the basis of gender.

Day care could have become a program that would have helped the most forgotten Americans, working-class women who were in the labor force. Though the income limit was set low enough to exclude most working women in two-parent families, the measure would have provided a foundation upon which to build a more comprehensive program.

Throughout the policymaking process, however, day-care legislation divided rather than united its potential supporters. Some programs promised support for working families as well as the welfare poor. However, limited funding meant that in practice day care became an income-targeted program, serving only welfare recipients. Other programs targeted poor children and excluded working- and middle-class taxpayers. Yet attempts to expand beyond this minimal base triggered the antagonism of social conservatives, who feared government intrusion in child rearing.

Debates over day care also revealed the issues that were to mobilize the Moral Majority: an antipathy to state intervention and a nostalgia for the traditional family. In vetoing the legislation, Nixon won the loyalty of this nascent constituency and began building a New Right center for Republican party politics of the 1970s and 1980s.

SEVEN

Universal Principles in Social Security

The War on Poverty initiated ambitious programs to improve communities, train workers, and increase housing for the poor. But because these programs also promoted racial equality, they created a backlash against the welfare state. Proposals for child care and welfare reform also failed because they became entangled in racial issues. These outcomes suggest that targeting, whether by income or by race, is an ineffectual strategy for expanding the welfare state.

Recognizing the political vulnerability of targeted programs, many social scientists propose basing eligibility for social benefits on universal criteria.[1] This is the standard argument of welfare state theorists and of most social scientists interested in devising strategies for new policy measures. Theda Skocpol, for example, contends that proponents of targeting have not faced the hard political questions: "Why should people struggling just above the poverty line . . . pay for programs that go exclusively to people below the poverty line? Why might not many Americans from the working and middle classes simply write off troubled inner city people and just call for the police and prisons to contain their threatening behavior?"[2] Perhaps no one has pled the case for universalism more eloquently than William Julius Wilson:

I am convinced that, in the last few years of the twentieth century, the problems of the truly disadvantaged in the United States will have to be attacked primarily through universal programs that enjoy the support and commitment of a broad constituency. Under this approach, targeted programs (whether based on the principle of equality of group opportunity or that of equality of life chances) would not necessarily be eliminated, but would rather be deemphasized— considered only as offshoots of, and indeed secondary to, the universal programs. *The hidden agenda is to improve the life chances of groups such as the ghetto underclass by emphasizing programs in which the more advantaged groups of all races can positively relate.*[3]

Despite these arguments, universalism has raised heated opposition from both liberals and conservatives. Liberals fear that universalism threatens racial advancement. In their view, advocates of universalism are reneging on the commitment to equality, optimistically pursuing a strategy that is not only too costly but also unlikely to guarantee that the least privileged will receive benefits. As Kenneth Tollett argues: "If white supremacy continues to be as strong as I am indicating, universal policies that also benefit blacks substantially will be resisted or undermined by whites if they perceive that the benefits going to blacks may dilute the benefits to them."[4] Yet conservatives, for whom the logic of universalism should be most appealing, criticize the nation's only universal program, Social Security, for favoring the elderly at the expense of children and for squandering the nation's limited resources.[5]

It is not surprising that both proponents and opponents of universalism point to Social Security to set the agenda. Social Security has reduced poverty among the elderly and created sustained majority support, making it a politically untouchable "sacred cow." The question, then, is whether Social Security provides an optimal model for resolving other social problems. This chapter weighs the advantages and disadvantages of basing other programs around the universal principles of Social Security.

Granting the Right to Benefits

While political theorists debate the merits of universalism, few bother to define the term. In the broadest sense, universalism means benefits granted as a right of citizenship. However, citizenship is often defined by participation in the paid labor force; indeed such a definition is inherent in T. H. Marshall's definition of democracy.[6] Thus, most universal social programs are forms of social *insurance* in which eligibility depends on labor force participation. As Walter Korpi explains: "Since the days of Bismarck and Lloyd George, in the European countries the concept of social rights tied to worklife participation or citizenship has played a central role in policy debates . . . the break between the old poor laws and the new welfare state was based precisely on the introduction of social rights via social insurance."[7] Social insurance is thus an extension of citizenship, because eligibility for benefits is based on work history. According to this definition, only wage workers are citizens and only wage workers are eligible for social rights.[8]

Social Security is a universal program in the more limited sense of social insurance. Eligibility for benefits is linked to work history. This arrangement has mixed results. On the one hand, linking the right to work with the right to income security has protected millions of Americans in old age. On the other hand, it has also perpetuated racial and gender inequality.

As Chapter 1 explained, the Social Security Act of 1935 created an old-age insurance program for wage workers. Not all workers could earn the right to benefits, however, for more than three-fifths of black workers, those employed in agricultural labor or domestic service, were excluded from coverage.[9] Social Security also excluded teachers, nurses, hospital employees, librarians, and social workers—all occupations heavily dominated by women. Of the 22 percent of women gainfully employed in 1930, 52 percent were not covered by Social Security.[10] Thus, the nation's first "social wage" provided little or nothing for most women and most African Americans.

Initially, Social Security contained no provisions for wives or widows, but in 1939 Congress added a spouse and widow's benefits. The eligibility rules for spouse and widow's benefits rewarded women who remained in stable marriages and were supported by their husbands but penalized women who became separated or divorced or who earned their own way.[11] The spouse benefit granted wives one-half of the full benefit if they were at least sixty-five and living with their husbands. Women separated from their husbands, even if they were still married, had no right to Social Security. Working wives were also ineligible if their own earned benefit was more than one-half the spouse benefit. Divorced women, even if they had been married for fifty years, had no right to a spouse benefit when their former husbands retired. Widows were only eligible for benefits if they were at least sixty-five, if they were living with the husband at the time of his death, and if they had never remarried. Like wives, widows were ineligible for benefits in their own names.[12]

What Social Security's early experience teaches us is that when rights to benefits are earned, the right to earn them is not automatically granted to all workers but rather is politically negotiable. Historically, the manipulation of the category "wage worker" led to the exclusion of black men and women engaged in paid employment. A second lesson is that when benefits are based on family status, the criteria for distributing them create an inferior form of citizenship.

Becoming More Universal

Over the next thirty years Social Security gradually was expanded to cover more occupations and to provide greater income security. In 1956 Congress allowed widows of insured workers to claim full benefits at age sixty-two and women workers to claim actuarially reduced benefits at age sixty-two. Legislation in 1954 and 1956 extended coverage to all farm and domestic workers and to nearly all professional groups, including nurses and teachers.[13] By 1960 Social Security covered most of the labor force. Still, one-third of older men and 40 percent of older women had incomes below poverty level.[14] And because Congress only increased benefits sporadically, usually right before an election, inflation persistently eroded the value of their benefits. Health-care expenses also placed an enormous financial burden on millions of the uninsured of all ages.

The Great Society provided one great gift for the elderly. In 1965 Congress enacted Medicare, a program of health insurance for covered workers over age sixty-five. It also improved women's benefits. Widows were allowed to take actuarially reduced benefits as early as age sixty, and divorced women who had been married for at least twenty years were now allowed one-half their former husbands' benefits.[15] Poverty rates among the elderly remained high, however.

Johnson was eager to raise Social Security benefits, which he viewed as part of his antipoverty strategy. In 1966 he asked Congress to increase benefits by 15 percent, to raise the wage base from $6,600 to $10,000 by 1970, and to raise minimum benefits. Congress granted part of his request. Benefits were increased 13 percent and the wage base raised to $7,800.[16]

The modest package seemed unlikely to be improved further after the Republican victory in 1968. But Nixon surprised nearly everyone by supporting the most generous increases in the program's history and, more important, by adding automatic cost-of-living adjustments. He proposed 10 percent increases in Social Security benefits and an automatic cost-of-living adjustment. These automatic increases, he argued, would "do much to remove the system from biennial politics" and "make fair treatment of beneficiaries a matter of certainty rather than a matter of hope."[17] Between 1969 and 1972 Congress raised benefits three times and finally in 1972 indexed benefits to inflation and maximum taxable wages to future wage movements.[18] The COLA (automatic cost-of-living increase) permanently protected the incomes of the elderly against inflation. The benefit for widows and (now) widowers was also increased to 100 percent of the insured worker's benefit.

Nixon's generosity reflected his political calculation that spending on so popular a program would help cement the loyalty of the forgotten Americans to the Republican party. In 1970 his speechwriter, Pat Buchanan, sent him a memo analyzing a book entitled *The Real Majority*. The book, Buchanan explained, argued that the Democrats had lost their populist base by caving in to the demands of vocal minorities, like African Americans and feminists. To put the Democrats on the defense, Nixon decided to preempt the "social issue." Instead of the "special interests" catered to by the Democrats, Nixon decided to "aim our strategy primarily at disaffected Democrats, at blue-collar working class white ethnics. We should set out to capture the vote of the forty-seven year-old Dayton housewife."[19]

Although congressional Democrats had opposed automatic

cost-of-living increases on the grounds that they fueled inflation, the campaign for the FAP and its ultimate failure lent momentum to Social Security reform. As Martha Derthick explains: "Because Social Security was popular and [reform] feasible, it won support when more controversial forms were stymied. . . . Incremental changes in well-established programs do not attract attention."[20] What also made Social Security expansion possible was that the trust fund was generating excess revenues estimated to produce cumulative reserves approaching a trillion dollars by 2025. To reduce the reserves, the 1971 Advisory Council on Social Security recommended automatic benefit adjustments, liberalization of the retirement test, and improved disability protection.

The 1972 amendments reduced the threat of old-age poverty significantly and provided income security against inflation. By the mid-1970s more than 80 percent of those over sixty-five were receiving some income from Social Security. Social Security also helped widows and widowers with dependent children and provided benefits to the disabled. Still, pockets of old-age poverty remained. And those most likely to remain poor in old age were women and minorities. Whereas poverty rates among white males over age sixty-five dropped to 10.4 percent by 1972, 16.5 percent of elderly women and 39.9 percent of elderly African Americans were still poor.[21]

Social Security also distributed costs and benefits unevenly. Rather than transferring income from rich to poor, it transferred income from African Americans to whites and from working women to homemakers.

Distributional Inequality in Social Security

Social Security penalizes African Americans in part because they have a lower life expectancy than whites. In 1970 the average life expectancy of nonwhites at age sixty was significantly lower than that of whites. Sixty-year-old white females could expect to live another 20.8 years and white males 16.1 years. By contrast, sixty-year-old nonwhite females had a life expectancy of only 19 years and nonwhite males only 15.4 years.[22] Whites received more benefits because they lived longer.

African Americans are also disadvantaged in the share of earnings they pay in taxes. This results from black/white differences in the proportion of wages subject to Social Security taxes. The 1972 amendments raised the wage base to $9,000. Any individual earning over that amount only paid taxes on the first $9,000. In 1972 white median family income was $11,549, while black median family income was only $6,864. Thus, white, but not black, median family income exceeded maximum taxable earnings. Social Security taxes are not levied on families, however, but on individuals. Taking the individual male head of household as the taxable unit, the median income of a black male household head in 1972 was only 66.1 percent of maximum taxable earnings, while the median income of the white male household head was 8.5 percent higher than maximum taxable earnings.[23] Thus, black men were taxed on 100 percent of their income, on average, while white men earned a considerable amount of untaxed income.

Social Security is a universal program in the sense that benefits are calculated on prior earnings. In 1972 the average Social Security benefit was $162.35 a month. However, the average benefit for blacks was only $130.76.[24] Although African Americans on average pay a disproportionate share of taxes on earnings, their low lifetime earnings mean they receive lower benefits. The distribution of benefits reflects market inequities.

Social Security sometimes bypasses the market in the distribution of benefits by rewarding women who marry, stay married, and don't work. Women who sustain a marriage for at least ten years, regardless of whether they have ever worked for wages, are eligible for a spouse benefit.[25] Working women pay full payroll taxes. Yet most working women find that when they retire, the spouse benefit pays more than their own earned benefit. The spouse benefit is a better deal, because women earn lower wages than men and have more sporadic work histories. Thus, Social Security transfers income from women in the labor force to homemakers.[26]

Black women are doubly disadvantaged by the subsidy to wives. One reason is that they are less likely than white women to qualify for a spouse benefit, because only women who have been married for at least ten years are eligible. In 1970 73.5 percent of white women aged forty-five to sixty-four were married compared to

54.1 percent of black women; 20.4 percent of black women were separated, divorced, or had a husband absent compared to only 7.3 percent of white women.[27] Another reason is that black women are more likely than white women to have paid employment. In 1970 only 39.5 percent of all married white women with a spouse present were in the labor force compared to 50 percent of married, nonwhite women with a spouse present.[28] Thus, their Social Security taxes subsidize the spouse benefits of white housewives.

Still, Social Security provides the most important and most stable income source in old age for most men and women, regardless of race. Between 1967 and 1984 average earned income declined for all families except the elderly whose income rose by 55 percent. Most of the improvement came from Social Security benefits, which increased from 28 percent of the total share of elderly income to 36 percent.[29]

By the early 1980s Social Security (including Medicare) had become the sole welfare program where the middle class as well as the poor received something tangible back for their taxes. Not surprisingly, public support was high. Virtually every public opinion poll between 1977 and 1990 indicated the American people supported Social Security.[30] These opinions illustrate the great virtue of universalism. Social Security was so well liked that it created its own political lobby.

The Growth of the Elderly Lobby

When Ronald Reagan was elected president, he promised to roll back the welfare state. His 1981 Omnibus Budget Reconciliation Act eliminated the entire public service jobs program, removed 400,000 individuals from the food stamp program, and reduced or eliminated welfare and Medicaid benefits for the working poor. It also eliminated the minimum benefit for low-income Social Security recipients, ended the modest death benefit, and phased out benefits for older children of deceased workers, who had no political voice. In addition, residents of public housing were required to pay 30 percent of their income toward rent instead of 25 percent.[31]

These cuts slid through Congress, but when Reagan proposed

more sweeping cuts in Social Security he sparked a storm of controversy. Reagan suggested a 10 percent cut in future benefits, a 31 percent cut in early-retirement benefits, and a further narrowing of the rules regulating disability eligibility. This second set of cuts attacked middle-class entitlements, and reprisals were swift and harsh. Days after Reagan's proposal appeared, his public approval rating dropped sixteen points.[32] And in two congressional elections Ohio congressman Michael Oxley barely held on to a seat Republicans had occupied since the 1930s and a secure Mississippi seat went to the Democrats.[33] The 1981 budget scenario demonstrated both the vulnerability of programs targeted to the poor and the invincibility of Social Security.

These events and subsequent coverage of old-age politics by the media suggest that the elderly have formed a powerful lobby. Does such a lobby exist, and if so, what are its weapons?

One myth, that nonetheless strikes fear in the hearts of politicians, is that older people have enormous influence at the ballot box. Older people *do* vote in greater proportions than any other age group. In 1988, for example, 19 percent of voters were sixty-five or older. Yet the elderly are quite heterogeneous in terms of health, income, social status, and education and rarely vote as a bloc. Rather, on most issues, including aging policy issues, older people are nearly indistinguishable from young adults. On some measures, in fact, they are *less* supportive of government benefits *for the elderly* than other age groups.[34] Class, rather than age-based interests, determines how older people vote, with prosperous older people being conspicuously unwilling to support increases in Social Security and Medicare.[35]

Rather than through voting, the elderly lobby has manifested its influence through senior-citizen organizations, which grew rapidly in the 1970s. These organizations have engaged in advocacy efforts, lobbying and monitoring the behavior of politicians, which they report to their constituents. The largest senior organization, indeed the largest voluntary membership organization in the United States, is the American Association of Retired Persons (AARP). Founded in 1958 mainly to provide insurance to retirees, by 1992 AARP had more than 28 million members. AARP lobbies actively on behalf of senior issues and scored a big success in eliminating mandatory retirement. It has a paid staff of 1,300 and an annual budget of approximately a quarter of a billion dollars. Its magazine, *Modern Maturity,* has the highest circulation of any magazine in the United States.[36] *Modern Maturity* publishes voter's guides on candidates' positions, runs a wire service that provides newspapers with reports on elderly issues, and sponsors a weekly television series. During the 1988 presidential election, in New Hampshire alone, AARP mailed out 250,000 pieces of literature detailing the candidates' positions on Social Security, long-term health care, and other issues of relevance to older people. Yet because it is so large and its membership so diverse, AARP can rarely take a position without angering someone, a dilemma that constrains its political power even as politicians overestimate its impact.

Other organizations are not hamstrung by these constraints. The National Council of Senior Citizens (NCSC) was founded by the AFL-CIO in 1962 to lobby for Medicare. It has approximately four and a half million members, primarily blue-collar workers and trade unionists, and retains a liberal Democratic bias. Organized around 4,000 active local clubs, NCSC has access to the full lobbying power of the AFL-CIO. Moreover, its smaller size and the shared background of its members make it more capable of taking a stance on particular issues than the unwieldy AARP.[37]

The National Committee to Preserve Social Security and Medicare was founded in 1982 and has more than five million members, a budget of $40 million, and a well-funded political action committee. As I will show below, it played a key role in killing the Medicare Catastrophic Coverage Act of 1988. Finally, the National Association of Retired Federal Employees has a membership of approximately half a million and is concerned primarily with issues of interest to retired federal employees. It has an annual budget of five million dollars and a large political action committee. This is not an exhaustive list of organizations that comprise the old-age lobby, but it gives some sense of those that are the most active and influential.

Despite their number these senior organizations played a secondary role at best in most of the major policy victories of the 1960s and 1970s. The enactment of Medicare, the Employee Retirement Income Security Act, the Older Americans Act, and Supplementary Security Income (SSI), the regulation of nursing homes and prescription drugs, and improvements in social security benefits were due to the efforts of other organizations—organized labor, social welfare groups, and consumer groups. Most old-age organizations emerged or became politically active *after* much of the pathbreaking legislation had been passed.[38] The old-age lobby didn't create the policies; rather, the policies created the lobby. This suggests that what makes programs based on universal criteria successful politically is their ability to unify the middle class behind the welfare state. As Esping-Anderson explains:

> The formula was to combine universal entitlements with high earnings-graduated benefits, thus matching welfare-state benefits and services to middle-class expectations. For the average worker, as social citizen the result was an experience of upward mobility. For the welfare state, the result was the consolidation of a vast popular majority wedded to its defence. "Middle class" universalism has protected the welfare state against backlash.[39]

Generational Equity and the Distribution of Wealth

Despite popular support and the presence of an elderly lobby that successfully prevented cuts at a time when nearly every other social program was wounded, some fatally, by the Reagan budget-cutting axe, attacks on Social Security appear periodically. In the 1980s these attacks were framed around the concept of generational equity. At first, generational equity meant that the generosity of entitlements to the old were harmful to children. "The old," Philip Longman wrote in the *Washington Monthly,* "have come to insist that the young not only hold them harmless for their past profligacy, but sacrifice their own prosperity to pay for it."[40] Social Security had significantly reduced poverty among the elderly, but 23 percent of children were poor. Why, Longman asked, had we cut programs for children while increasing our expenditures on the aged? Rather than investing in future economic growth, Longman argued, Social Security squandered the nation's limited wealth on an unproductive segment of the population.

Few bought the depiction of the elderly as greedy, selfish, and unproductive. Unlike the poor, hidden from sight in bleak inner cities, the elderly were highly visible, present in every American family. People had only to look at their own parents and grand-parents to know that most older people were living comfortably but not grandly and that if the federal government stopped providing income security and health care, they—their children and grandchildren—would have to bear the burden.

As the generational equity debate failed to make a dent in public support for Social Security, conservatives who wished to see benefits cut began linking the idea of generational equity to broader economic and social issues. Eerily prescient, just a month before the 1987 stock market crash Peter G. Peterson published an *Atlantic Monthly* article warning that feeble productivity growth had created "a widening split between the elderly, among whom poverty is still declining, and children and young families, among whom poverty rates have exploded." [41] According to Peterson, Americans endorsed smaller and leaner government, but between 1979 and 1986 federal spending increased significantly. Most of the growth was concentrated in entitlement programs, which increased from 5.4 percent of gross national product (GNP) to 11.5 percent. [42] By contrast, spending on the public infrastructure for research and development in industry, education, job skills, and remedial social services had been cut. [43] Not only were children the victims of elderly greed, the entire economy was held hostage to the programs that protected the elderly but no one else from the ravages of the marketplace.

The theme of generational equity capitalized on the economic issues that had split the Democratic party and turned working-class Democrats to the Republicans. By focusing on middle-class discontent over the growing tax burden, the theme had appeal for young, educated Republicans. At the same time the emphasis on the penalty poor children were paying aroused the resentment of low-income groups in traditional Democratic strongholds over cuts in welfare benefits. For example, congressman Jim Moody (D-WI), who hailed from a working-class district, told the Allied Council of Senior Citizens in Milwaukee that "Many people receiving Social Security benefits are better off than those taxed to pay them. The federal deficit is out of control, and the young are too heavily taxed; everyone must sacrifice; Social Security must be curbed." [44]

What lent credence to the idea that the elderly had become a privileged class was the reorientation of federal policy that occurred in the 1980s, as a shifting of the income-tax burden downward and rising income inequality seemingly placed Social Security in competition with other domestic programs.

Between 1977 and 1988 America's richest 1 percent experienced a 7.8 percent decline in the effective tax rate, whereas the bottom decile of the income scale experienced a 2.5 percent increase.[45] The redistribution of the tax burden from rich to poor resulted from two changes in the tax structure. The first was the 1981 Economic Recovery Tax Act. While the Act cut taxes across the board for individuals, it reduced the top bracket on unearned income from 70 percent to 50 percent, an enormous boon to the small proportion of the population deriving most of its income from rents and interest. Then, the 1987 tax reforms reduced the top rate on earned income from 50 percent to 28 percent.

The inequity of the tax burden on lower-income families is compounded by the fact that they are least likely to have health insurance. In 1987 two-thirds of the working poor, families with incomes less than double the poverty level, had no health insurance.[46] Yet poor, working people with no health insurance of their own pay 1.5 percent of their income for health insurance for the elderly through the Medicare portion of the Social Security tax. Thus, as lower-income Americans absorbed a higher share of the tax burden and suffered further losses through cuts in social programs, the guaranteed automatic cost-of-living increases protected the standard of living of the elderly.

It wasn't only the poor who paid a higher tax burden but also the middle class. As the tax burden on both earned and unearned income dropped, Social Security tax rates climbed upward, from 6.05 percent in 1978 to 7.65 percent in 1990. The leap in the tax rate occurred in 1983 when Congress enacted amendments to the Social Security Act to increase the trust fund reserves, which had been drained in the 1970s due to high levels of unemployment and inflation. The amendments increased the Social Security tax rate and accelerated the pace of future increases.

Congress increased Social Security tax rates to build the trust fund reserve and guarantee future generations a secure old age. Instead, because income taxes were cut and made less progressive, the tax burden shifted from general revenues to regressive Social

Security taxes. Between 1980 and 1988 total tax receipts remained relatively stable—19.4 percent of GNP in 1980; 19 percent of GNP in 1990. But the portion of federal taxes from Social Security rose from 31 percent to 37 percent, while income-tax revenues dropped from 60 percent to 55 percent.[47] Middle- and upper-middle-income households with two earners were the big losers.

Most analysts ignore the fact that the middle- and the upper-middle income elderly were also losers. In 1992 the maximum taxable income was 28 percent for all wage earners. However, middle-income elderly were subject to considerably higher tax rates. Two effects were involved. The first derived from the 1983 amendments, which not only increased the tax rate but also taxed Social Security benefits. Single persons with incomes above $25,000 and couples with incomes above $32,000 now had 50 percent of their benefits subject to taxation. The second was the existing limitation on other earned income. Social Security recipients under age seventy lost one dollar for every three dollars earned above $10,000 a year. These taxes made the effective tax rate for older people potentially as high as 80 percent.[48] The 1993 federal budget further increased taxes paid by the elderly by raising the taxable share of Social Security income from 50 percent to 85 percent.

Still, despite growing inequality and a reduction in the standard of living of young families, public support for Social Security remained strong. A 1987 survey conducted for the American Association of Retired Persons concluded that there are "no signs of waning support for programs targeted for the elderly." Rather, even among young adults (21 to 29) 77 percent believe the government should spend more money on Medicare, 74 percent favor higher Social Security benefits, and 76 percent say the government is "not doing enough for older people."[49] Nonetheless, entitlement programs are not invincible. A recent policy issue, framed in generational equity terms, demonstrates how readily social programs that don't spread the costs and benefits across the entire population can erode public support.

The Medicare Catastrophic Coverage Act of 1988

On July 1, 1988, with the hearty endorsement of Congress, the Medicare Catastrophic Coverage Act of 1988 was signed into law.

Just three months later, it was repealed. The events that transpired in the interim provide some lessons about the balance that must be maintained between universal and targeted programs.

In 1985 Otis Bowen, secretary of Health and Human Services, drafted a proposal to provide insurance against catastrophic health expenses. Catastrophic health needs were still not covered by Medicare, and a serious illness, especially if it meant a long stay in a nursing home, could devastate an elderly person, wiping out all savings and leaving him or her saddled with debt. Initially the proposal was shelved, but in 1987 President Reagan, stung by criticism of his proposal to delay the scheduled cost-of-living increases in Social Security benefits, asked Bowen to revive it. However, Reagan agreed to support Bowen's proposal only if the program was financed entirely by the elderly.[50]

The following year a much revised proposal emerged from the Health Subcommittee of the Senate Finance Committee. The Medicare Catastrophic Coverage Act of 1988 represented the largest expansion of the Medicare program since 1965. All Medicare recipients would pay a flat premium of $4.00 a month for extensive benefits including long-term hospital stays (365 days of coverage after payment of a one-time deductible of $560), a prescription-drug benefit for medication not covered by pre-existing Medicare policies, mammography screening, hospice care, caregiver support for anyone caring for a sick relative, and the extension of Medicaid benefits to poor pregnant women and infants.[51] But the program failed to alleviate the burdensome cost of nursing-home care, merely extending nursing-home coverage under Medicare from 100 to 150 days.

In addition to the flat premium, about one-third of Medicare recipients—those who pay at least $150 in annual income taxes—would pay a surtax. The surtax would have worked in this fashion: for every $150 paid in federal income tax, a person receiving Medicare would pay an additional $37.50 surtax. A tax liability of $1,500 would trigger a surtax of $375; a tax liability of $3,000 would mean a surtax of $750 and so on up to a ceiling of $800, which would increase to $1,050 by 1993. If a husband and wife were both on Medicare, both would pay the surtax.[52]

Because of the surtax, the costs for middle-income taxpayers would have been substantial, while the potential benefits would have been paltry. There are several reasons why the middle class would actually have gained little from a program that seemed to offer so much. First, only a small fraction of Medicare recipients (less than 1.5 percent) would exceed the 150-day limit on covered hospital care, and only 16.8 percent would have benefited from the prescription-drug coverage. Second, because Medicare leaves many medical costs uncovered, a large portion of older people purchase Medigap policies from private insurance companies. These policies provide benefits similar to those covered by the Catastrophic Coverage Act and fill many of the holes in health-care coverage that the new legislation would not have filled.[53] Finally, the only present source of public funding for extended nursing-home care is Medicaid, a means- and asset-tested welfare program. The middle-class elderly still would have no help in financing nursing-home care, except by spending down their income and assets to become impoverished enough to qualify for Medicaid. Thus, middle- and upper-income elderly would have had to pay increased taxes for insurance coverage they did not need, while receiving no help with the one terrifyingly large health-care expense they still faced.

Not surprisingly, the Catastrophic Coverage Act triggered an explosive reaction from the elderly lobby. Across the country petition drives and other protests arose almost instantaneously. In just sixty days the Nevada-based Senior Coalition Against the Catastrophic Act claimed to have gathered 410,000 signatures on a repeal petition.[54] According to newspaper reports, six thousand older people canceled their membership in AARP, which supported the legislation and opposed its repeal. And Washington legislators had their offices flooded with letters and calls from constituents, many triggered by a mail campaign begun by the National Committee to Preserve Social Security and Medicare, infuriated that the middle-income elderly would be paying the highest tax rates in the nation as a result of the legislation.[55] What they wanted was either repeal of the legislation, a significant reduction of the tax burden to the middle class, or the right to withdraw from the new benefits (and costs) with no penalty on other health-care coverage.

Historically, Medicare has been funded through payroll taxes, which socialized its costs. The legislation represented the first successful attempt to "de-socialize" an entitlement program. Instead of spreading the costs across the entire working population, it placed them solely on the shoulders of the elderly with the middle class paying the most.

On October 4, 1989, the House voted to repeal the program it had approved just 16 months earlier. Two days later the Senate voted to repeal the surtax and retain only the long-term hospital benefits, eliminating the ceiling on doctors' bills, the expanded nursing-home benefits, and the drug benefits. Thus, a program that would have provided needed health benefits to the least prosperous aged, to the disabled of all ages, and to poor women and children was destroyed because it was financed solely by middle- and upper-income elderly.

The Catastrophic Care Act illustrates that middle-class support for social programs hinges on shared costs and shared returns for tax dollars. When programs are socialized across the entire population, the cost for any individual is relatively small compared to the benefits received. But when upper- and middle-income individuals, in this case the aged, are asked to sustain a program that primarily benefits the poor, the relationship between costs and benefits is reversed.

Theda Skocpol argues that universal programs are preferable to racially targeted social programs because they "create new symbolic and political space for more targeted efforts on behalf of disadvantaged people."[56] The sad fate of the Catastrophic Care Act illustrates how little "political space" exists when the middle class has to pay for the poor. It makes one wonder how much targeting within universal programs is possible before the middle class revolts.

The Legacy of Universalism

Proponents of universalism believe that only such programs can mobilize sufficient political support. By this measure Social Security is the United States' most successful social program. Yet this political support did not immediately commence, and, aside from protecting the program from cuts, it is not clear what import this support actually has. It certainly does not produce the groundswell of opinion necessary to make large improvements in the program. It is also not clear that the same amount of political support could be generated for other social programs. Unlike income support in old age, not everyone needs job training or welfare, and housing policy already has a universal component in the tax break it provides to the middle class. There is no guarantee that people would willingly pay for programs unlikely to benefit them.

The more salient issue is whether universal programs can rescue the ghetto underclass. Advocates of targeted programs maintain that universal programs are too costly and that the problems faced by the nation's most impoverished families "can only be ameliorated by highly concentrated comprehensive benefits and social services devised especially for the poor."[57] For example, Nicholas Lemann argues that the only solution to the woes of the ghettos is to direct social programs where they will do the most good and have the most chance of reaching those who need them.[58] Similarly, Isabel Sawhill contends that "if there is one lesson that we have learned from all the evaluations and research that has been conducted since the War on Poverty began, it is that service programs that provide limited benefits to many people, although politically popular, are not effective in responding to the problems of the most seriously disadvantaged."[59] Proponents of targeting also claim that some targeted programs have been remarkably successful in withstanding budget cuts and in providing basic services, such as health care, to the poor.[60]

The problem with these debates is that they fail to distinguish between targeting by income and targeting by race, which raise separate issues in the minds of most people. Opinion polls show a sizeable difference in public support for programs targeted to the poor and programs targeted to African Americans. As Table 7.1 shows, white Americans are significantly more likely to favor tax breaks for businesses to locate in poor areas than in black ghettos, to favor spending more money on schools in poor areas than in black ghettos, and to favor special scholarships for poor children than for black children.[61] Although a majority of Americans are willing to support some targeted measures, the differential responses suggest that racial considerations do affect support for social programs.

So what can universal programs accomplish? Certainly they can

Table 7.1.   *Comparison of Responses of White Americans Indicating Support for Programs for the Poor and for Blacks*

Would you favor or oppose giving business and industry special tax breaks for locating

	in poor and high-unemployment areas	in largely black areas
strongly favor	18.4	7.7
favor	52.2	35.5
neither	16.2	25.0
oppose	9.9	24.6
strongly oppose	3.3	7.2

Would you favor or oppose spending more money on the schools, especially for pre-school and early education programs

	in poor and high-unemployment areas	in largely black areas
strongly favor	29.4	17.4
favor	56.8	50.6
neither	7.9	15.3
oppose	4.5	12.3
strongly oppose	1.5	4.3

Would you favor or oppose providing special college scholarships for children who maintain good grades who are

	from economically disadvantaged backgrounds	black children
strongly favor	36.7	16.6
favor	54.7	53.1
neither	5.7	14.1
oppose	1.6	11.5
strongly oppose	1.3	4.8

Source: 1992 General Social Survey

enhance income security for all people. However, the inequities in Social Security benefits reflect race and gender inequities in the labor market. Universal programs cannot eliminate inequality as long as universality is equated with labor force participation. When work opportunities are constrained by race or by gender, benefit levels reflect these inequities.

But perhaps Americans don't want their welfare state to eliminate inequality. The question, then, is what does the nation expect from its social programs? I address this issue in Chapter 8.

EIGHT

Rebuilding the Welfare State

In less than a decade Johnson's War on Poverty was over. Its nucleus, the Office of Economic Opportunity, was abolished and its programs either transferred to other agencies or directed toward other goals. The Job Corps went to the Department of Labor; literacy training and Headstart to the Department of Health, Education and Welfare; job training was steered away from the poor; a program to help the poor buy their own homes was halted; and community action was eliminated altogether.

Undeniably, the War on Poverty did not end poverty in America. Indeed, it was not designed to do so. Only $800 million was appropriated for its first year of operation, and the programs were not designed to redistribute wealth or fundamentally restructure the economy.[1] Still, the antipoverty effort accomplished much. The number of poor Americans fell from about 18 percent in 1960 to only 9 percent by 1972, the result of a substantial expansion of all social welfare programs including Social Security, unemployment compensation, Medicare, food stamps, and public assistance.[2] Among children, poverty rates declined from 27 percent in 1960 to 15 percent in 1974, a decisive (though short-lived) victory.[3]

The black middle class gained more. Federal grants helped bring the percentage of black 18- to 24-year-olds enrolled in college from 13 in 1965 to 22.6 by 1975, a trend that if continued would have produced parity by 1983. Further, affirmative action programs provided black college graduates opportunities that had previously eluded them. Whereas before World War II 73 percent of college-educated African Americans chose either the ministry or teaching, where even then they served almost exclusively black communities, by 1989 the number holding white-collar jobs increased by 522 percent. Affirmative action also reduced wage differentials. By the mid-1970s black men earned more than two-thirds of what white men earned and black and white women drew even.[4]

On the other hand, during this same period on nearly every indicator the quality of life for poor African Americans declined. Between the early 1970s and the late 1980s the percent of two-parent black families fell from 63.4 to 40.6; the labor force participation rates of black high school dropouts fell by 25 percentage points, rates of joblessness among black men rose from 4.7 to 13.6 percent, and the percent of children born out of wedlock increased from 35.1 to 62.6 percent.[5]

Conservatives had a ready explanation for inner city decline. They blamed the liberal welfare state of the 1960s. This argument first appeared in George Gilder's book *Wealth and Poverty*. Gilder contends that poverty resulted not only from such individual traits as indolence and cynicism but also from the demoralizing impact of public policy. What demoralized the poor most, according to Gilder, was a perverse welfare system that eroded work and family values and eliminated incentives to move up the ladder of equal opportunity.[6]

Charles Murray pursues this argument in greater depth. In *Losing Ground*, he argues that the antipoverty programs of the 1960s reduced incentives to marriage, decreased the attractiveness of low-wage work, and increased the benefits of bearing children out of wedlock. The Horatio Alger ethic—starting at the bottom, acquiring job skills, and then moving "into a relatively secure job with decent wages"—was undermined by "the reforms of the 1960s. They discouraged poor young people, and especially poor young males, from pursuing this slow, incremental approach." Instead, Murray claims, the reforms "increased the size of the welfare package and transformed the eligibility rules so as to make welfare a more available and attractive *temporary* alternative to a job." They also "diminished the stigma associated with welfare and simultaneously devalued the status associated with working at a menial, low-paying job—indeed, holding onto a menial job became in some communities a *source* of stigma."[7]

Critics readily demolished the argument that rising unemployment among young, black men and declining marriage rates was caused by liberal social programs. Murray's analysis was based on the increase in the value of the welfare package, especially AFDC and other programs targeted to the very poor, which by 1972 nearly equaled a minimum-wage job. The problem with attributing inner-city decline to the welfare package is that after 1972 eligibility rules tightened. By 1984 the real value of AFDC plus food stamps had declined more than 20 percent.[8] Further, in 1976 Congress enacted the Earned Income Tax Credit (EITC), which provided low-income families with tax credits for each dollar they earned.[9] How, then, could a decline in welfare benefits and the addition of a program with built-in work incentives explain the increase in female-headed households and unemployment among young black men? Why did the trend toward black joblessness and family dissolution not reverse itself when the relative advantage of work over welfare increased sharply?[10]

More important, Gilder and Murray ignore the fact that racial segregation remains an enduring feature of urban life in America. From 1970 to 1990, rates of racial concentration in thirty metropolitan areas remained virtually unchanged. In northern cities in 1970 the average level of racial concentration was 84.5. By 1990 it had declined only slightly to 77.8. In southern cities racial concentration declined from 75.3 to 66.5, better than in the North but still high.[11] The costs are high. Segregation systematically builds deprivation into the residential structure of black communities and increases the susceptibility of the neighborhood to spirals of decline. A harsh and extremely disadvantaged environment also creates an oppositional culture that further separates ghetto residents from the majority of society. In isolating African Americans geographically, segregation undermines political support for jobs and services to the ghetto. As Douglas Massey and Nancy Denton explain: "That blacks are the only ones to benefit from resources

allocated to the ghetto—and are the only ones harmed when resources are removed—makes it difficult for them to find partners
for political coalitions. . . . Segregation prevents blacks from participating in pluralist politics based on mutual self-interest." [12]

Despite anomalies in Murray's evidence and the persistence of
racial segregation, the argument that the welfare state was responsible for urban decay resonated with the public. It provided the
rationale for draconian budget cuts in social programs when Ronald Reagan became president. In 1981 he began rolling back the
welfare state. Funds for job training declined from more than 6
million in 1980 to less than 2.5 million by 1984.[13] Funds to state
and local governments were also reduced from a flood to a trickle.
In 1981 deep cuts in federal aid to states and localities reduced
funding to 1968 levels. These cuts forced cities to rely more on
their own diminishing tax bases.[14]

Federal support for housing was also devastated. New low-
income housing starts financed by HUD dropped from 183,000 in
1980 to only 28,000 in 1985.[15] Housing aid dwindled from more
than 50 million in 1977 to less than 9 million in 1988. As a result,
the proportion of households receiving federal assistance to own
their own homes declined from 34 percent to less than 20 percent
by 1988. Hardest hit were young families struggling to buy their
first homes. Among people aged 25 to 34, the rate of home ownership plummeted from 53.3 percent in 1980 to 45.1 percent in
1987.[16]

The Postwar Welfare State and the Declining Middle Class

The attack on the welfare state has had an insidious and negative
effect on the inner cities, but it has also hurt the poor outside of
ghettos and the middle class. In the continuing furor over the quality of life in the cities, it is easy to forget that the percent of poor
people who live in ghettos is relatively small. In 1980 only 8.9
percent of all poor, 21.1 percent of black poor, and 15.9 percent
of Hispanic poor lived in ghetto areas.[17] Other poor Americans
live in mixed-income and nonpoor neighborhoods. Poverty is not
confined to urban ghettos, though its worst features are more visible there.

Nor is poverty confined to members of minority groups. Rather, minorities face economic risks that most Americans confront: the risk of slipping into poverty through the loss of a job, a decline in earnings, or the breakup of a marriage.[18] In the past two decades these risks have spread beyond the near-poor and working class. Middle-class families can no longer presume that their standard of living will improve, for they, too, are vulnerable to the economic insecurity that their parents' generation had seemingly overcome.

The parents of today's middle class were blessed by being born into an era of unprecedented economic prosperity, which not only enhanced family income but also produced the excess economic capacity for expanding the welfare state. The decades following World War II brought a rising standard of living, even to those with little education. From 1947 to 1973 real income grew at a rate of 2.5 to 3.0 percent per year. Median family income (in constant dollars) increased by 42 percent between 1949 and 1959 and by 38 percent between 1959 and 1969.[19] Improved living standards were accompanied by an expanding welfare state that helped stabilize wages over the life course and that provided a refuge for those who fell between the cracks. By 1973, the average income of young (25 to 34 years old) men with a high school education exceeded $24,500 (in 1988 dollars), a postwar high.[20]

Then after nearly thirty years of improving living standards, the wages of American workers entered a period of real decline. The year 1973 marked the end of rapid growth, as mean earnings for all white males fell from $19,619 to $19,307 (in 1984 dollars).[21] By 1983 the proportion of full-time, male workers earning enough to provide their families a middle-class lifestyle decreased from 56 to 47 percent with two-thirds of the shrinkage shifting to the lower class.[22]

These losses did not occur across the board but fell most heavily on entering workers. Between 1973 and 1987 the median real earnings of full-time younger workers fell, while the incomes of older workers rose. Unskilled young workers were especially hard hit, as median real earnings of 25 to 34-year-old male high school graduates working full-time fell by 12 percent.[23] Although entering workers always begin at the bottom of the jobs-and-income ladder, the acceleration in income inequality has meant that the youths of the 1970s are aging in place.[24]

Despite real declines in wages, initially family income remained stable, as the entry of women into the labor force compensated for the loss of male earning power. Between 1970 and 1990 the percent of women under age 65 in the labor force rose from 50 to nearly 70 percent.[25] Women's incomes became crucial to family security. By 1990 more than 60 percent of all families had two earners. This is not surprising for only families in which both husband and wife were working could maintain a middle-class lifestyle. The traditional American family, the nostalgic "Leave It To Beaver" family of the 1950s, had all but disappeared. But even in families where both husband and wife worked, declining real wages reduced family income. As a result the proportion of American families who were middle class fell from 60 percent in 1969 to only 53 percent by 1986.[26]

Declining wages are not solely responsible for the shrinking middle class. The increased divorce rate and increased number of children born out of wedlock has also reduced the standard of living of many women and put their children at risk of living in poverty. According to the 1990 Census, 26.4 percent of white female-headed households and 51.2 percent of black female-headed households were below poverty level.[27] Divorced women usually experience downward mobility simply because wives cannot match the earning capacities of their former husbands. Although women have gained relatively to men, in 1987 women's median earnings were still only 67 percent of male earnings.[28] The earnings disadvantage divorced women face in the labor market is compounded by erratic or inadequate child-support payments from ex-husbands.

The risks young families and divorced women experience reverberate across the generations, as middle-aged parents reduce their own standards of living to help their children and grandchildren. Parents loan children money, give them down payments for a house, and continue to share their homes long after their children are grown. More young families are now living with their middle-aged parents because they can't make it on their own. Between 1964 and 1988, the percent of persons aged twenty to thirty-nine living in their own households with their own children decreased from 66 to 47 while the proportion living in the household of another primary family member increased from 15 to 23 percent.[29] Although young families are most affected by declining family income, the economic pressures they feel are shared across generations.

The postwar welfare state was constructed around a model of a two-parent family with a blue-collar, male wage earner. Social-insurance programs like Social Security, worker's compensation, unemployment insurance, and disability insurance were designed to provide income security over the life course and to take care of the widows and orphans of these working men. This two-parent, male wage earner household is no longer the model family type. According to the 1990 census, only 21 percent of households consisted of married couples with children.[30] Further, even in families with two parents in the household the majority of mothers are in the labor force. Single mothers have even higher rates of labor-force participation: in 1990 64 percent of never-married mothers with school-aged children and 83.4 percent of divorced mothers with school-aged children were working. Even mothers of pre-school children and infants were working at increasing rates: 58.4 percent of women with children under six were in the labor force, 36.9 percent full-time.[31] The market cannot adequately provide for these vulnerable families; neither can existing social programs.

The Postindustrial Working Class

Since the New Deal, the composition of the working class has changed. It is now comprised more of women employed in service jobs than of men in manufacturing jobs.[32] Programs that adequately protected the families of fully employed male workers in manufacturing industries from risks associated with cyclical fluctuations in business and from loss of employment in old age are insufficient to protect part-time employees in low-wage service industries characterized by high labor turnover and the absence of fringe benefits.[33] What these workers need is a reconstructed welfare state to protect them, and their children, from falling into poverty.

Despite the need for safe and affordable child care, especially among those welfare mothers the American public would most like to see working, the federal government is only minimally involved in providing services to children and in regulating child care in the private sector. In 1981 less than 5 percent of the children from low-income families who were potentially eligible for child-care support actually received it. The 1981 budget cuts forced thirty-two states to reduce funding for child care and thirty-three states to reduce enforcement standards and staff.[34] Support that does exist consists of two streams: direct support for low-income families and a tax subsidy for middle- and upper-income families. A bleak picture, indeed.

This situation exists even though the greatest increase in working women in the past decade has taken place among mothers with young children. Research shows that the ability of mothers of young children to work is constrained by the availability of reasonably priced child care.[35] Women who pay high costs for child care have higher rates of job turnover. When child-care costs are too high, women, especially poor women, withdraw from the labor force. The paucity of child care penalizes women who need employment support most—the young mother, the unmarried mother, the black mother, and the poor mother.[36]

What programs will help protect these families? Mandatory are health insurance, child care, the right to *paid* leave from work after the birth of a child, and to care for ill children and parents. What is also needed, given the absence of any viable policy to increase wages, is further expansion of the EITC to subsidize those low-wage jobs that almost guarantee a life of impoverishment. In 1993 a first step was taken in this direction. More is needed. Work should pay.

In 1988 Congress also sought to reform the welfare system with the passage of the Family Support Act. The Act requires all states to broaden their eligibility criteria for AFDC to provide at least six months' coverage each year to two-parent families where one member is unemployed. The working poor who receive a refund from the EITC will henceforth not have that amount subtracted from their AFDC benefits. And child care and other work expenses of AFDC recipients are to be covered more generously.

Yet job training is still minimal and largely aimed at two-parent families, i.e., at men; only 20 percent of single-parent families (women) will receive training and placement assistance by 1995, and, by all accounts, most states have done little to implement the new measures.[37] Even if fully implemented, the measure is unlikely to bring poor women off the welfare rolls, because it is based on the assumption that "the principal determinant of poverty is

unemployment."[38] Reform oriented toward such a view ignores
the fact that women can work full-time and still fall below poverty
level.[39] Encouraging women to work without making work pay
will do little to lead women out of poverty. Though welfare reform coupled with job training, child care subsidies, and health
care will improve AFDC, these measures overlook the more fundamental issue of inequality in the labor market.

Is all this too much to ask? The experience of other, less affluent
nations suggests that it is not. Compared to other countries, the
United States has a sorry record. In the mid-1980s the poverty
rate of young families with children in the United States was 39.5
percent compared to 29.5 percent in Canada, 23.2 percent in the
United Kingdom, 18.8 percent in Germany, 31.1 percent in the
Netherlands, 9.1 percent in France, and 5.3 percent in Sweden.[40]
As Figure 8.1 shows, these countries have successfully used gov-

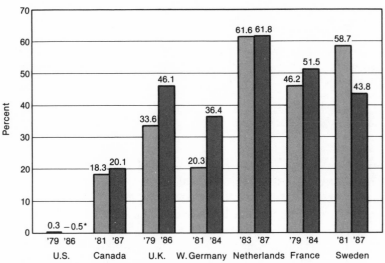

Figure 8.1. *Percent of poor households (before taxes and transfer income) that were lifted out of poverty as a result of government tax and
transfer systems. Poverty is defined as 50 percent of the median income
for households with heads 20–55 years old in each country.* (**Source:**
Katherine McFate, *Poverty, Inequality and the Crisis of Social Policy,*
Washington, D.C.: Joint Center for Political and Economic Studies,
1991.)

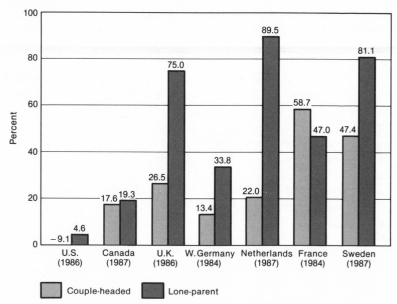

Figure 8.2. *Percentage of all poor families with children lifted out of poverty by government interventions. Poverty is defined as 50 percent of the median income for households with heads 20–55 years old in each country.* (**Source:** Katherine McFate, *Poverty, Inequality and the Crisis of Social Policy,* Washington, D.C.: Joint Center for Political and Economic Studies, 1991.)

ernment tax and transfer systems to lift families out of poverty. The United States is a dismal exception. More households had income reduced by taxes than increased by transfer payments.

The lack of support has been especially punishing to children in single-parent families. As Figure 8.2 shows, the Netherlands, Sweden, and the United Kingdom have used tax and transfer programs to lift more than three-quarters of all poor, single-parent families out of poverty. In the United States, by contrast, such programs helped less than 5 percent.

A further irony is that American policy does least for those whom anti-spending conservatives hold up as the model for all families, the two-parent household. In every industrialized country except the United States, government tax and transfer systems help a significant percentage of poor, couple-headed families with children attain minimum-income levels. Sweden helps almost half of this group rise above poverty, and France helps almost six of every ten couple-headed families rise above poverty. The United States is unique in its failure to use social policy to improve the economic circumstances of families with children.

Reviving the Vital Center

The New Deal tied benefits to work effort, spread the costs of social provision across the entire working population, and created a base of support upon which to build real income security for the working class. It also left an enduring legacy of racial division that had to be undone. The War on Poverty sought to create instead an "equal opportunity" welfare state to integrate African Americans into the national political economy. Although most Americans believed these objectives were just, the "equal opportunity" welfare state created a zero-sum game. It asked the working class to make compromises but offered no incentives to do so.

Any effort to revive support for social provision must recognize that programs must reward those who pay their costs. Still, that fundamental fact provides only minimal guidelines for constructing a second New Deal. What else is needed? Some policy analysts argue that new social programs must be constructed around the principles that have made Social Security popular. In *Gaining Ground,* for example, Charles Lockhart contends that Social Security has succeeded because it fits nicely with American political culture. The political culture consists of six prominent values: liberty, economic efficiency, equality, democracy, community and social solidarity, and human dignity. Although no social program can be entirely compatible with all core values, Social Security comes closest because it rewards constructive activity, that is, exertion or effort in the paid labor market.[41]

Certainly, Americans respect programs that reward work effort. The popularity of Social Security, however, results not only from its implicit value system but, more important, because it protects the family across generations. Social Security pays benefits to men and women of working age who become disabled, to children of deceased workers, and to widows and widowers. It also protects the family indirectly by taking the burden of supporting elderly parents off their children and grandchildren.

As postindustrial society faces the dilemma of creating economic security for the new working class, the key lesson is that the family is the core societal unit, regardless of the form it takes, and that protecting the family is an objective nearly everyone believes is worthwhile. Yet the United States cannot protect its families as long as racial segregation remains a blemish on the American conscience and a contradiction of the American ethos. A comprehensive welfare state that enhances the rights of citizenship cannot be erected on the foundation of racial segregation.

NINE

Explaining American Exceptionalism

Half a century ago the Carnegie Foundation invited the Swedish economist, Gunnar Myrdal, to take a hard look at American race relations. Myrdal was not only an eminent scholar but also a foreigner, capable of scrutinizing American society with an objectivity no native could muster. Captivated by a nation he saw as simultaneously energetic, moral, rational, pragmatic, and above all, optimistic, Myrdal nonetheless discerned a disturbing contradiction between what he termed "the American creed" and the treatment of blacks.[1] Rooted in an abiding liberal ethos, the American creed embodied ideals of liberty, justice, and equality of opportunity. Americans espoused this creed with a remarkable unanimity, regardless of national origin, race, or social class. Their country, they proudly told Myrdal, was the land of the free, the cradle of liberty, the home of democracy. How then, Myrdal puzzled, could these champions of liberty and equality of opportunity engage in rigid racial discrimination that negated every aspect of the creed? How could a nation that espoused a democratic ideology and adhered to a constitution that provided the most democratic state structure in the world establish political, social, and economic institutions around a deep racial divide? For Myrdal,

"The subordinate position of the Negro [was] perhaps the most glaring conflict in the American conscience and the greatest unsolved task for American democracy." [2]

Although Myrdal, a foreigner, readily identified this fundamental characteristic of American society, it has been disregarded by most other observers. Political theorists who attempt to trace the grand panorama of American politics generally fail to recognize how racial inequality has continually reshaped the nation's social, economic, and political institutions. James Morone, for example, argues that the central dynamic of American society is the expansion of the state bureaucracy and the resultant democratic impulse to limit this threat to civic liberty. [3] For Walter Dean Burnham, it is the arrested development of political parties. [4] For Kevin Phillips, it is an intensification in the concentration of wealth. [5]

I believe that only Gunnar Myrdal has correctly identified the more important motor of change, the governing force from the nation's founding to the present: the politics of racial inequality. The upheavals that periodically alter the nation's institutional arrangements stem from the contradictions between an egalitarian ethos and anti-democratic practices that reproduce racial inequality.

The pattern can be observed during the decades from the Revolutionary War to the Civil War. In those years, an industrialized North with an expanding base of free labor contained within its borders a separate nation, a cotton-producing South dependent for profit on slave labor. After the Civil War officially ended slavery, American state formation remained fettered by the unique configuration of North and South. The North had an organized working class, full political democracy (after 1920), and a competitive two-party system. A nation within a nation, the South remained primarily agricultural, distinguished politically by a one-party system and disfranchisement of blacks and economically by sharecropping, an arrangement that guaranteed planters control over a subservient, primarily black labor force. Few workers in the South organized into unions, and the unions that did exist were greatly weakened by their refusal to admit black workers.

The New Deal represented a breakthrough toward a more social democratic, Keynesian welfare state. It also set in motion a great migration of blacks out of the South. The migration undermined the political compromise that had allowed the South to function as a separate nation and forced all Americans to confront the impediments to racial equality that had previously been considered "the southern problem." That confrontation occurred during the 1960s when the civil rights movement demanded that Americans live up to their political ideology and guarantee full democratic rights to all, regardless of race. In the following section, I analyze what happened during the nation's one attempt to reconstruct its racial politics in the context of other theories of American exceptionalism.

Race and Theories of American Exceptionalism

The Polity-Centered Approach

Polity-centered theorists view the sequence of democratization and bureaucratization as crucial to understanding the timing and structure of the welfare state. They argue that in nations where government bureaucracies were installed before citizens won the right to vote, state bureaucrats instituted regulations that protected their positions from partisan use. As a result, when the working class began to mobilize politically, party activists could not use the "spoils of office" to attract voters. Instead parties had to rely on programmatic appeals to the emerging electorate.[6] Because national welfare provisions had wide programmatic appeal, they became a resource for securing party loyalty.

By contrast, in the United States electoral democratization preceded state bureaucratization. The civil administration was not protected from partisan use, and parties and factions used government jobs and resources to mobilize their personal clienteles and reward activists. Instead of attracting the electorate through programmatic appeals such as national welfare benefits, politicians waged battles over the spoils of office, which were distributed in a particularistic manner to loyal constituents.[7]

This argument helps explain the late onset of a national welfare state in the United States. During the first three decades of the twentieth century, patronage abuses in Civil War pensions made Americans suspicious of allowing the federal government to administer any national spending programs. The legacy of patronage

abuses continued to haunt New Deal reformers, who only partially succeeded in instituting civil service reforms and extending
the bureaucracy. Some programs of the Social Security Act of
1935 did set national regulations and national eligibility criteria
but significant departures from these standards were allowed in
other programs. Ann Orloff argues that this failure to create uni-
formity

> reflected the inability of Roosevelt administration officials to over-
> come the deep resistance of Congress and some congressional consti-
> tuencies to reform and, ultimately, the large obstacles represented by
> the legacies of American state-building and state structure. . . . The
> patronage practices initially encouraged by early mass democracy
> and the lack of bureaucratic state-building deprived reformers of
> readily available institutional capacities for carrying out new social
> spending activities.[8]

The federal bureaucracy's incomplete authority over the New Deal
welfare state was not primarily a legacy of patronage politics,
however, but rather a legacy of incomplete democracy. The confrontations between the New Deal bureaucracy and the states
were not struggles over regulating patronage *per se* but struggles
over the way patronage inhibited basic democratic rights. A limited bureaucracy allowed the southern states to operate autono-
mously from central government authority and to deprive African
Americans of the social rights extended to other citizens. Programs
with national regulations and national eligibility criteria excluded
African Americans; programs for which blacks were eligible remained under the jurisdiction of local welfare authorities. Other
New Deal programs actively used the federal bureaucracy to sup-
press democracy. Federal housing programs tacitly endorsed racial
segregation, while federal labor laws ignored racial discrimination
by employers and trade unions.

The second phase of bureaucratic state-expansion occurred during the 1960s. Instead of building upon the New Deal, the War
on Poverty challenged its bureaucratic legacies. It established new
patronage networks that by-passed anti-democratic political structures. In distributing federal funds for job training, housing, and
community improvement, the War on Poverty helped extend so-

cial rights to African Americans. However, these resources also unintentionally fueled struggles over civil and political rights—the right to work and the right to participate in politics. Ironically, then, whereas bureaucracy repressed democracy, patronage provided the means for democratic institutions to emerge.

Polity-centered theorists rightly argue that the development of the welfare state must be analyzed in the context of broader processes of state formation. But in concentrating on the war against patronage abuse, they neglect the war waged for democracy. Among the distinctive features of American state formation, none is more salient than the failure to extend full citizenship to African Americans. It is this characteristic, more than any other, that has influenced the development of the welfare state. The battle over racial equality delayed national welfare programs, limited the reach of the federal bureaucracy, and shaped the structure of the programs that were developed in the two key periods—the New Deal and the War on Poverty

Working Class Weakness

A second explanation of American exceptionalism is the legacy of a weak working class. Andrew Martin captures the essence of this argument:

> [T]he failure of organized labor to develop sufficiently to provide the basis for a union-party formation . . . has been a decisive factor in the failure of cohesive parties to develop. In the absence of such parties, it is difficult to see what can substantially overcome the fragmented, or archaic, character of public authority in the United States. Under the circumstances, it can hardly be surprising that the role of the public sector in the American economy has lagged behind that in the industrially advanced West European countries.[9]

But when we consider the unique role race has played in American working-class politics, it becomes clear that this view ignores the importance of racial conflict in weakening the labor movement and undermining support for the welfare state.

From the Civil War to the New Deal, workers fought a losing battle to organize into trade unions. Factors that weakened labor included the consolidation of corporate power, the emergence of new industries—rubber, automobiles, chemicals—that depended largely on unskilled labor, and the migration of older industries to the South.[10] During the New Deal, resistance by skilled workers to integrating trade unions thwarted working-class solidarity and divided the labor movement. Trade union discrimination festered for decades until complaints from civil rights advocates forced the AFL to confront its discriminatory policies. Even then the skilled trades refused to yield.

These practices made it impossible for trade unions to institute a pro-labor political agenda during its one historic opportunity. That opportunity arose during the 1960s when, according to J. David Greenstone, organized labor's political influence most closely approximated the European model:

> [T]he American labor movement's role in the national Democratic party represented a partial equivalence to the Social Democratic [formerly socialist] party-trade union alliances in much of Western Europe. This equivalence obtained with respect to its activities as a party campaign [and lobbying] organization, its influence as a party faction, and its welfare state objectives.[11]

Yet instead of realizing a full employment policy and new social programs to fill in the gaps in the welfare state, organized labor made no gains in the 1960s. Instead, the government first instituted tax cuts and then embarked on an anti-poverty effort targeted to African Americans.

The failure of the working class to unite behind the welfare state resulted from racial tensions that surfaced over job training programs and housing policy. The skilled trade unions opposed federal job training programs for several reasons. The programs not only provided an alternative to union apprenticeships, they also became the means by which the government could pressure the skilled trades to integrate. The consequences were harmful to the long-term vitality of the union movement. In taking the indefensible position of defending racist policies, the skilled trade unions undermined union solidarity and provided a Republican administration with a weapon to further intervene in union prerogatives.

Racial tension also sapped working class strength in another more subtle way. In the United States working-class politics have largely been played out in the community rather than at the work-place.[12] From the 1930s to the present, high levels of neighborhood racial concentration have eroded the basis for a racially integrated working-class politics. Yet when the federal government sought to integrate housing, resistance to the programs undermined working-class support for national housing policy. The result was increased racial concentration in urban ghettos, or hyperghettos, and further isolation of poor blacks. As sociologists Loic Wacquant and William Julius Wilson write:

> If the "organized" or institutional ghetto of forty years ago described so graphically by Drake and Cayton imposed an enormous cost on blacks collectively, the "disorganized" ghetto, or hyperghetto, of today carries an even larger price. For now, not only are ghetto residents, as before, dependent on the will and decisions of outside forces that rule the field of power—the mostly white, dominant class, corporations, realtors, politicians, and welfare agencies—they have no control over and are forced to rely on services and institutions that are massively inferior to those of the wider society.[13]

The creation of hyperghettos, in turn, has isolated black political leaders, prevented them from keeping federal funds flowing to the cities, and destroyed possibilities for wider political coalitions between the city and suburbs. Thus, when the federal government abandoned efforts to integrate the suburbs, a new era of racial politics was established, one based on concentrated isolation of the poor.

Has the weakness of the American labor movement allowed opponents of big government to thwart efforts to expand the welfare state? Certainly, some evidence supports this argument. During the War on Poverty, however, labor's own resistance proved to be the greater impediment to welfare state expansion. Organized labor's opposition originated in racial divisions, which made the movement hostile to programs that pursued equality of opportunity. One outcome of the confrontation over social policy was the loss of working-class support for job training and for housing programs. Another outcome was further fragmentation of the labor movement.

The weakness of the American labor movement has thus been both a product and a producer of racial divisions. And a divided labor movement has been less capable of promoting social programs that enhance working-class solidarity.

Liberal Values

There is a long tradition in political theory that states that Americans oppose government intervention of all forms because of a legacy of strong, liberal values. According to the "values" argument, America's classic liberal tradition was born in rebellion against British rule, as the lack of strong class divisions or a feudal heritage nurtured an encompassing liberal culture. In liberal thought individual rights are sacred, private property is honored, and state authority is distrusted. It is this distrust of state authority that has been the chief obstacle to the development of American social programs.[14]

But as I noted previously, Americans have often supported massive government intervention in the form of social programs such as veteran's pensions, Social Security, and Medicare. Conflicts over the welfare state derive not from a deeply ingrained distrust of the state but from competing definitions of liberty: liberty as the positive freedom to act on one's conscious purposes versus the negative freedom from external constraints on speech, behavior, and association.[15]

The experience of the War on Poverty shows that public antagonism to most of the anti-poverty programs only minimally concerned opposition to government intervention *per se*. Reducing government intervention became a rallying point only when social programs threatened the negative liberties of white Americans. But the evidence also indicates a more complex historical transformation, a redefinition of the very meaning of liberalism.

The Democrats took office in 1932 with a popular mandate to develop a new approach to economic and social problems that the Depression had brought painfully into focus. As government began monitoring malpractice among corporations, supporting the rights of workers to organize into unions, and using the state to alleviate the suffering of poor children, the unemployed, the elderly, and the disabled, the New Deal liberalism of the Democratic party came to mean active, positive intervention for the public good. Public support was high for programs that protected the many against the abuses of the few and taxed the few for the benefit of the many.[16]

During the 1960s, liberalism was redefined. Instead of government intervention for the common good, what defined the new liberalism, racial liberalism, was the premise of government intervention for civil rights. Government intervention for civil rights meant that the struggle for equal opportunity came to permeate issues of social policy. Nearly every social program—welfare, job training, community action, housing—became more than components of the welfare state that one supported or reviled depending upon whether one favored government intervention (a liberal) or opposed it (a conservative). Rather, because the reconstruction of race relations became inextricably woven into the very fabric of the Great Society, support for social programs came to mean support for integration. It also meant that if one opposed government intervention on behalf of civil rights, then one also opposed the social programs that helped enforce them.

This reconstruction of liberalism had concrete political consequences, for the War on Poverty activated the inherent conflict between positive and negative liberty. The positive liberties it extended to African Americans were viewed by the working class as infringements on their negative liberties, the liberty for trade unions to discriminate in the selection of apprentices and to control job training programs; the liberty to exclude minorities from representation in local politics; the liberty to maintain segregated neighborhoods. The resentment these infringements triggered destroyed the New Deal coalition of northern wage workers and southern racial conservatives, the stable Democratic party base for three decades.

As this coalition splintered over the racial issue, Republicans learned to capitalize on the racial hostilities civil rights enforcement had generated. In the 1964 election Barry Goldwater opposed federal intervention to end segregation and won only five states. Just four years later, Richard Nixon staked out a middle ground, remaining publicly committed to racial equality while opposing forceful implementation of civil rights legislation. By 1980

Republicans had artfully forged racial hostility with conservative economic policy into a New Right coalition, and their candidate Ronald Reagan "articulated a public philosophy directed at drawing into the Republican party citizens with the kinds of economic, social and racial concerns that could be addressed in terms of a free-market conservative doctrine."[17] Republicans became the party of racial conservativism, while Democrats retained the liberal label inherited from their New Deal grandparents, expanded to include racial connotations.[18]

Over the past three decades, opponents of government spending for social welfare have found an anti-government ideology effective in undermining support for the welfare state. But opposition to government invention is not the central element in public antagonism to social programs. Initially, public approval of the War on Poverty was high. It was not until the anti-poverty programs became linked to the pursuit of civil rights that support waned. The idea that liberal values have inhibited the development of the American welfare state remains, at best, an overly simple explanation of how values are connected to the formation of social programs. An anti-government ideology has generated most antagonism to the welfare state when it has been associated with racial issues.

America's Welfare Regimes

Over the past century the United States has instituted three "welfare state regimes." Each has had different consequences for racial equality. The first national welfare programs of the New Deal protected the working class against the exigencies of old age and unemployment. The price of this protection was a compromise with the American creed. As this compromise proved unworkable, the programs of the War on Poverty provided the means to undo the New Deal legacy and extend equal opportunity. Instead of finally instituting full democratic rights, however, the policies enacted in that turbulent decade left a disturbing legacy of "what might have been."

The community action programs that might have provided a precedent for extensive intervention in the inner cities and prevented the spiral of decline so painfully visible to observers on all sides of the political spectrum became instead embroiled in the task of extending political rights to African Americans. That proved their undoing. Rather than responding to the need for jobs, housing, and social services that the black migration brought to the urban centers, the nation turned its back on the cities.

The job training programs might have bolstered a full employment policy. They could have established a partnership between the federal government and given the trade unions a solid footing in national policymaking. Instead, job training became the source of internecine warfare within the trade union movement and between skilled workers and African Americans, hastening the decline of trade unionism. The irony of this historical outcome is that a nation that most abhors government handouts does least to prepare its citizens for work.

The funds for housing that briefly poured into the inner cities might have improved the quality and expanded the quantity of the nation's housing supply. However, the racial backlash that ensued when integration became linked to housing undermined public support for a national housing agenda.

No social programs could better have served the families of the emerging postindustrial order than a guaranteed annual income and national child care. Yet demands for welfare reform were triggered by the expanding welfare rolls and the threat of urban disorder. And child care was inextricably linked to welfare reform. When the policy agenda turned from the expansion of the welfare state to the repression of disorder, this grand opportunity to protect the family, especially, families headed by women, was lost. Instead of initiating a new era of race relations, the War on Poverty became a transitional phase on the road to benign neglect. The equal opportunity welfare state was replaced by a welfare state that encouraged racial isolation and the concentration of the black poor in inner cities.

The failure of America's domestic policy agenda reflects a failure to live up to the values of the American creed, to create a nation that not only guarantees liberty but also democratic rights—the right to work, the right to participate in the political process, and the right to economic security. In the 1960s Americans sought to resolve the American dilemma and grant these basic rights. Three decades later that task remains unfinished.

NOTES

Preface

1. Quoted in Kathleen Hall Jamieson, *Dirty Politics: Deception, Distraction and Democracy* (New York: Oxford University Press, 1992), p. 86.

2. Thomas Byrne Edsall and Mary D. Edsall, *Chain Reaction: The Impact of Race, Rights, and Taxes on American Politics* (New York: W.W. Norton, 1991), p. 148.

3. Richard A. Cloward and Frances Fox Piven, "Punishing the Poor, Again: The Fraud of Workfare." *The Nation* (May 24, 1993): 693.

Introduction: The American Dilemma Revisited

1. Roy Lubove, *The Struggle for Social Security, 1900–1935* (Pittsburgh: University of Pittsburgh Press, 1986), p. 2; Gaston Rimlinger, *Welfare Policy and Industrialization in Europe, America and Russia* (New York: John Wiley, 1971), p. 62; A summary of this perspective appears in Theda Skocpol, *Protecting Soldiers and Mothers: The Political Origins of Social Policy in the United States* (Cambridge: Harvard University Press, 1992), p. 62; see also Ann Orloff, *The Politics of Pensions: A Comparative Analysis of Britain, Canada, and the United States, 1880–1940* (Madison: University of Wisconsin Press, 1993), pp. 52–55.

2. Seymour Martin Lipset, *The Continental Divide: The Values and Institutions of the United States and Canada* (London: Routledge, 1990), p. 136.

3. Skocpol, *Protecting Soldiers and Mothers*, pp. 16–17.

4. James Morone, *The Democratic Wish: Popular Participation and the Limits of American Government* (New York: Basic Books, 1990), p. 7.

5. C. B. Macpherson, *Democratic Theory: Essays in Retrieval* (Oxford: Oxford University Press, 1973), pp. 201–216; Charles Lockhart, *Gaining Ground: Tailoring Social Programs to American Values* (Berkeley: University of California Press, 1989), p. 48.

6. John Stephens, *The Transition from Capitalism to Socialism* (London: Macmillan, 1979); John Myles, *Old Age in the Welfare State* (Lawrence: University Press of Kansas, 1989). There is also substantial evidence that other forces are equally influential in establishing generous social benefits. See Evelyne Huber Stephens, Charles Ragin, and John Stephens, "Social Democracy, Christian Democracy, Constitutional Structure and the Welfare State." (Paper presented to Research Committee 19, conference on Comparative Studies in Welfare State Development, Bremen, Germany, Sept. 3–6, 1992); Kees van Kersbergen, *Social Capitalism: A Study of Christian Democracy and the Postwar Settlement of the Welfare State* (Ph.D diss., Florence, Italy: European University Institute, 1991).

7. The position of the labor movement toward social welfare legislation is less consistent than how it is portrayed in many accounts. Early in the history of the labor movement, national leaders did oppose many welfare measures, but local labor groups often supported them. Later the AFL-CIO worked for national health insurance and improved Social Security benefits. See Christopher Anglim and Brian Gratton, "Organized Labor and Old Age Pensions." *International Journal of Aging and Human Development,* 25 (1987): 91–107; Martha Derthick, *Policymaking for Social Security* (Washington, D.C.: The Brookings Institute, 1979).

8. G. William Domhoff, *The Power Elite and the State: How Policies are Made in America* (New York: Aldine de Gruyter, 1990), pp. 45–64.

9. Ira Katznelson, *City Trenches: Urban Politics and the Patterning of Class in the United States* (Chicago: University of Chicago Press, 1981), p. 19; Jerome Karabel, "The Reason Why." *New York Review of Books,* 26 (February, 1976): 22–25.

10. Ann Orloff and Theda Skocpol, "Why Not Equal Protection: Explaining the Politics of Public Social Spending in Britain, 1900–1911, and the United States, 1880–1920." *American Sociological Review,* 49 (1984): 741–742; Skocpol, *Protecting Soldiers and Mothers,* p. 44.

11. Goran Therborn, "The Rule of Capital and the Rise of Democracy." *New Left Review,* 103 (June, 1977): 43.

12. T. H. Marshall, *Class, Citizenship and Social Development* (Chicago: University of Chicago Press, 1964), p. 83.

13. Gosta Esping-Anderson, *The Three Worlds of Welfare Capitalism* (Princeton: Princeton University Press, 1990), p. 23; see also, Gosta Esping-Anderson, "The Comparison of Policy Regimes: An Introduc-

tion." In *Stagnation and Renewal in Social Policy: The Rise and Fall of Policy Regimes*, ed. Martin Rein, Gosta Esping-Anderson, and Lee Rainwater (Armonk, New York: M. E. Sharpe, 1987), pp. 3–12.

14. Gosta Esping-Anderson and Walter Korpi, "From Poor Relief to Institutional Welfare States: The Development of Scandinavian Social Policy." In *The Scandinavian Model: Welfare States and Welfare Research*, ed. Robert Erikson, Erik Hansen, Stein Ringen, and Hannu Uusitalo (New York: M. E. Sharpe, 1987), pp. 39–74; Peter Baldwin, *The Politics of Social Solidarity: Class Bases of the European Welfare State, 1875–1976* (New York: Cambridge University Press, 1990), p. 26.

15. Esping-Anderson, *The Three Worlds of Welfare Capitalism*, p. 64.

16. Gosta Esping-Anderson, "The Three Political Economies of the Welfare State." *The Canadian Review of Sociology and Anthropology*, 26 (February 1989): 23–24.

17. Esping-Anderson, *The Three Worlds of Welfare Capitalism*, p. 60.

18. Gunnar Myrdal, *An American Dilemma* (New York: McGraw Hill, 1944), p. 3.

19. Skocpol, *Protecting Soldiers and Mothers*, p. 59; Orloff, *The Politics of Pensions*, p. 91.

20. Skocpol, *Protecting Soldiers and Mothers*, p. 58.

21. Kevin Phillips, *The Emerging Republican Majority* (New York: Doubleday, 1970), p. 24.

Chapter 1: Unfinished Democracy

1. T. H. Marshall, *Class, Citizenship and Social Development* (Chicago: University of Chicago Press, 1964), pp. 82–87.

2. Goran Therborn, "The Rule of Capital and the Rise of Democracy." *New Left Review*, 103 (June, 1977): 43.

3. Dietrich Rueschemeyer, Evelyne Huber Stephens, and John D. Stephens, *Capitalist Development and Democracy* (Chicago: University of Chicago Press, 1992), p. 41.

4. Marshall, *Class, Citizenship and Social Development*, p. 78.

5. John Myles, "States, Labor Markets and Life Cycles." In *Beyond the Marketplace: Rethinking Economy and Society*, ed. Roger Friedland and A. F. Robertson (New York: Aldine de Gruyter, 1990), p. 280.

6. *Social Security Programs Throughout the World, 1983*. Research Report No. 59 (Washington, D.C.: U.S. Department of Health and Human Services, 1984); Peter Flora, *Growth to Limits: The Western European Welfare States Since World War II*, Vol. 4 (Berlin: Walter de Gruyter, 1987); Jennifer Schirmer, *The Limits of Reform: Women, Capi-*

tal and Welfare (Cambridge, MA: Schenkman, 1982); Dennis Guest, *The Emergence of Social Security in Canada* (Vancouver: University of British Columbia Press, 1985).

7. Quoted in Myrdal, *The American Dilemma,* p. 9.

8. James Morone, *The Democratic Wish: Popular Participation and the Limits of American Government* (New York: Basic Books, 1990), p. 36.

9. Morone, *The Democratic Wish,* p. 59.

10. Jane Jenson, "Representations of Gender: Policies to 'Protect' Women Workers and Infants in France and the United States before 1914." In *Women, the State and Welfare,* ed. Barbara Nelson (Madison: University of Wisconsin Press, 1990), p. 154; Jill Quadagno, *The Transformation of Old Age Security: Class and Politics in the American Welfare State* (Chicago: University of Chicago Press, 1988), p. 11: Theda Skocpol, *Protecting Soldiers and Mothers: The Political Origins of Social Policy in the United States* (Cambridge: Harvard University Press, 1992), p. 9.

11. Edward Berkowitz, *America's Welfare State: From Roosevelt to Reagan* (Baltimore: Johns Hopkins University Press, 1991), p. 13.

12. Edward G. Carmines and James A. Stimson, *Issue Evolution: Race and the Transformation of American Politics* (Princeton: Princeton University Press 1989), pp. 31, 190.

13. James Patterson, *America's Struggle Against Poverty* (Cambridge: Harvard University Press, 1986), p. 72; see also Berkowitz, *America's Welfare State,* p. 37.

14. Marshall, *Class, Citizenship and Social Development,* p. 82.

15. V. O. Key, *Southern Politics in State and Nation* (New York: Alfred Knopf, 1949), p. 20; C. Vann Woodward, *Origins of the New South, 1877–1913* (New Haven: Yale University Press, 1951), p. 345; Quadagno, *The Transformation of Old Age Security,* pp. 15–17.

16. Nicholas Lemann, *The Promised Land, The Great Black Migration and How It Changed America* (New York: Alfred Knopf, 1991), p. 8.

17. Margaret Weir, *Politics and Jobs: The Boundaries of Employment Policy in the United States* (Princeton: Princeton University Press, 1992), p. 81.

18. G. William Domhoff, *The Power Elite and the State: How Policy is Made in America* (New York: Aldine de Gruyter, 1990), p. 65.

19. Philip Foner, *Organized Labor and the Black Worker 1619–1981* (New York: International Publishers, 1981), pp. 168–70.

20. Ibid., p. 213.

21. Charles V. Hamilton and Dona C. Hamilton, "Social Policies, Civil Rights and Poverty." In *Fighting Poverty: What Works and What*

Doesn't, ed. Sheldon H. Danziger and Daniel H. Weinberg (Cambridge: Harvard University Press, 1986), p. 291.

22. National Archives (hereafter NA), Record Group (hereafter RG) 207, correspondence files, Robert Weaver, Secretary of Housing and Urban Development, Box 240, File: U.S. Commission on Civil Rights, Race and Education Report, p. 11.

23. J. Paul Mitchell, "Historical Context for Housing Policy." In *Federal Housing Policy and Programs,* ed. J. Paul Mitchell (New Brunswick, NJ: Center for Urban Policy Research, 1988), p. 8.

24. Norman Peel, Garth Pickett, and Stephen Buehl, "Racial Discrimination in Public Housing Site Selection." In *Housing,* ed. George Sternlieb and Lynne Sagalyn (New York: AMS Press, 1972), p. 322.

25. Marshall, *Class, Citizenship and Social Development,* p. 78.

26. Quadagno, *The Transformation of Old Age Security,* p. 142; Arthur M. Ford, *Political Economies of Rural Poverty in the South* (Cambridge: Ballinger, 1973), p. 39.

27. Gerald David Jaynes and Robin Williams, eds. *A Common Destiny: Blacks and American Society* (Washington, D.C.: National Academy Press, 1989), p. 60.

28. Kevin Phillips, *The Emerging Republican Majority* (New York: Doubleday, 1970), p. 39.

29. Harvard Sitkoff, *The Struggle for Black Equality* (New York: Hill and Wang, 1981), pp. 23–24.

30. Jack Bloom, *Class, Race and the Civil Rights Movement* (Bloomington: Indiana University Press, 1987), p. 139.

31. Bloom, *Class, Race and the Civil Rights Movement,* p. 155.

32. Doug McAdam, *Political Process and the Development of Black Insurgency: 1930–1970* (Chicago: University of Chicago Press, 1982), p. 138.

33. McAdam, *Political Process and the Development of Black Insurgency,* pp. 79–80; Frances Fox Piven and Richard Cloward, *Poor People's Movements: Why They Succeed, How They Fail* (New York: Vintage, 1979), p. 272.

34. Steven F. Lawson, *Black Ballots: Voting Rights in the South, 1944–1969* (New York: Columbia University Press, 1976), p. 256.

35. Allen Matuso, *The Unraveling of America: A History of Liberalism in the 1960s* (New York: Harper and Row, 1984), p. 105.

36. Robert Haveman, *A Decade of Federal Anti-Poverty Programs* (New York: Academic Press, 1977), p. 121.

37. Piven and Cloward, *Poor People's Movements,* p. 27; see also Barbara Ehrenreich, *Fear of Falling: The Inner Life of the Middle Class* (New York: Harper, 1990), p. 47.

38. Piven and Cloward, *Poor People's Movements*, p. 270.

39. Margaret Weir, "The Federal Government and Unemployment: The Frustration of Policy Innovation from the New Deal to the Great Society." In *The Politics of Social Policy in the United States*, ed. Margaret Weir, Ann Shola Orloff, and Theda Skocpol (Princeton: Princeton University Press, 1988), p. 68.

40. Hugh Davis Graham, *The Civil Rights Era: Origins and Development of National Policy* (New York: Oxford University Press, 1990), p. 152.

41. Gary Orfield, "Race and the Federal Agenda: The Loss of the Integrationist Dream, 1965–1974." *Working Paper 7, Project on the Federal Social Role* (Washington, D.C.: National Conference on Social Welfare, 1965), p. 19.

42. Quoted in Edward D. Berkowitz, *America's Welfare State: From Roosevelt to Reagan* (Baltimore: Johns Hopkins University Press, 1991), p. 111.

43. Morone, *The Democratic Wish*, p. 217.

44. Weir, "The Federal Government and Unemployment," p. 183.

45. Peter Marris and Martin Rein, *Dilemmas of Social Reform*. (Chicago: Aldine, 1973), p. 50.

46. Marris and Rein, *Dilemmas of Social Reform*, pp. 49–52.

47. Lyndon Baines Johnson, *The Vantage Point: Perspectives of the Presidency, 1963–1969* (New York: Popular Library, 1971), p. 327.

48. Quoted in Lemann, *The Promised Land*, p. 156.

Chapter 2: Fostering Political Participation

1. James Patterson, *America's Struggle Against Poverty 1900–1985* (Cambridge: Harvard University Press, 1986), p. 103.

2. Vernon Alden (oral history, Lyndon Baines Johnson Library, Austin, Texas), p. 12.

3. James Sundquist, *On Fighting Poverty* (New York: Basic Books, 1969), p. 72.

4. Paul Schulman, *Large Scale Policy Making* (New York: Elsevier, 1980), p. 5.

5. David Zarefsky, *President Johnson's War on Poverty, Rhetoric and History* (University City, AL: University of Alabama Press, 1986), p. 131.

6. Quoted in Patterson, *America's Struggle Against Poverty 1900–1985*, pp. 140, 147.

7. Zarefsky, *President Johnson's War on Poverty*, p. 107.

8. Richard Zweigenhaft and G. William Domhoff, *Blacks in the White*

Establishment, A Study of Race and Class in America (New Haven: Yale University Press, 1991), p. 161.

9. Oscar Lewis, *La Vida, A Puerto Rican Family in the Culture of Poverty—San Juan and New York* (New York: Random House, 1966), pp. xlv–xlvii.

10. Lewis, *La Vida,* pp. xlviii–xlix.

11. Zweigenhaft and Domhoff, *Blacks in the White Establishment,* pp. 166–167.

12. Nicholas Lemann, *The Promised Land: The Great Black Migration and How It Changed America* (New York: Alfred Knopf, 1991), p. 151.

13. NA, RG 381, Office of Economic Opportunity, Box 40, File: Star Inc, Harassment.

14. Frank Parker, *Black Votes Count, Political Empowerment in Mississippi after 1965* (Chapel Hill: University of North Carolina Press, 1990), pp. 22–23.

15. David Campbell and Joe Feagin, "Black Politics in the South: A Descriptive Analysis." *Journal of Politics,* 37 (1975): 129–139.

16. David James, "The Transformation of the Southern Racial State: Class and Race Determinants of the Local-State Structures." *American Sociological Review,* 53 (1988): 191–208.

17. Jay R. Mandle, *The Roots of Black Poverty: The Southern Plantation Economy After the Civil War* (Durham, N.C.: Duke University Press, 1978), p. 46.

18. Jack Bloom, *Class, Race and the Civil Rights Movement* (Bloomington: Indiana University Press, 1987), p. 167.

19. Jack Bass and Walter DeVries, *The Transformation of Southern Politics* (New York: New American Library, 1977), p. 201.

20. John C. Donovan, *The Politics of Poverty* (Washington, D.C.: University Press of America, 1980), p. 85.

21. Bass and DeVries, *The Transformation of Southern Politics,* p. 194.

22. Parker, *Black Votes Count,* p. 22.

23. Ibid., p. 29.

24. Bass and DeVries, *Transformation of Southern Politics,* p. 203.

25. Parker, *Black Votes Count,* p. 24.

26. Bass and DeVries, *Transformation of Southern Politics,* pp. 204–205.

27. NA, RG 381, Box 40, File: Oct.–Dec. 1965. Mississippi Economic Opportunities Inc., Oct. 1, 1965.

28. NA, RG 381, Box 40, File: May, 1966. "List of complaints from Negro citizens of Columbia, Mississippi."

29. NA, RG 381, Box 40, File: Oct.–Dec. 1965. "Central Mississippi Incorporated, Winona, Mississippi."

30. NA, RG 381, Box 40, File: Star Inc., Jackson, 1965, "Highlights of a demonstration grant."

31. Ibid.

32. NA, RG 381, Box 40, File: Star Inc. Activities Report, May 16, 1966.

33. NA, RG 381, Box 40, File: Star Inc., Report for Cycle 1.

34. NA, RG 381, Box 40, File: Star Inc., "A few current highlights of the Star program, April 12, 1966."

35. NA, RG 381, Box 40, File: Star Inc., Harassment. Weekly situation and incident report, May 17, 1966. In other Mississippi communities opposition to civil rights activities was equally intense, and the accompanying violence—cross burnings, threats, harassment of recruiters—affected Star as well. When a Star employee in Meridian, a Klan stronghold, went out one evening to move her car, she found a man standing on her back porch. Another employee found that "the carter pin had been removed from each wheel on his car and the nut turned back to where there were only two or three threads holding the nut on." The Natchez Center Director received a call warning that "her body would be found in a creek just like Ben White's, a Negro recently murdered by three members of the Ku Klux Klan." NA, RG 381, Box 40, File: Star Inc., Harassment. "Threatening phone call, June 29, 1966."

36. NA, RG 381, Box 40, File: Star Inc., Harassment. Further information of the incidents of violence, May 4, 1966.

37. NA, RG 381, Box 40, File: Star Inc. Memo from Robert Martin to Edgar May, Jan. 15, 1966.

38. Ibid.

39. NA, RG 381, Box 40, File: Star Inc., Harassment. Memo on Threatening Phone Call, June 29, 1966.

40. NA, RG 174, Department of Labor, Files of Arnold Weber, Box 2, File: Concentrated Employment Program.

41. NA, RG 174, Box 2, File: Community Work and Training Program. "Memorandum of Agreement," April 11, 1968.

42. NA, RG 174, Box 2, File: Concentrated Employment Program. Special Report on Five Day Meeting with Mississippi State ES.

43. NA, RG 174, Box 2, File: Concentrated Employment Program. "Questions concerning the operation of the Mississippi Delta CEP, August 26, 1969."

44. NA, RG 381, Inspection Reports, Box 39, File: Corinth. Memo from Bill Hadden to Ken Smilen, March 15, 1965, p. 15.

45. NA, RG 381, Box 39, File: Corinth. Letter from W.A. Stevens, President, Local 707, ACWA to Mrs. Herbert McKay, April 19, 1965.

46. Manning Marable, *Race, Reform and Rebellion: The Second Re-*

construction in Black America 1945–1982 (Jackson: University of Mississippi Press, 1984), p. 182.

47. National Advisory Commission on Civil Disorders, *Report* (New York: E.P. Dutton, 1968), p. 233.

48. Ibid., p. 57.

49. NA, RG 381, Inspection Reports, Box 46, File: Newark, July–Dec. 1967. "Newark On-Site Evaluation," August 25, 1967, p. 1.

50. Ibid., p. 2.

51. NA, RG 381, Box 46, File: Newark, Essex City. "United Community Corporation, 8/5/66."

52. NA, RG 381, Box 46, File: Newark, Essex City. "Newark On-Site Evaluation" p. 4.

53. Phyllis Wallace, "A Decade of Policy Developments in Equal Opportunities in Employment and Housing." In *A Decade of Federal Anti-Poverty Programs,* ed. Robert Haveman (New York: Academic Press, 1973), p. 351.

54. NA, RG 381, Box 46, File: New Jersey General. "Report of A. Donald Bourgeois Re On Site Visit to Newark, N.J.," p. 4.

55. NA, RG 381, Box 46, File: New Jersey Essex City. Memo from Jack William to Edgar May, February 14, 1967, p. 8.

56. National Advisory Commission on Civil Disorders, *Report,* p. 56.

57. NA, RG 381, Box 46, File: New Jersey Crisis. "Telegram from Dominick Spina to Clifford Case," May 26, 1967.

58. NA, RG 381, Box 46, File: Newark, Essex City. "Letter from Albert Quie to Sergeant Shriver," June 13, 1967.

59. NA, RG 381, Box 46, File: New Jersey General. "Report of A. Donald Bourgeois Re On Site Visit to Newark, N.J.," p. 4.

60. National Advisory Commission on Civil Disorders, *Report,* p. 61.

61. Ibid., p. 62.

62. NA, RG 381, Box 46, File: New Jersey General. "Newark On-Site Evaluation," pp. 6–9.

63. NA, RG 381, Box 46, File: Newark, July–Dec., 1967. Confidential OI Report on Newark, 11/2/67, p. 1.

64. NA, RG 381, Box 46, File: Newark, July–Dec. 1967. "Evaluation of United Community Corporation," August 25, 1967, p. 2.

65. NA, RG 381, Box 46, File: Newark, July–Dec. 1967. "*Newark Evening News,* Nov. 9, 1967," p. 5.

66. Nicholas Lemann, *The Promised Land: The Great Black Migration and How It Changed America* (New York: Alfred A. Knopf, 1991), p. 344.

67. Paul Peterson and J. David Greenstone, "Racial Change and Citizen Participation: The Mobilization of Low-Income Communities through

Community Action." In *A Decade of Federal Anti-Poverty Programs,* ed. Robert Haveman (New York: Academic Press, 1973), pp. 241–278.

68. Lemann, *The Promised Land,* p. 75.

69. Ibid., pp. 81, 356.

70. William J. Grimshaw, *Bitter Fruit: Black Politics and the Chicago Machine, 1931–1991* (Chicago: University of Chicago Press, 1992), pp. 106–107.

71. NA, RG 381, Box 22, File: Feb. 67–June 67. Charles Percy, House Republican Task Force on Economic Opportunity, August 19, 1966.

72. NA, RG 381, Box 22, File: Feb. 67–June 67. Report of Individual Observations On-Site Monitoring of Chicago Committee on Urban Opportunity.

73. NA, RG 381, Box 22, File: June 66–April 66. Report on Evaluation of Chicago Community Action Program, February 25, 1966.

74. NA, RG 381, Box 22, File: Feb. 67–June 67. Affidavit by Kathleen Morris, State of Illinois, County of Cook, August 12, 1966.

75. NA, RG 381, Box 22, File: June 66–April 66. Report on Evaluation of Chicago Community Action Program, February 25, 1966.

76. NA, RG 381, Box 22, File: June 66–April 66. Evaluation of CCUO Applications.

77. NA, RG 381, Box 22, File: June 66–April 66. Chicago Sign Off.

78. NA, RG 381, Box 22, File: April 66–June 66. "Poor to have bigger voice, Chicago poverty chiefs say." *Chicago Daily News,* March 7, 1966.

79. Quoted in Lemann, *The Promised Land,* p. 165.

80. James Morone, *The Democratic Wish* (New York: Basic Books, 1990), p. 248.

81. Margaret Weir, "Urban Political Isolation and the Politics of Marginality in the United States." (Presented to the Workshop on Comparative Studies of Welfare State Development, Research Committee on Poverty, Social Welfare, and Social Policy, Helsinki, Finland, August, 1991), p. 16.

82. Margaret Weir, *Politics and Jobs* (Princeton: Princeton University Press, 1991), p. 82.

Chapter 3: Extending Equal Employment Opportunity

1. Philip Foner, *Organized Labor and the Black Worker* (New York: International Publishers, 1982), p. 339.

2. Ibid., p. 334.

3. Foner, *Organized Labor and the Black Worker,* p. 340.

4. Theodore White, *The Making of the President 1960* (New York: Athenaeum, 1961), p. 354.

5. Ray Marshall, "Union Racial Practices." In *The Negro and Employment Opportunity, Problems and Practices,* ed. Herbert Northrup and Richard L. Rowan (Ann Arbor: Bureau of Industrial Relations, 1965), p. 179.

6. Mary Keyserling (oral history, Lyndon Baines Johnson Oral History Collection, Austin, Texas), p. 21.

7. Marshall, "Union Racial Practices," p. 179; Foner, *Organized Labor and the Black Worker,* p. 346.

8. NA, RG 381, Box 780, File: 5.02 Field Reports. Task Force Meeting with Mayor Ralph Locher of Cleveland, April 28, 1965.

9. NA, RG 174, Box 38, File: National Industry Promotion, 1967.

10. Quoted in Foner, *Organized Labor and the Black Worker,* p. 348.

11. NA, RG 174, Box 144, File: July–August, 1964. Letter from Percy Green to Willard Wirtz, March 18, 1964.

12. James H. Jones, "Human Rights and the Labor Movement." In *The Negro and Employment Opportunities,* ed. Herbert Northrup and Richard L. Rowan (Ann Arbor: Bureau of Industrial Relations, 1965), p. 187; Marshall, "Union Racial Practices," p. 181.

13. NA, RG 174, Box 235, File: State and Local Promotion, Jan.–April 1965. Letter from Donald Jacobs to Willard Wirtz, April 13, 1965.

14. NA, RG 174, Box 235, File: State and Local Promotion, Jan.–April 1965. Letter from William Young to Willard Wirtz, April 7, 1966.

15. Benjamin Wolkinson, *Blacks, Unions and the EEOC, A Study of Administrative Failure* (Lexington, MA: Lexington Books, 1973), p. 13.

16. Foner, *Organized Labor and the Black Worker,* p. 368.

17. Julius F. Rothman, "A Look At the War on Poverty." *American Federationist,* 74 (November, 1967): 8.

18. Ibid., p. 5.

19. David Sullivan, "Labor's Role in the War on Poverty." *American Federationist,* 73 (April, 1966): 10.

20. Ramsey Clark (oral history, Lyndon Baines Johnson Library, Austin, Texas), p. 22.

21. Cited in Michael B. Katz, *The Undeserving Poor: From the War on Poverty to the War on Welfare* (New York: Pantheon, 1989), p. 93.

22. Margaret Weir, "The Federal Government and Unemployment: The Frustration of Policy Innovation from the New Deal to the Great Society." In *The Politics of Social Policy in the United States,* ed. Margaret Weir, Ann Orloff, and Theda Skocpol (Princeton: Princeton University Press, 1988), p. 169.

23. The Manpower Development and Training Act (MDTA) of 1962 preceded the War on Poverty. MDTA required the Secretary of Labor to assess what skills the economy needed and to develop policies for equip-

ping the nation's workers with them. The secretary decided to retrain educated, skilled men who were unemployed family heads with strong labor force attachment and merely victims of automation. Because unemployment was low in the early 1960s, few skilled workers sought retraining. MDTA instead recruited young men, who were twice as likely as adults to be unemployed. As literacy and basic work skills were added to the program, its constituents became younger, less educated black males.

24. NA, RG 381, Box 802, File: Labor. "Job Corps Contractor Labor Relations—Statement of Policy," July 7, 1966.

25. Ibid., p. 3.

26. Ibid. p. 5.

27. NA, RG 381, Box 802, File: Labor. "Guidelines for the Conduct of Center Labor-Management Relations."

28. Weir, "The Federal Government and Unemployment," p. 169.

29. Ibid., p. 116.

30. Jill Quadagno, *The Transformation of Old Age Security, Class and Politics in the American Welfare State* (Chicago: University of Chicago Press, 1988), p. 12.

31. Mike Davis, *Prisoners of the American Dream* (London: Verso, 1986), p. 132.

32. NA, RG 174, Box 144, File: National Industry Promotion, 1964. MDTA Training and Apprenticeship, April 1, 1964.

33. NA, RG 381, Box 802, File: Labor. "Proposed Training Program by Armstrong Cork Company," March 16, 1966.

34. NA, RG 381, Box 802, File: Labor. "Training of Flooring Mechanics in Cooperation with the Armstrong Cork Co.," April 4, 1966.

35. NA, RG 174, Box 144, File: State and Local Promotion, Jan.–Feb. 1964. Memo to Joseph Mire, National Institute of Labor Education, February 4, 1964.

36. NA, RG 174, Box 144, File: State and Local Promotion, Jan.–Feb. 1964. Memorandum to the Under Secretary, February 17, 1964.

37. Ibid.

38. NA, RG 174, Box 144, File: State and Local Promotion, Jan.–Feb. 1964. Letter from the President of the United Association of Journeymen and Apprentices of the Plumbing and Pipe Fitting Industry to Willard Wirtz.

39. Paul Burstein, *Discrimination, Jobs, and Politics, The Struggle for Equal Employment Opportunity in the United States Since the New Deal* (Chicago: University of Chicago Press, 1985), p. 37.

40. Joseph Meranze, "Negro Employment in the Construction Industry." In *The Negro and Employment Opportunity, Problems and Practices,* ed. Herbert Northrup and Richard L. Rowan (Ann Arbor: Bureau

of Industrial Relations, 1965), p. 202; F. Ray Marshall and Vernon Briggs, *The Negro and Apprenticeship* (Baltimore: Johns Hopkins Press, 1967), p. 195.

41. NA, RG 174, Box 144, File: May–June 1964. Letter from Clement Zablocki to Willard Wirtz, May 26, 1964.

42. Wolkinson, *Blacks, Unions and the EEOC,* pp. 3–4.

43. NA, RG 174, Box 38, File: National Industry Promotion, March/ Unions. Construction Labor Report.

44. Foner, *Organized Labor and the Black Worker,* p. 368.

45. Marshall and Briggs, *The Negro and Apprenticeship,* pp. 197–200.

46. Ibid., p. 43.

47. NA, RG 174, Box 35, File: National Industry Promotion, 1968. "Discrimination and the Trade Unions," p. 7.

48. NA, RG 174, Box 6, File: Job Corps. Letter from Royce Hulsey to Arnold Weber, April 17, 1969.

49. Marshall and Briggs, *The Negro and Apprenticeship,* pp. 83–84.

50. Jean Gould and Lorene Hickok, *Walter Reuther: Labor's Rugged Individualist* (New York: Dodd, Mead, 1972), pp. 334–335; Walter Cormier and William J. Eaton, *Reuther* (Englewood Cliffs: Prentice Hall, 1970), pp. 384–386; John Barnard, *Walter Reuther and the Rise of the Auto Workers* (Boston: Little Brown, 1983), pp. 197–198.

51. Foner, *Organized Labor and the Black Worker,* p. 397.

52. George Meany Archives, Legislative Reference Files, Box 6, File: 20. "Labor and the Philadelphia Plan."

53. "17,200 Given Construction Job Training." *AFL-CIO News,* January 20, 1968, p. 10.

54. "D.C. Crafts Launch Youth Joint Training." *AFL-CIO News,* February 3, 1968, p. 12.

55. "Plan Joint Effort With Negro Groups." *AFL-CIO News,* February 17, 1968, p. 1.

56. Daniel B. Cornfield, *Workers, Managers and Technological Change, Emerging Patterns of Labor Relations* (New York: Plenum, 1987), p. 18.

57. NA, RG 174, Box 235, File: State and Local Promotion, May–August, 1965. File: Letter from J. Michael Turner, July 9, 1965.

58. Philip E. Converse, Warren E. Miller, Jerrold G. Rusk, and Arthur C. Wolfe, "Continuity and Change in American Politics: Parties and Issues in the 1968 Election." *American Political Science Review,* 63 (December 1969): 1084.

59. Ibid., p. 1085.

60. Ibid, p. 1102; J. Michael Ross, Reeve D. Vanneman, and Thomas

Pettigrew, "Patterns of Support for George Wallace: Implications for Racial Change." *Journal of Social Issues,* 36 (1976): 78.

61. Quoted in "Women and Federal Job Training Policy." In *Job Training for Women,* ed. Sharon L. Harlan and Ronnie J. Steinberg (Philadelphia: Temple University Press, 1989), p. 60.

62. Hugh Graham. *The Civil Rights Era: Origins and Development of National Policy* (New York: Oxford University Press, 1990), p. 304.

63. Meany Archives, LRF, Box 6, File: 20. Memo, Conference with Gloster Current, Director of Organization, National Association for the Advancement of Colored People, March 18, 1970.

64. Meany Archives, LRF, Box 6, File: 20. "John Herling's Labor Letter."

65. Quoted in Thomas Edsall and Mary Edsall, *Chain Reaction: The Impact of Race, Rights and Taxes on American Politics* (New York: W.W. Norton, 1991), p. 87.

66. Meany Archives, LRF, Box 6, File: 20. "The Philadelphia Plan."

67. Meany Archives, LRF, Box 6, File 20. "The Philadelphia Plan: Forcing Labor's Hand."

68. Ibid.

69. Davis, *Prisoners of the American Dream,* p. 132.

70. Meany Archives, LRF, Box 6, File: 20. "The Philadelphia Plan."

71. Russell K. Schutt, "Craft Unions and Minorities: Determinants of Change in Admission Practices." *Social Problems,* (1987): 396.

72. Robert Glover, "Apprenticeship: A Route to the High-Paying Skilled Trades for Women?" In Harlan and Steinberg, *Job Training for Women,* pp. 269, 276; Meany Archives, LRF, Box 6, File: 20. "Legality of 'Philadelphia Plan' Upheld by U.S. Appeals Court."

73. Christopher Jencks, *Rethinking Social Policy* (Chicago: University of Chicago Press, 1992), p. 57.

74. NA, RG 207, Box 24, File: Equal Opportunity. Recommendations for the Reduction of Construction Costs.

75. NA, RG 207, Box 74, File: Memorandum to President. The need for a more direct attack on the wage-price spiral.

76. NA, RG 174, Box 2, File: Construction Industry. Memo to Arnold Weber, "Construction Industry Programs," April 18, 1969.

77. NA, RG 174, Box 2, File: Construction Industry. "Use of Apprenticeships and/or Trainees on Federal Construction," Manpower Administration, May 7, 1970.

78. NA, RG 174, Box 2, File: Construction Industry, Report on Manpower Needs. "Statement by the President on Combating Construction Inflation and Meeting Future Construction Needs," March 17, 1979, p. 1.

79. NA, RG 207, Box 75, File: White House Correspondence. Statement by the President, March 29, 1971.

80. NA, RG 207, Box 75, File: White House Correspondence. Construction Industry Stabilization Committee.

81. NA, RG 207, Box 2, File: Housing Crisis and Housing Goals. Draft Message on Construction.

82. NA, RG 174, Box 2, File: Construction Industry: Report on Manpower Needs. Memo to All Regional Manpower Administrators, April 1, 1970.

83. NA, RG 174, Box 2, File: Construction Industry. U.S. Department of Labor Report, June 10, 1970.

84. Ibid., p. 4.

85. NA, RG 174, Box 2, File: Construction Industry. "Plans for Expanding Construction Skills Training in MDTA Institutional Programs."

86. NA, RG 174, Box 2, File: Construction Industry. "Progress Report on Pilot Program for Construction Labor Market Information System in Large Metro Area," June 16, 1970.

87. NA, RG 174, Box 2, File: Construction Industry. "Pilot Program for Construction Labor Market Information System in Large Metro Area."

88. Meany Archives, LRF, Box 6, File 20. Letter from Nat Goldfinger, Dept. of Research, AFL-CIO, to Walter Heller, Oct. 4, 1974.

89. Gilbert Burke, "A Time of Reckoning for the Building Trades." *Fortune* (June, 1979): 83.

90. Harlan and Steinberg, "Women and Federal Job Training Policy," p. 61.

91. William Julius Wilson, *The Truly Disadvantaged* (Chicago: University of Chicago Press, 1987), pp. 112–113.

92. Weir, "The Federal Government and Unemployment," pp. 182–183.

Chapter 4: Abandoning the American Dream

1. Quoted in T. H. Marshall, *Class, Citizenship and Social Development* (Chicago: University of Chicago Press, 1964), p. 83.

2. Thomas J. Sugrue, "The Structures of Urban Poverty: The Reorganization of Space and Work in Three Periods of American History." In *The Underclass Debate,* ed. Michael Katz (Princeton: Princeton University Press, 1993), p. 112; see also David W. Bartelt, "Housing the Underclass." In Katz, *The Underclass Debate.*

3. Barry Jacobs, Kenneth Harney, Charles Edson, and Bruce Lane,

Guide to Federal Housing Programs (Washington, D.C.: Bureau of National Affairs, 1986), p. 162.

4. NA, RG 207, Box 305, File: National Committee Against Discrimination in Housing. "Rap Group Raps Weaver."

5. Quoted in J. Paul Mitchell, "The Historical Context for Housing Policy." In *Federal Housing Policy and Programs* (New Brunswick, NJ: Center for Urban Policy Research, 1985), p. 4.

6. Lawrence Friedman, *Government and Slum Housing* (Chicago: Rand McNally, 1968), p. 49.

7. Marc Weiss, "The Origins and Legacy of Urban Renewal." In J. Paul Mitchell, *Federal Housing Policy and Programs* (New Brunswick, NJ: Center for Urban Policy Research, 1985), p. 254.

8. J. Paul Mitchell, "Historical Overview of Direct Federal Housing Assistance." In *Federal Housing Policy and Programs,* p. 194.

9. Gerald David Jaynes and Robin M. Williams, Jr., *A Common Destiny, Blacks and American Society* (Washington, D.C.: National Academy Press, 1989), p. 89.

10. NA, RG 207, Box 240, Race and Education Report, p. 39; Martin Meyerson and Edward Banfield, *Politics, Planning and the Public Interest: The Case of Public Housing in Chicago* (New York: MacMillan, 1965), p. 25; Devereux Bowly, Jr., *The Poorhouse: Subsidized Housing in Chicago, 1895–1975* (Carbondale: Southern Illinois University Press, 1978), p. 112.

11. NA, RG 207, Box 240. File: National Commission. Letter from Jack Wood to the President, 3/7/67.

12. Nicholas Lehmann, *The Promised Land, The Great Black Migration and How It Changed America.* (New York: Alfred A. Knopf, 1991), p. 116.

13. NA, RG 207, Box 240, Race and Education Report, p. 11.

14. NA, RG 207, Box 253, File: Aug.–Dec. 1967, Memorandums. Housing Segregation and Governmental Process in the United States, p. 4.

15. Robert Wood (oral history, Lyndon Baines Johnson Library, Austin, Texas), p. 8.

16. Ibid., p. 16.

17. U.S. Commission on Urban Problems, *Building the American City* (Washington, D.C.: U.S. Government Printing Office, 1969), p. 146.

18. Joseph A. Califano, Jr., *The Triumph and Tragedy of Lyndon Johnson* (New York: Simon and Schuster, 1991), p. 127.

19. NA, RG 207, Weaver, Box 136, File: Rent Supplement. Rent Supplement Program.

20. Marlan Blissett, "Untangling the Mess: The Administrative Legacy

of President Johnson." In *Lyndon Baines Johnson and the Uses of Power,* ed. Bernard Firestone and Robert Vogt (New York: Greenwood Press, 1988), p. 66.

21. Robert C. Weaver (oral history, Lyndon Baines Johnson Library, Austin, Texas), p. 25.

22. Ibid., p. 67.

23. Wood (oral history), p. 19.

24. Ibid., p. 15.

25. NA, RG 207, Box 253, File: Intergroup Relations, Aug.–Dec. 1967. Memo. "Housing Desegregation and Private Industry Leadership."

26. Stephen B. Oates, *Let the Trumpet Sound: The Life of Martin Luther King Jr* (New York: Harper and Row, 1982), p. 406.

27. NA, RG 207, Box 305, File: National Committee Against Discrimination in Housing. Press release, January 19, 1966.

28. NA, RG 207, Box 305, File: National Commission on Discrimination in Housing. "Rights Group Raps Weaver," *Evening Star,* Feb. 9, 1967.

29. NA, RG 207, Box 186, File: President's Commission on Equal Opportunity in Housing. Summary Report No. 5.

30. NA, RG 207, Box 186, File: President's Commission on Equal Opportunity in Housing. Summary Report No. 3.

31. NA, RG 207, Box 253, File: Intergroup Relations, Aug.–Dec. 1967. Article in *Sun Times,* 5/7/67.

32. Ibid, p. 3.

33. Robert A. Sauer, "Free Choice in Housing." *New York Law Forum* (December, 1964), p. 541.

34. Sauer, "Free Choice in Housing," pp. 544–545.

35. Thomas Edsall and Mary Edsall, *Chain Reaction, The Impact of Race, Rights, and Taxes on American Politics* (New York: W.W. Norton, 1991), p. 139.

36. Edmund Gerald Brown (oral history, Lyndon Baines Johnson Library, Austin, Texas), p. 4.

37. NA, RG 207, Box 186, File: President's Commission on Equal Opportunity. Memo on significant events and activities, Sept. 30, 1965.

38. NA, RG 207, Box 253, File: Aug.–Dec. 1967, Memorandums. Housing Segregation, p. 13.

39. Califano, *The Triumph and Tragedy of Lyndon Johnson,* p. 276.

40. Gary Orfield, "Race and the Liberal Agenda: The Loss of the Integrationist Dream, 1965–1974." In *The Politics of Social Policy in the United States,* ed. Margaret Weir, Ann Shola Orloff, and Theda Skocpol (Princeton: Princeton University Press, 1988), p. 338.

41. Califano, *The Triumph and Tragedy of Lyndon Johnson,* p. 276.

42. NA, RG 207, Subject files of Richard Van Dusen, Box 10, File: Open Communities. "A Strategy for Metropolitan Open Communities"; NA, RG 207, Box 24, File: Equal Opportunity. HUD news release, Dec. 31, 1969.

43. Jacobs, Harney, Edson, and Lane, *Guide to Federal Housing Programs,* p. 19.

44. Weaver (oral history), p. 42.

45. NA, RG 207, Box 253, File: Aug.–Dec. 1967. Memorandums. "Departmental Equal Opportunity Activities," p. 4.

46. NA, RG 207, Box 253, File: Intergroup Relations, Aug.–Dec. 1967. Confidential memo, January 11, 1967.

47. NA, RG 207, Box 242, File: Equal Opportunity in HUD Operations. Memo, Oct. 17, 1967, p. 10.

48. NA, RG 207, Box 242, File: Equal Opportunity in HUD Operations. Tenant Selection and Assignment Plans.

49. NA, RG 207, Box 242, File: Equal Opportunity in HUD Operations and Programs, p. 4.

50. NA, RG 207, Box 240, File: Race and Education Report, p. 37.

51. NA, RG 207, Box 305, File: National Committee Against Discrimination in Housing. Letter from Neil Gold to Robert Wood, 6/18/67.

52. NA, RG 207, Box 240, File: Race and Education Report, p. 37.

53. NA, RG 207, Box 305, File: National Committee Against Discrimination in Housing. Letter from Wood to President.

54. Ramsey Clark (oral history, Lyndon Baines Johnson Library, Austin, Texas), p. 6.

55. NA, RG 207, Weaver, Box 191, File: Intergroup Relations. Intergroup Relations Task Force on Aggressive Action.

56. In 1964 Reuther had written a letter outlining a method for rebuilding urban slums in six major cities. See Michael Reopel and Lance Bardsley, "Strategies for Governance: Domestic Policy Making in the Johnson Administration." In *Lyndon Baines Johnson and the Uses of Power* (New York: Greenwood Press, 1988), p. 24.

57. Califano, *The Triumph and Tragedy of Lyndon Johnson,* p. 115.

58. Bernard J. Frieden and Marshall Kaplan, *The Politics of Neglect: Urban Aid from Model Cities to Revenue Sharing* (Cambridge: MIT Press, 1975), pp. 35–39.

59. NA, RG 207, Box 242. File: Equal Opportunity in HUD Operations, p. 7.

60. Weaver (oral history), p. 7.

61. NA, RG 207, Box 253. File: Equal Opportunity in HUD Operations, p. 6.

62. NA, RG 207, Weaver, Box 241, File: Model Cities. Telegram from Rev. W. J. Hodge.

63. NA, RG 207, Box 253, File: Aug.–Dec. 1967. Memorandums. Departmental Equal Opportunity Activities, p. 6.

64. NA, RG 207, Box 384, File: Urban Tension Monthly Reports.

65. Mitchell, "Historical context for Housing Policy," p. 12.

66. U.S. Department of Housing and Urban Development, *Housing in the Seventies: A Report of the National Housing Policy Review* (Washington, D.C.: U.S. Government Printing Office), p. 105.

67. Brian Boyer, *Cities Destroyed for Cash* (Chicago: Follett, 1973), p. 170.

68. NA, RG. 207, Box 24, File: Equal Opportunity. Recent Actions Filed by Attorney General Relating to Fair Housing.

69. NA, RG 207, Van Dusen, Box 10, File: Open Communities. Statement of George Romney to the United States Commission on Civil Rights, June 15, 1981, p. 4.

70. NA, RG 207, Box 10, File: Open Communities. Memo from John Chapin to George Romney, August 15, 1969.

71. NA, RG 207, Box 10, File: Open Communities. *The National Observer*, Oct. 20, 1969.

72. NA, RG 207, Box 10, File: Open Communities. Memo for the Secretary from Open Communities Group.

73. NA, RG 207, Box 10, File: Open Communities. "President Reaffirms Opposition to Forced Suburban Integration." Article in *The New York Times*, February 18, 1971.

74. NA, RG 207, Van Dusen, Box 77, File: President's Statement on Federal Policies. "Housing Policy Battle Lines Drawn. Article in *The Detroit Free Press*, June 17, 1971.

75. NA, RG 207, Box 77, File: President's Statement on Federal Policies. White House Press Conference, June 11, 1971.

76. NA, RG 207, Box 77, File: Housing Crisis and Housing Goals. Statement by the President on Federal Policies Relative to Equal Housing Opportunity.

77. Edsall and Edsall, *Chain Reaction*, p. 76.

78. Interview with George Romney, quoted in Boyer, pp. 226–227.

79. Boyer, *Cities Destroyed for Cash*, p. 25.

80. NA, RG 207, Box 75, File: White House Correspondence. "St. Louis Housing Debacle." Article in *St. Louis Globe Democrat*, March 11, 1972.

81. Boyer, *Cities Destroyed for Cash*, p. 182.

82. Jacobs, Harney, Edson, and Lane, *Guide*, p. 21.

83. Paul Dimond, *Beyond Busing: Inside the Challenge to Urban Segregation* (Ann Arbor: University of Michigan Press, 1985), p. 185.

84. Joel Blau, *The Visible Poor.* (New York: Oxford University Press, 1992), p. 74.

85. Helene Slessarev, "Racial Tensions and Institutional Support: Social Programs during a Period of Retrenchment." In *The Politics of Social Policy in the United States* (Princeton: Princeton University Press, 1988), p. 358.

86. Ibid., pp. 358–359.

87. Ibid., pp. 360.

88. Gary Orfield, "The Movement for Housing Integration." In *Housing Desegregation and Federal Policy,* ed. John Goering (Chapel Hill: University of North Carolina Press, 1986), p. 23.

Chapter 5: The Politics of Welfare Reform

1. See George Gilder, *Wealth and Poverty* (New York: Basic Books, 1981); Charles Murray, *Losing Ground: American Social Policy, 1950–1980* (New York: Basic Books), 1984.

2. Linda Gordon, "The New Feminist Scholarship on the Welfare State." In *Women, the State and Welfare,* ed. Linda Gordon (Madison: University of Wisconsin Press, 1990), p. 12; Theodore R. Marmor, Jerry Mashaw, and Philip L. Harvey, *America's Misunderstood Welfare State* (New York: Basic Books, 1990, p. 95); David Ellwood, *Poor Support: Poverty in the American Family* (New York: Basic Books, 1988), p. 41.

3. T. H. Marshall, *Class, Citizenship and Social Development* (Chicago: University of Chicago Press, 1964), p. 83.

4. "Nixon: The First Year of His Presidency." *Congressional Quarterly* (1970): 75–A.

5. Mildred and Claude Pepper Library, RG 309B, Box 56, File 7. "The Bill to Revamp the Welfare System," legislative analysis, American Enterprise Institute, April 6, 1970, analysis no. 4.

6. Ann Orloff, "Gender and the Social Rights of Citizenship: State Policies and Gender Relations in Comparative Perspective." (Paper presented at the Conference on Comparative Studies of Welfare Development, University of Bremen, Germany, September 3–6, 1992), p. 1; Carol Pateman, "The Patriarchal Welfare State." In *Democracy and the Welfare State,* ed. Amy Gutman (Princeton: Princeton University Press, 1988), pp. 235–236; Jane Jenson, "Representations of Gender: Policies to Protect Women Workers and Infants in France and the United States before 1914." In *Women, the State and Welfare,* ed. Linda Gordon (Madison: University of Wisconsin Press, 1990), p. 153.

7. Gwendolyn Mink, "The Lady and the Tramp: Gender, Race, and the Origins of the American Welfare State." In *Women, the State and Welfare,* ed. Linda Gordon (Madison: University of Wisconsin Press, 1990), p. 110.

8. Theda Skocpol, *Protecting Soldiers and Mothers* (Cambridge: Harvard University Press, 1992), pp. 424–479; Winifred Bell, *Aid to Dependent Children* (New York: Columbia University Press, 1965), p. 6. Barbara Nelson, "The Gender, Race and Class Origins of Early Welfare Policy and the Welfare State: A Comparison of Workmen's Compensation and Mothers' Aid." In *Women, Politics and Change,* ed. Louise Tilly and Patricia Gurin (New York: Sage, 1990), p. 429.

9. Jill Quadagno, *The Transformation of Old Age Security: Class and Politics in the American Welfare State* (Chicago: University of Chicago Press, 1988), p. 115.

10. Arthur Altmeyer, *The Formative Years of Social Security* (Madison: University of Wisconsin Press, 1966), pp. 16, 28.

11. Bell, *Aid to Dependent Children,* p. 46.

12. Irene Lurie, *An Economic Evaluation of Aid to Families with Dependent Children* (Washington, D.C.: The Brookings Institute, 1968), pp. 5, 14.

13. Catherine Fobes, "Solidarity Among Women in Social Protest: The Case of the National Welfare Rights Organization." (Paper presented to the American Sociological Association, Miami, FL, August, 1993, p. 7.

14. Frances Fox Piven and Richard Cloward, *Poor People's Movements, Why They Succeed, How They Fail* (New York: Random House, 1979), p. 272.

15. "How the Relief System Works Now." *U.S. News and World Report,* Sept. 22, 1969, 76.

16. Piven and Cloward, *Poor People's Movements,* p. 274.

17. "Why the Welfare Bill is Stuck," *Newsweek,* Dec. 7, 1970, 23.

18. National Advisory Commission on Civil Disorders, *Report* (New York: E. P. Dutton, 1968), p. 461.

19. Vincent J. Burke and Vee Burke, *Nixon's Good Deed, Welfare Reform* (New York: Columbia University Press, 1974), p. 25.

20. Lurie, *An Economic Evaluation of Aid to Families with Dependent Children,* p. 20.

21. "Behind Rising Alarm Over Welfare Costs." *U.S. News and World Report,* Nov. 30, 1970, 32.

22. "The Welfare Backlash." *Newsweek,* April 14, 1969, p. 17.

23. National Advisory Commission on Civil Disorders, *Report,* p. 6.

24. Milton Friedman, *Capitalism and Freedom* (Chicago: University of

Chicago Press, 1962), pp. 190–195; See also Christopher Green, *Negative Taxes and the Poverty Problem*. (Washington: Brookings Institute, 1967); Martin Anderson, *Welfare: The Political Economy of Welfare Reform in the United States* (Stanford, CA: Hoover Institution Press, 1978), pp. 72–73.

25. Cited in James Sundquist, "The End of the Experiment." In *On Fighting Poverty: Perspectives from Experience*, ed. James Sundquist (New York: Basic Books, 1969), pp. 235–251.

26. Piven and Cloward, *Poor People's Movements*, p. 273.

27. James Patterson, *Struggle Against Poverty* (Cambridge: Harvard University Press, 1986), p. 190.

28. Michael Katz, *The Undeserving Poor: From the War on Poverty to the War on Welfare* (New York: Pantheon, 1989), p. 104.

29. Burke and Burke, *Nixon's Good Deed*, p. 170.

30. National Advisory Commission on Civil Disorders, *Report*, pp. 203–204.

31. Joan Hoff-Wilson, "Outflanking the Liberals on Welfare." In *Richard M. Nixon: Politician, President, Administrator*, ed. Leon Friedman and William F. Levantrosser (New York: Greenwood Press, 1991), p. 102.

32. Quoted in Jonathan Rieder, "The Rise of the Silent Majority." In *The Rise and Fall of the New Deal Order, 1930–1980*, ed. Steve Fraser and Gary Gestle (Princeton: Princeton University Press, 1989), pp. 260–261.

33. Among those who assess Nixon's strategy in these terms are Rowland Evans and Robert Novak, *Nixon in the White House: The Frustration of Power* (New York: Random House, 1971), p. 227; Herbert S. Parmet, *Richard Nixon and his America* (Boston: Little Brown, 1990), p. 549; William Safire, *Before the Fall: An Inside View of the Pre-Watergate White House* (Garden City, NY: Doubleday, 1975), p. 309.

34. In 1969 AFDC payments in Mississippi averaged $468 per year compared to more than $2,500 in New York. Editorial, *The Nation*, August 25, 1969, 31.

35. "Nixon's New Deal." *Newsweek*, Aug. 18, 1969, 17; Nixon's New Tory identity reversed his previous conservative stance on social spending, which he had consistently maintained throughout his career. See Roger Morris, *Richard Milhous Nixon: The Rise of an American Politician* (New York: Henry Holt, 1990); For a similar evaluation of the FAP as an electoral strategy, see Michael A. Genovese, *The Nixon Presidency: Power and Politics in Turbulent Times* (New York: Greenwood Press, 1990), p. 79.

36. Daniel Patrick Moynihan, *The Negro Family: The Case for National Action* (U.S. Department of Labor: Office of Policy Planning and Research, 1965), pp. 12–13.

37. Lee Rainwater and William Yancey, *The Moynihan Report and the Politics of Controversy* (Cambridge: The Massachusetts Institute of Technology Press, 1967), p. 6.

38. Moynihan, *The Negro Family*, p. 25, 29.

39. Ibid., p. 93; Rainwater and Yancey, *The Moynihan Report*, p. 29.

40. The National Advisory Commission on Civil Disorders, *Report*, pp. 13–14.

41. Ibid., p. 457.

42. Ibid., p. 466.

43. George Shultz, "The Nixon Welfare Plan." *New Generation*, (1970): 6.

44. Federal Archives and Record Center (hereafter FARC), RG 235, Box 1, "Suggested Modification in H.R. 1." Paper prepared by the Office of Equal Opportunity for NEW Secretary Elliot Richardson, August 6, 1971. Tables prepared by HEW on the estimated impact of the FAP also emphasized male employment. See "What A Working Man Must Earn to be as Well Off as a Welfare Family." The FAP was revised several times to counter criticisms that the minimum was too low, that the work requirements could be abused, that payments would favor the South at the expense of the northern industrial states, and that cutting off food stamps would leave many families worse off. "Welfare: Second Thoughts." *Newsweek,* July 28, 1969, 18.

45. FARC, RG 235, Box 1, Internal HEW memo from Jim Edwards to John Montgomery, Sept. 22, 1971.

46. FARC, RG 235, Box 2, "Issue Memo Re Departmental Jurisdiction for Payment of FAP Benefits to Families," March 18, 1971, p. 3.

47. U.S. Congress, Senate, Committee on Finance. *Hearings on H.R. 16311.* (Washington, D.C.: U.S. Government Printing Office, 1970), p. 321.

48. Ibid., p. 384.

49. Ibid., pp. 242, 305, 1742.

50. "It Pays to Work—Agnew Explains the President's Welfare Plan." *U.S. News and World Report,* March 23, 1970, 84.

51. FARC, RG 235, Box 2, Prepared testimony of the Secretary of Health, Education and Welfare before the Committee on Finance, July 21, 1970, p. 4. AFDC-UI paid benefits to unemployed fathers.

52. FARC, RG 235, Box 2, Letter from Elliot Richardson to Tom Vail, July 8, 1970, p. 3.

53. U.S. Congress, *Hearings on H.R. 16311*, p. 1940.

54. Richard Nixon, "Welfare Reform, Shared Responsibility." *Vital Speeches of the Day*, 35 (1969): 675. Although Nixon promised in his speech on welfare reform that "in no case could anyone's present benefits be lowered," when the FAP was revised to meet Senate Finance Committee objections, those residing in high payment states would have lost benefits. U.S. Congress, *Hearings on H.R. 16311*, p. 340.

55. Reg Murphy and Hal Gulliver, *The Southern Strategy* (New York: Charles Scribner's Sons, 1971), p. 3.

56. U.S. Congress, *Hearings on H.R. 16311*, p. 292.

57. FARC, RG 235, Box 2, John F. Kain and Robert Schafer, "Regional Impacts of the Family Assistance Plan." Office of Economic Research, Department of Commerce, 1971, p. 24.

58. Richard Armstrong, "The Looming Money Revolution Down South." *Fortune* December (1970): 66, 151.

59. U.S. Congress, *Hearings on H.R. 16311*, p. 1510.

60. Lester M. Salamon, "The Stakes in the Rural South." *The New Republic* (1971): 18.

61. Ibid.

62. U.S. Congress, *Hearings on H.R. 16311*, p. 1511.

63. Ibid., p. 1518.

64. Salamon, "The Stakes in the Rural South," p. 17.

65. David James, "The Transformation of the Southern Racial State: Class and Race Determinants of Local-State Structures." *American Sociological Review*, 53 (1988): p. 205.

66. Salamon, "The Stakes in the Rural South," p. 18; U.S. Congress, *Hearings on H.R. 16311*, p. 1512.

67. Salamon, "The Stakes in the Rural South," p. 18.

68. U.S. Congress, *Hearings on H.R. 16311*, p. 254. Estimates of the cost and coverage of the FAP were continually revised as changes were made in the bill or better data became available.

69. U.S. Congress, *Hearings on H.R. 16311*, pp. 981–984.

70. Daniel Patrick Moynihan, *The Politics of a Guaranteed Income: The Nixon Administration and the Family Assistance Plan* (New York: Random House, 1973), p. 137.

71. U.S. Bureau of the Census, *Census of Population* (Washington, D.C.: U.S. Government Printing Office, 1970), Table 209. For white male household heads in Mississippi, the poverty rate was 8.1 percent.

72. Armstrong, "The Looming Money Revolution," p. 67.

73. U.S. Congress, *Hearings on H.R. 16311*, Chart 2.

74. Armstrong, "The Looming Money Revolution," p. 154.

75. Ibid., p. 68.

76. Ibid., pp. 66–69, 151–159.

77. Ibid., p. 152.

78. Tom Herman, "Welfare Reform: The Southern View." *Wall Street Journal*, December 15, 1970, 4.

79. Moynihan, *The Politics of a Guaranteed Income*, p. 257.

80. *Congressional Record*, House (Washington, D.C.: U.S. Government Printing Office, April 16, 1970), pp. 12105–12106.

81. FARC, RG 235, Box 1, Internal Memo, Department of HEW, August 18, 1971: Report of our efforts to determine the positions of state and local Chambers of Commerce on proposed welfare reform legislation. See also "The Great Welfare Debate," *Nation's Business*, April 1970: 56–59.

82. U.S. Congress, *Hearings on H.R. 16311*, p. 1886.

83. George Meany Memorial Archives, Silver Spring Maryland, Legislative Reference Files (LRF), Box 25, File: 62. "The Negative Income Tax Dilemma, Welfare Reform and Possible Alternatives," p.2.

84. U.S. Congress, *Hearings on H.R. 16311*, pp. 1729, 1947.

85. Ibid., p. 1730.

86. "Income by Right," *New Yorker*, 48 (1973): 73; "Why the Welfare Bill is Stuck," *Newsweek*, Dec. 7, 1970, 23.

87. NA, RG 381, Box 22, File: Aug. 66–Oct. 66. Poverty/Rights Action Center.

88. Vincent J. Burke and Vee Burke, *Nixon's Good Deed* (New York: Columbia University Press, 1974), p. 163.

89. Quoted in Parmet, *Richard Nixon and his America*, p. 560.

90. Hoff-Wilson, "Outflanking the Liberals on Welfare," p. 102.

Chapter 6: The Politics of Motherhood

1. Joint Hearings before the Subcommittee on Employment, Manpower and Poverty and the Subcommittee on Labor and Public Welfare, 92nd Congress, First Sess., S. 1512, May 13 and 20, 1971, p. 758.

2. Gilbert Y. Steiner, *The Children's Cause* (Washington, D.C.: Brookings Institute, 1976), p. 5.

3. Ibid., p. 9.

4. Ibid., p. 10.

5. Patricia G. Zelman, *Women, Work and National Policy: The Kennedy–Johnson Years* (Ann Arbor: UMI Research Press, 1980), p. 9.

6. Mary D. Keyserling (oral history, Lyndon Baines Johnson Library Oral History Collection, Austin, Texas, October 22, 31, 1968), p. 30.

7. Margaret O'Brien Steinfels, *Who's Minding the Children?* (New York: Simon and Schuster, 1973), pp. 66–70; Victoria L. Getis and Maris

Vinovskis, "History of Child Care in the United States Before 1950." In *Child Care in Context: Cross-Cultural Perspectives,* ed. Michael Lamb, Kathleen Sternberg, Carl-Philip Hwang, and Anders G. Broberg (Hove and London: Lawrence-Erlbaum, 1992), pp. 199–202.

8. Erika Streuer, "Current Legislative Proposals and Public Policy Questions for Child Care." In *Child Care, Who Cares,* ed. Pamela Roby (New York: Basic Books, 1973), p. 59.

9. NA, RG 102, Box 832, File: Day Care of Children of Working Mothers. Draft of Position Statement on Day Care, March 9, 1962.

10. Keyserling (oral history), p. 22.

11. Steinfels, *Who's Minding the Children,* p. 72.

12. NA, RG 102, Box 832, File: Day Care of Children of Working Mothers. Letter from Jacob Javits to Katherine Oettinger, May 6, 1958.

13. For a discussion of welfare expansion and public reaction, see Chapter 5.

14. NA, RG 102, Box 832, File: Day Care of Children of Working14. Mothers. Discussion of Day Care Legislation at Women's Bureau, December 6, 1961.

15. NA, RG 102, Box 832, File: Day Care of Children of Working Mothers. Detailed Summary of Public Welfare Amendments of 1962. Letter from Gertrude Hoffman to Theresa Jackson, February 6, 1961.

16. NA, RG 102, Box 832, File: Day Care of Children of Working Mothers. Letter from Elinor Guggenheimer to Raymond Gallagher, February 28, 1962.

17. NA, RG 102, Box 832, File: Day Care of Children of Working Mothers. Day Care Services, Form and Substance by Gertrude Hoffman.

18. NA, RG 102, Box 832, File: Day Care of Children of Mothers. Letter from Margaret Wainwright to the President, February 14, 1962; letter from G.H. Randles to the President, April 9, 1962; letter from Raymond Stauble to the President, February 26, 1962.

19. *Congressional Record,* July 9, p. 12052.

20. NA, RG 102, Box 1150, File: Aug. 67. Federal Funds for Day Care Projects.

21. NA, RG 102, Box 1150, File: March 68–Oct. 68. Narrative on Day Care Developments.

22. NA, RG 102, Box 1005, File: March 65–Jan. 66. Memo on Day Care Services, February 20, 1963.

23. NA, RG 102, Box 833, File: Day Care May 1966. Highlights of Maryland Program for Day Care Services.

24. NA, RG 102, Box 1150, File: Aug. 67. Daytime Programs for Children.

25. Ben Bagdikian, "Who Is Sabotaging Day Care for Our Children?" *Ladies Home Journal* (November, 1966): 86.

26. Ibid.

27. For a discussion of the transition from Watson to Spock, see William M. Tuttle, Jr., *Daddy's Gone to War: The Second World War in the Lives of America's Children* (New York: Oxford University Press, 1993), chap. 6; see also J. McVicker Hunt, *Intelligence and Experience* (New York: Ronald Press, 1961).

28. Benjamin S. Bloom, *Stability and Change in Human Characteristics* (New York: Wiley, 1964).

29. NA, RG 102, Box 1005, File: March 65–Jan. 66. Background for discussion of day care services, April 9, 1965.

30. Sheldon Danziger and Daniel Weinberg, *Fighting Poverty: What Works and What Doesn't* (Cambridge: Harvard University Press, 1986), p. 157. See also state records of the community action programs from the Office of Economic Opportunity in the National Archives.

31. NA, RG 102, Box 1150, File: Aug. 67. Daytime Programs for Children.

32. Steiner, *The Children's Cause*, p. 54.

33. NA, RG 102, Box 1150, File: March 68–Oct. 68. Letter from Gertrude Hoffman to Mrs. Franc Balzer, September 23, 1968.

34. NA, RG 102, Box 1150, File: March 68–Oct. 68. "Another Mom Takes Over While Mother's at School."

35. NA, RG 102, Box 1150, File: March 68–Oct. 68. Program Memo on Income Maintenance and Social Services Programs.

36. NA, RG 102, Box 1150, File: Aug. 67. Bills Introduced Relating to Day Care.

37. NA, RG 102, Box 1150, File: March 68–Oct. 68. Conference with Mary Keyserling, March 8, 1968.

38. NA, RG 102, Box 1150, File: Aug. 67. Letter from Bert Seidman to John Gardner, August 9, 1967; Stevanne Auerback, "Federally Sponsored Child Care." In *Child Care, Who Cares?*, ed. Pamela Roby (New York: Basic Books, 1973), p. 180.

39. NA, RG 102, Box 1150, File: March 68–Oct. 68. Day Care Services Outside the Win Program, August 6, 1968.

40. NA, RG 102, Box 1150, File: March 68–Oct. 68. Comments on Standards of Care for Infants.

41. NA, RG 102, Box 1150, File: Aug. 67. Memo from Gertrude Hoffman, April 27, 1967.

42. NA, RG 102, Box 1150, File: March 68–Oct. 68. Federal Interagency Requirements for Day Care.

43. Quoted in Irvin D. Solomon, *Feminism and Black Activism in Contemporary America* (New York: Greenwood Press, 1989), p. 44.

44. Ethel Klein, *Gender Politics* (Cambridge: Harvard University Press, 1984), p. 23.

45. Kim M. Blankenship, "Bringing Gender and Race In: U.S. Employment Discrimination Policy." *Gender and Society,* 7 (1993): 204–226.

46. See Chapter 3 for a more detailed discussion of the employment provisions of the Civil Rights Act.

47. Jo Freeman, *The Politics of Women's Liberation* (New York: David McKay, 1975), p. 55.

48. Ibid., p. 80.

49. Ibid., p. 118.

50. Doug McAdam, "Gender as a Mediator of the Activist Experience: The Case of Freedom Summer." *American Sociological Review,* 5 (1992): 1211–1240.

51. Linda Gordon, "Functions of the Family." In *Voices From Women's Liberation,* ed. Leslie Tanner (New York: New American Library, 1970), pp. 182–184.

52. Vickie Pollard, "Producing Society's Babies." In Tanner, *Voices From Women's Liberation,* pp. 197.

53. Louise Gross and Phyllis MacEwan, "On Day Care." In Tanner, *Voices From Women's Liberation,* p. 199–200.

54. Elizabeth Hagen, "Child Care and Women's Liberation." In *Child Care, Who Cares?,* ed. Pamela Roby (New York: Basic Books, 1973), p. 284; Evelyn Leo, "Saturday Afternoon at the Congress to Unite Women." In *Voices From Women's Liberation,* ed. Leslie Tanner (New York: New American Library, 1970), p. 127.

55. Freeman, *Politics of Women's Liberation,* p. 76.

56. *Joint Hearings before the Subcommittee on Employment, Manpower and Poverty and the Subcommittee on Labor and Public Welfare,* 92nd Congress, First Sess., S. 1512, May 13 and 20, 1971, p. 758.

57. "Nixon: The First Year of His Presidency." (*Congressional Quarterly* 1970): 75A, 77A.

58. Erika Streuer, "Current Legislative Proposals and Public Policy Questions for Child Care." In Roby, *Child Care, Who Cares?,* pp. 52, 56.

59. Steiner, *The Children's Cause,* p. 105.

60. Rochelle Beck and John Butler, "An Interview with Marian Wright Edelman." *Harvard Educational Review,* 44 (February, 1974): 68; Marian Wright Edelman, "A Political-Legislative Overview of Federal Child Care Proposals." In *Raising Children in Modern America: Problems and Prospective Solutions,* ed. Nathan B. Talbot (Boston: Little Brown, 1974), pp. 304–318.

61. *Hearings on S. 1512,* pp. 367–368.

62. Testimony of Evelyn Moore at Hearings on S. 1215, pp. 366–369.

63. There was considerable controversy over the income limit, and as the bill moved through Congress, the limit was revised several times. On September 30, 1971, when debate was held in the House, the income

limit was $6,970, the low budget for an urban family of four set by the Bureau of Labor Statistics. *Congressional Record*, Sept. 30, 1971, p. 34293. For a detailed discussion of the income controversy, see Steiner, *The Children's Cause*, pp. 110–113.

64. Testimony of Stephen Kurzman, Assistant Secretary for Legislation, Department of Health, Education and Welfare, on S. 1512, pp. 761–763.

65. Quoted in Margaret O'Brien Steinfels, *Who's Minding the Children?* (New York: Simon and Schuster, 1973), p. 19.

66. Carol Joffe, "Why the United States has no Child Care Policy." In *Families, Politics and Public Policy*, ed. Irene Diamond. (New York: Longman, 1983), p. 171; Gary Allen, *Nixon's Palace Guard* (Boston: Western Islands, 1971), p. 112; John Osborne, *The Third Year of the Nixon Watch* (New York: Liveright, 1972), p. 195.

67. *Congressional Record*, Sept. 30, 1971, p. 34290.

68. Ibid., p. 34305.

69. Ibid., p. 31305.

70. U.S. Congress, Senate, 1st Sess., *Economic Opportunity Amendments of 1971*, Report to accompany S. 2007, July 30, 1971, p. 12.

71. Charles Hamilton and Dona Hamilton, "Social Policies, Civil Rights and Poverty." In *Fighting Poverty: What Works and What Doesn't*, ed. Sheldon H. Danziger and Daniel H. Weinberg (Cambridge: Harvard University Press, 1986), p. 301; Carl Lieberman, "Legislative Success and Failure: The Social Welfare Policies of the Nixon Administration." In *Richard M. Nixon: Politician, President, Administrator*, ed. Leon Friedman and William Levantrosser (New York: Greenwood Press, 1991), p. 108.

72. Veto of Economic Opportunity Amendments of 1971. The President's Message to the Senate Returning S.2007 Without His Approval. December 9, 1971. *Weekly Compilation of Presidential Documents*, December 13, 1971, p. 1634.

Chapter 7: Universal Principles in Social Security

1. Charles Lockhart, *Gaining Ground: Tailoring Social Programs to American Values* (Berkeley: University of California Press, 1989), p. 2.

2. Theda Skocpol, "Sustainable Social Policy: Fighting Poverty Without Poverty Programs." *The American Prospect*, 2 (Summer, 1990): 59.

3. William Julius Wilson, *The Truly Disadvantaged: The Inner City, the Underclass and Public Policy* (Chicago: University of Chicago Press, 1987), p. 120.

4. Kenneth S. Tollett, "Racism and Race-Conscious Remedies." *The American Prospect* 3 (Spring 1991): 91.

5. Jill Quadagno, "Generational Equity and the Politics of the Welfare State." *Politics and Society,* 17 (1989): 363.

6. T. H. Marshall, *Class, Citizenship and Social Development* (Chicago: University of Chicago Press, 1964), pp. 83–86.

7. Walter Korpi, "Power, Politics and State Autonomy in the Development of Social Citizenship: Social Rights During Sickness in Eighteen OECD Countries Since 1930." *American Sociological Review,* 54 (1989): 310.

8. Carole Pateman, "The Patriarchal Welfare State." In *Democracy and the Welfare State,* ed. Amy Gutmann (Princeton: Princeton University Press, 1988), p. 237.

9. Jill Quadagno, "Welfare Capitalism and the Social Security Act of 1935." *American Sociological Review,* (1984): 632–647.

10. Fifteenth Census of the United States, 1930. *Population, General Report of Occupations,* 5: 40, 49.

11. Men were ineligible for both the spouse and widow's benefit except those who were at least sixty-five, could prove that they had been totally dependent on their wives' income, and were parents of a child under the age of eighteen. Ibid., p. 7.

12. Title I—Amendments to Title I of the Social Security Act, Public Law No. 379, 76th Cong., Chap. 666, 1st Sess. H.R. 6635, pp. 5, 6.

13. Walter Reuther Archives of Labor History and Urban Affairs, Collection of Katherine Ellickson, Box 96, File: Older Women and Social Security. "Social Security Benefit Awards to Older Women, 1954–65" by Lenore Epstein.

14. Greg Duncan and Ken Smith, "The Rising Affluence of the Elderly: How Far, How Fair, and How Frail?" *Annual Review of Sociology,* 15 (1989): 262.

15. Gerald Nash, Noel Pugach, and Richard Tomasson, *Social Security: The First Half Century* (Albuquerque: University of New Mexico Press, 1988), p. 318.

16. Martha Derthick, *Policymaking for Social Security* (Washington, D.C.: Brookings Institute, 1979), pp. 342–345.

17. "Nixon: The First Year of His Presidency." (*Congressional Quarterly* 1970): 87–A.

18. Derthick, *Policymaking for Social Security,* p. 259.

19. Richard Nixon, *Memoirs of Richard Nixon* (New York: Grosset and Dunlap, 1978), p. 491.

20. Derthick, *Policymaking for Social Security,* pp. 35–42.

21. *Statistical Abstracts of the United States* (Washington, D.C.: U.S. Government Printing Office, 1975), p. 403.

22. Vital Statistics of the United States, 1980. Life Tables (Washington, D.C.: U.S. Dept. of Health and Human Services).

23. Frank Davis, *The Black Community's Social Security* (Washington, D.C.: University Press of America, 1978), p. 84.

24. Ibid., p. 77.

25. Ninety-nine percent of those receiving the spouse benefit are women. Until 1977, women had to be married for 20 years to receive the spouse benefit. See Madonna Harrington Meyer and Marcia Bellas, "U.S. Old Age Policy and the Family." *Handbook of Aging and the Family,* ed. Victoria Bedford and Rosemary Blieszner (New York: Academic Press, 1994).

26. Madonna Harrington Meyer, "Family Status and Poverty Among Older Women: The Gendered Distribution of Retirement Income in the United States." *Social Problems,* 37 (November, 1990): 555; see also Madonna Harrington Meyer, "Gender, Race, Class and the Social Security Spousal Benefit: Explaining the Resilience of the Patriarchal Welfare State." (Paper presented to the Gerontological Society of America, New Orleans, November, 1993).

27. William J. Wilson, *The Truly Disadvantaged, The Inner City, the Underclass and Public Policy* (Chicago: University of Chicago Press, 1987), p. 69.

28. U.S. Bureau of the Census, *Census of Population: 1970.* Employment Status and Work Experience (Washington, D.C.: U.S. Government Printing Office, 1973), p. 68.

29. Duncan and Smith, "The Rising Affluence of the Elderly," pp. 268–269.

30. Jill Quadagno, "Interest-Group Politics and the Future of U.S. Social Security." In *States, Labor Markets and the Future of Old Age Policy,* ed. John Myles and Jill Quadagno (Philadelphia: Temple University Press, 1991), p. 49.

31. Thomas Byrne Edsall, *The New Politics of Inequality* (New York: W.W. Norton, 1984), p. 17.

32. Paul Light, *Artful Work: The Politics of Social Security Reform* (New York: Random House, 1985), p. 124.

33. Quadagno, "Interest-Group Politics," p. 36.

34. Christine Day, *What Older Americans Think: Interest Group Politics and Aging Policy* (Princeton: Princeton University Press, 1990), p. 47.

35. Ibid., p. 53.

36. Ibid.

37. Light, *Artful Work,* p. 77.

38. Day, *What Older Americans Think,* p. 95.

39. Gosta Esping-Anderson, *The Three Worlds of Welfare Capitalism* (Princeton: Princeton University, 1990), p. 69.

40. Philip Longman, "Taking America to the Cleaners." *Washington Monthly* (November 1982): 24.

41. Peter G. Peterson, "The Morning After." *Atlantic Monthly* (October 1987): 44.

42. Ibid., pp. 44, 60.

43. Ibid., p. 60.

44. Paula Schwed, "A Dirty Little Secret." *Campus Voice* (Aug./Sept., 1986): 16.

45. Kevin Phillips, *The Politics of Rich and Poor: Wealth and the American Electorate in the Reagan Aftermath* (New York: Random House, 1990), p. 83.

46. The Pepper Commission. *A Call for Action* (Washington, D.C.: U.S. Bipartisan Commission on Comprehensive Health Care, 1990), p. 2.

47. Kevin Phillips, *Boiling Point: Democrats, Republicans, and the Decline of Middle-Class Prosperity* (New York: Random House, 1993), p. 44.

48. Phillips, *Boiling Point*, p. 46.

49. AARP News Bulletin (April 1987).

50. Martin Tolchin, "Health Act Doomed from Outset," *Kansas City Times*, October 9, 1989, p. A-1.

51. The premium was scheduled to increase to $10.20 a month in 1993. For a detailed discussion of the repeal of the Act, see Debra Street, "Maintaining the Status Quo: The Impact of Old Age Interest Groups on the Medicare Catastrophic Coverage Act of 1988." *Social Problems*, 40 (1993): 501–514.

52. James Kilpatrick, "Catastrophic was a Catastrophe." *Tallahassee Democrat*, August 24, 1089, p. 10A.

53. Among the gaps presently covered by Medigap policies that the new legislation doesn't cover are the one-time deductible for Part A hospital coverage, the daily co-payment for the first eight days of skilled nursing home care, the 20 percent portion of out-of-pocket expenses for doctor's visits and other outpatient services, and the difference between Medicare's allowable charges and the amount a doctor actually charges. Gregory Spears, "Medicare Payments Go Up." *Tallahassee Democrat*, January 1, 1989, p. 1A.

54. Spears, "Medicare Payments Go Up," p. 1A; "Catastrophic Care Act Headed for Revision." *Tallahassee Democrat*, August 4, 1989, p. 10A.

55. Joan Beck, "Catastrophic Needs to be Repealed." *Tallahassee Democrat*, July 29, 1989, p. 12A.

56. Skocpol, "Sustainable Social Policy," p. 67.

57. Theda Skocpol, "Targeting Within Universalism: Politically Viable Policies to Combat Poverty in the United States." In *The Urban Un-*

derclass, ed. Christopher Jencks and Paul E. Peterson (Washington, D.C.: The Brookings Institute, 1991), p. 413.

58. Nicholas Lemann, *The Promised Land: The Great Black Migration and How It Changed America* (New York: Alfred Knopf, 1991), p. 349.

59. Quoted in Robert Greenstein, "Universal and Targeted Approaches to Relieving Poverty: An Alternative View." In Christopher Jencks and Paul E. Peterson, *The Urban Underclass* (Washington, D.C.: The Brookings Institute, 1991), p. 457.

60. Ibid., p. 438.

61. I thank Leslie Innis for calculating these statistics for me.

Chapter 8: Rebuilding the Welfare State

1. S.M. Miller and Martin Rein, "The War on Poverty: Perspectives and Prospects." In *Poverty as a Public Issue,* ed. Ben Seligman (New York: The Free Press, 1965), pp. 272–320.

2. John E. Schwarz, *America's Hidden Success: A Reassessment of Public Policy from Kennedy to Reagan* (New York: W.W. Norton, 1986), p. 27; James T. Patterson, *America's Struggle Against Poverty, 1900–1985* (Cambridge: Harvard University Press, 1986), p. 164. These figures include in-kind transfers, which are excluded in many measures of poverty.

3. By 1986 they had climbed back to 21 percent, the result of an increase in female-headed households as well as a decline in the real value of the AFDC-food stamp package. See Katz, *The Undeserving Poor,* p. 127.

4. Christopher Jencks, *Rethinking Social Policy, Race, Poverty and the Underclass* (Cambridge: Harvard University Press, 1992), p. 57; Thomas Edsall and Mary Edsall, *Chain Reaction: The Impact of Race, Rights and Taxes on American Politics* (New York: W.W. Norton, 1991), pp. 246–250.

5. Christopher Jencks, "Is the American Underclass Growing?" In Jencks and Peterson, *The Urban Underclass,* pp. 44, 88; Edsall and Edsall, *Chain Reaction,* p. 231–232, 241.

6. George Gilder, *Wealth and Poverty* (New York: Basic Books, 1981), p. 41.

7. Charles Murray, *Losing Ground: American Social Policy, 1950–1980* (New York: Basic Books, 1984), p. 121.

8. David Ellwood, *Poor Support: Poverty in the American Family* (New York: Basic Books, 1988), p. 59.

9. Ellwood, *Poor Support,* p. 114.

10. William J. Wilson, *The Truly Disadvantaged, The Inner City, the Underclass and Public Policy* (Chicago: University of Chicago Press, 1987), p. 17.

11. Douglas S. Massey and Nancy A. Denton, *American Apartheid: Segregation and the Making of the Underclass* (Cambridge MA: Harvard University Press, 1993), p. 222.

12. Massey and Denton, *American Apartheid*, p. 14.

13. *Statistical Abstract of the United States* (Washington, D.C.: U.S. Government Printing Office, 1966–90).

14. Advisory Commission on Intergovernmental Relations, *Significant Features of Fiscal Federalism*, Vol 2. Revenues and Expenditures (Washington, D.C.: Advisory Commission on Intergovernmental Relations, 1990), p. 42.

15. Katz, *The Undeserving Poor*, p. 189.

16. Peter Dreier and J. David Hulchanski, "Affordable Housing: Lessons from Canada." *The American Prospect* (Spring, 1990): 119–25. Other factors, particularly housing inflation, have made it difficult for first time homebuyers to enter the market.

17. Paul Jargowsky and Mary Jo Bane, "Ghetto Poverty in the United States, 1970–1980." In Peterson and Jencks, *The Urban Underclass*, p. 259.

18. Katherine McFate, *Poverty, Inequality and the Crisis of Social Policy* (Washington,D.C.: Joint Center for Political and Economic Studies, 1991), p. 12.

19. Frank Levy, *Dollars and Dreams: The Changing American Income Distribution* (New York: W.W. Norton, 1988), pp. 78–82.

20. Frank Levy, "U.S. Earnings Levels and Earnings Inequality: A Review of Recent Trends and Proposed Explanations." *Journal of Economic Literature*, 30 (September, 1992): 1342.

21. Levy, *Dollars and Dreams*, p. 128.

22. Levy, "U.S. Earnings Levels and Earnings Inequality," p. 1356. The Bureau of Labor Statistics defines the "middle class" as families between 68 and 190 percent of median income.

23. Ibid.

24. Mickey Kaus, *The End of Equality* (New York: Basic Books, 1992), p. 31.

25. Barbara R. Bergmann, *The Economic Emergence of Women* (New York: Basic Books, 1986), p. 21.

26. Ibid.

27. *Poverty in the United States: 1991* (Washington, D.C.: U.S. Department of Commerce, 1991), p. 1.

28. Levy, "U.S. Earnings Levels and Earnings Inequality," p. 1357.

29. Richard A. Easterlin, Diane J. Macunovich, and Eileen M. Crimmins, "Economic Status of the Young and Old in the Working Age Population, 1964 and 1987." In *The Changing Contract Across Generations,* ed. Vern Bengtson (New York: Aldine de Gruyter, 1993), p. 69.

30. *1990 Census of Population,* Table 3 (Washington, D.C.: U.S. Bureau of the Census, 1990).

31. U.S. Bureau of Labor Statistics, USDL 85–381, Table 1 (September 19, 1985), USDL 84–321 (July 26, 1984), Table 1; and Howard Hayghe, "Rise in Mothers' Labor Force Activity Includes Those with Infants," *Monthly Labor Review,* 109 (February 1986): 43–45; *Statistical Abstract of the United States* (Washington, D.C.: U.S. Government Printing Office, 1992), p. 388; "Who Is a Good Mother?" *The New York Times,* October 4, 1992, p. 18

32. Here "class" is defined in regard to relationship to the means of production, not by lifestyle. The working class consists of individuals who neither own the means of production nor command the labor power of others. Wallace Clement and John Myles, *Relations of Ruling* (Montreal: McGill Queens University Press, 1994), p. 24.

33. Ibid., pp. 249–250.

34. Alfred J. Kahn and Sheila Kamerman, *Child Care: Facing the Hard Choices* (Dover, MA: Auburn House, 1987), p. 22.

35. David Maume, "Child-Care Expenditures and Women's Employment Turnover." *Social Forces,* 70 (December, 1991): 495; Kahn and Kamerman, *Child Care,* p. 11.

36. Harriet Presser and Wendy Baldwin, "Child Care as a Constraint on Employment: Prevalence, Correlates and Bearing on the Work and Fertility Nexus." *American Journal of Sociology,* 85 (1980): 1202–1213.

37. Theodore Marmor, Jerry Mashaw, and Philip Harvey, *America's Misunderstood Welfare State* (New York: Basic Books, 1990), p. 122.

38. Marmor, Mashaw and Harvey, *America's Misunderstood Welfare State,* p. 121.

39. Diana Pearce, "Welfare Is Not for Women: Why the War on Poverty Cannot Conquer the Feminization of Poverty." In *Women, the State and Welfare,* ed. Linda Gordon (Madison: University of Wisconsin Press, 1990, pp. 265–279); Teresa Amott, "Black Women and AFDC: Making Entitlement Out of Necessity." In Gordon, *Women, the State and Welfare,* pp. 280–298.

40. McFate, *Poverty, Inequality and the Crisis of Social Policy,* p. 17.

41. Charles Lockhart, *Gaining Ground: Tailoring Social Programs to*

American Values (Berkeley: University of California Press, 1989), pp. 83–101.

Chapter 9: Explaining American Exceptionalism

1. Gunnar Myrdal, *An American Dilemma* (New York: McGraw Hill, 1944), Chapter 1.

2. Myrdal, *An American Dilemma,* p. 21.

3. James Morone, *The Democratic Wish: Popular Participation and the Limits of American Government* (New York: Basic Books, 1990).

4. Walter Dean Burnham, *Critical Elections and the Mainsprings of American Politics* (New York: W. W. Norton, 1970).

5. Kevin Phillips, *The Politics of Rich and Poor: Wealth and the American Electorate in the Reagan Aftermath* (New York: Random House, 1990).

6. Ann Shola Orloff, *The Politics of Pensions: A Comparative Analysis of Britain, Canada, and the United States, 1880–1940* (Madison: University of Wisconsin Press, 1993), p. 88.

7. See Ann Shola Orloff and Theda Skocpol, "Why Not Equal Protection: Explaining the Politics of Public Social Spending in Britain, 1900–1911 and the United States, 1880s–1920s." *American Sociological Review,* 49 (December, 1984): 726–750; Theda Skocpol, *Protecting Soldiers and Mothers: The Political Origins of Social Policy in the United States* (Cambridge: Harvard University Press, 1992).

8. Orloff, *The Politics of Pensions,* p. 298.

9. Andrew Martin, "The Politics of Economic Policy in the United States: A Tentative View from a Comparative Perspective." *Comparative Politics Series,* Sage Professional Papers in Comparative Politics (Beverly Hills, CA: Sage Publications, 1973), p. 47.

10. Jill Quadagno, *The Transformation of Old Age Security: Class and Politics in the American Welfare State* (Chicago: University of Chicago Press, 1988), p. 55.

11. J. David Greenstone, *Labor in American Politics* (New York: Alfred A. Knopf, 1969), p. 361.

12. Ira Katznelson, *City Trenches: Urban Politics and the Patterning of Class in the United States* (Chicago: University of Chicago Press, 1981), p. 19.

13. Loic J. D. Wacquant and William Julius Wilson, "The Cost of Racial and Class Exclusion in the Inner City." *Annals of the American Academy of Political and Social Science,* 501 (January, 1989), p. 15.

14. An excellent summary of this perspective appears in Skocpol, *Protecting Soldiers and Mothers,* pp. 15–23.

15. Charles Lockhart, *Gaining Ground: Tailoring Social Programs to American Values* (Berkeley: University of California Press, 1989), p. 48.

16. Kevin Phillips, *The Emerging Republican Majority* (New York: Doubleday, 1970), p. 38.

17. Thomas Edsall and Mary Edsall, *Chain Reaction: The Impact of Race, Rights, and Taxes on American Politics* (New York: W. W. Norton, 1991), p. 138.

18. Edsall and Edsall, *Chain Reaction*, p. 198; Chandler Davidson, *Race and Class in Texas Politics* (Princeton: Princeton University Press, 1990); E. J. Dionne, *Why Americans Hate Politics* (New York: Simon and Schuster, 1991).

BIBLIOGRAPHIC NOTES

Readers interested in pursuing research on the War on Poverty will find ample materials in the National Archives. Record Group (RG) 381 contains the records of the Office of Economic Opportunity. RG 381 is a rich source of information on the implementation of the community action programs. It contains correspondence between bureaucrats in OEO and other federal agencies and between federal authorities and local officials, newspaper clippings, task force and field reports, planning documents, and statistics evaluating various programs. The one difficulty in working with this RG is that the documents are organized by state so that the national perspective must be pieced together indirectly.

RG 174 contains the records of the Department of Labor. What I found most useful were the detailed evaluations of federal job-training programs, analyses of strategies for dealing with the trade unions, and correspondence between federal officials and labor leaders. The George Meany Archives also contained some useful materials on the role of the trade unions in the War on Poverty and particularly detailed evidence regarding the union's perspective on its struggles against quotas.

RG 207 is a gold mine on the early trials of the Department of Housing and Urban Development. It contains correspondence, newspaper reports, evidence on housing discrimination compiled by federal task forces and by the National Committee Against Discrimination in Housing, and monthly Urban Tension Reports documenting HUD's role in fomenting unrest. I located materials on the battle for national day care in RG 102, the records of the Children's Bureau. These records were rather sparse, but I was able to obtain a more complete picture when I located additional materials in the records of the Women's Bureau and in several oral histories from the Lyndon Baines Johnson Library in Austin, Texas. The LBJ Library's extensive oral history collection was especially valuable. A list of all oral histories held in the collection can be obtained by calling the library. I found the archivists at the LBJ Library always willing to answer questions about holdings and extremely efficient in mailing copies of oral histories.

In seeking materials on Richard Nixon's proposal for a guaranteed annual income, I found that the records had been moved to the Federal Archives and Record Center in Suitland, Maryland. When I asked how I might obtain access to them, no one knew where they were. After more than ten fruitless phone calls, I found myself referred back to the first person I had spoken to. Aloha South then advised me that I could unearth the records by making a written request under the Freedom of Information Act. That worked. For one week I sat in an office of the Department of Health and Human Services surrounded by three cardboard boxes of uncatalogued materials, containing all the plans, aspirations, and obstacles to Nixon's Family Assistance Plan.

Following is a selected list of books and articles on the War on Poverty that provided useful background detail on the various programs I examined:

Auerback, Stevanne. 1973. "Federally Sponsored Child Care." In *Child Care, Who Cares?*, edited by Pamela Roby. New York: Basic Books.

Berkowitz, Edward. 1991. *America's Welfare State: From Roosevelt to Reagan*. Baltimore: Johns Hopkins University Press.

Blau, Joel. 1992. *The Visible Poor*. New York: Oxford University Press.

Blissett, Marlan. 1988. "Untangling the Mess: The Administrative Legacy of President Johnson." In *Lyndon Baines Johnson and the Uses of Power*, edited by Bernard Firestone and Robert Vogt. New York: Greenwood Press.

Burke, Vincent J. and Vee Burke. 1974. *Nixon's Good Deed, Welfare Reform*. New York: Columbia University Press.

Donovan, John C. 1980. *The Politics of Poverty*. Washington, D.C.: University Press of America.

Gilder, George. 1981. *Wealth and Poverty*. New York: Basic Books.

Graham, Hugh Davis. 1990. *The Civil Rights Era: Origins and Development of National Policy*. New York: Oxford University Press.

Grimshaw, William J. 1992. *Bitter Fruit: Black Politics and the Chicago Machine, 1931–1991*. Chicago: University of Chicago Press.

Hamilton, Charles V. and Dona C. Hamilton. 1986. "Social Policies, Civil Rights and Poverty." In *Fighting Poverty: What Works and What Doesn't*, edited by Sheldon H. Danziger and Daniel H. Weinberg. Cambridge: Harvard University Press.

Haveman, Robert. 1973. *A Decade of Federal Anti-Poverty Programs.* New York: Academic Press.

Johnson, Lyndon Baines. 1971. *The Vantage Point: Perspectives of the Presidency, 1963–1969.* New York: Popular Library.

Katz, Michael. 1989. *The Undeserving Poor, From the War on Poverty to the War on Welfare.* New York: Pantheon.

Lemann, Nicholas. 1991. *The Promised Land: The Great Black Migration and How It Changed America.* New York: Alfred Knopf.

Marmor, Theodore, Jerry Mashaw and Philip L. Harvey. 1990. *America's Misunderstood Welfare State.* New York: Basic Books.

Marris, Peter and Martin Rein. 1973. *Dilemmas of Social Reform.* Chicago: Aldine.

Matuso, Allen. 1984. *The Unraveling of America: A History of Liberalism in the 1960s.* New York: Harper and Row.

Miller, S. M. and Martin Rein. 1965. "The War on Poverty: Perspectives and Prospects." In *Poverty as a Public Issue,* edited by Ben Seligman, pp. 272–320. New York: The Free Press.

Morone, James. 1990. *The Democratic Wish: Popular Participation and the Limits of American Government.* New York: Basic Books.

Moynihan, Daniel Patrick. 1965. *The Negro Family: The Case for National Action.* U.S. Department of Labor: Office of Policy Planning and Research.

Murray, Charles. 1984. *Losing Ground: American Social Policy, 1950–1980.* New York: Basic Books.

Patterson, James. 1986. *America's Struggle Against Poverty.* Cambridge: Harvard University Press.

Piven, Frances Fox and Richard Cloward. 1979. *Poor People's Movements, Why They Succeed, How They Fail.* New York: Random House.

Rainwater, Lee and William Yancey. 1967. *The Moynihan Report and the Politics of Controversy.* Cambridge: The Massachusetts Institute of Technology Press.

Schulman, Paul. 1980. *Large Scale Policy Making.* New York: Elsevier.

Schwarz, John E. 1986. *America's Hidden Success: A Reassessment of Public Policy from Kennedy to Reagan.* New York: W.W. Norton.

Sugrue, Thomas J. 1993. "The Structures of Urban Poverty: The Reorganization of Space and Work in Three Periods of American History." In *The Underclass Debate,* edited by Michael Katz. Princeton: Princeton University Press.

Sundquist, James. 1969. *On Fighting Poverty.* New York: Basic Books.

Weir, Margaret. 1988. "The Federal Government and Unemployment: The Frustration of Policy Innovation from the New Deal to the Great Society." In *The Politics of Social Policy in the United States,* edited by Margaret Weir, Ann Orloff and Theda Skocpol. Princeton: Princeton University Press.

Weir, Margaret. 1992. *Politics and Jobs: The Boundaries of Employment Policy in the United States.* Princeton: Princeton University Press.

Zarefsky, David. 1986. *President Johnson's War on Poverty: Rhetoric and History.* University City, AL: University of Alabama Press.

INDEX